Youth Culture and Sport

Critical Youth Studies

Series Editor: Greg Dimitriadis

Beyond Resistance! Youth Activism and Community Change: New Democratic Possibilities for Practice and Policy for America's Youth
Edited by Shawn Ginwright, Pedro Noguera, and Julio Cammarota

Youth Learning On Their Own Terms: Creative Practices and Classroom Teaching
Leif Gustavson

Youth Moves: Identities and Education in Global Perspective
Edited by Nadine Dolby and Fazal Rizvi

Next Wave Cultures: Feminism, Subcultures, Activism
Edited by Anita Harris

Youth Culture and Sport: Identity, Power, and Politics
Edited by Michael D. Giardina and Michele K. Donnelly

Youth Culture and Sport

Identity, Power, and Politics

Edited by

Michael D. Giardina • Michele K. Donnelly

Routledge
Taylor & Francis Group
New York   London

Routledge
Taylor & Francis Group
270 Madison Avenue
New York, NY 10016

Routledge
Taylor & Francis Group
2 Park Square
Milton Park, Abingdon
Oxon OX14 4RN

© 2008 by Taylor & Francis Group, LLC
Routledge is an imprint of Taylor & Francis Group, an Informa business

Printed in the United States of America on acid-free paper
10 9 8 7 6 5 4 3 2 1

International Standard Book Number-13: 978-0-415-95581-2 (Softcover) 978-0-415-95580-5 (Hardcover)

Library of Congress Cataloging-in-Publication Data

Youth culture and sport : identity, power, and politics / edited by Michael D. Giardina, Michele K. Donnelly.
    p. cm.
Includes bibliographical references and index.
ISBN 978-0-415-95580-5 (hb : alk. paper) -- ISBN 978-0-415-95581-2 (pb : alk. paper)
    1. Sports--Social aspects. 2. Sports--Social aspects--United States. 3. Sports for children--Social aspects--United States. 4. Youth--United States--Social conditions. 5. Subculture--United States. I. Giardina, Michael D., 1976- II. Donnelly, Michele K.

GV706.5.Y57 2008
306.4'83--dc22
        2007014496

Visit the Taylor & Francis Web site at
http://www.taylorandfrancis.com

and the Routledge Web site at
http://www.routledge.com

Contents

Section III: Racialized Pedagogies

Series Editor Introduction

As the editors of *Youth Culture and Sport: Identity, Power, and Politics* note in the volume's introduction, more than 35 million North American youth participate in some kind of organized sport activity. Many millions more consume sports through some other mass mediated form. Clearly, sports are a critical pedagogical site for youth—a space where their bodies and minds are formed in complex and often uniquely co-constituted ways. Yet, as the editors and authors in this volume make clear, critical work on youth sport has been largely missing—or at least, disproportionately so. This volume looks toward a corrective. And the stakes could not be any higher.

In particular, *Youth Culture and Sport: Identity, Power, and Politics* invites a critical, cultural interrogation of sport. In doing so, it both contests mainstream approaches to sports science and looks to extend the project of cultural studies in new and powerful directions. This dual intervention is important. Limited as it is, most work on sports to date has been narrowly empirical and functional, taken up in a range of medical and traditional social scientific disciplines. In all these cases, the deeply social, political, and cultural nature of these sporting practices tends to be elided in favor of pointedly technical concerns—about the athletic body, about the distribution of these practices in society, and so forth. Very little work has looked at the cultural meanings attached to sports—various manifestations, iterations, and all. Engaging with the best impulses of cultural studies, the editors and authors in this volume look toward a more fully contextualized approach to sport.

This point is important. Cultural studies has always been concerned with the dynamics of cultural practices, the ways in which such practices are radically situated by a host of contextual forces and trajectories. While much of the earliest work in cultural studies was concerned with youth culture, it often highlighted so-called spectacular practices—for example, the music, style, and fashion of "punks," as in the work of Dick Hebdige—a legacy that has largely endured. Surprisingly, there has been little work to date that looks similarly at the role of sport and sport culture in the lives of youth, either at the level of practice or text. Perhaps this elision has to do with a general marginalization of, and discomfort with, "the body" itself in much cultural work. Whatever the reason, the massive and growing popularity of sport can no longer be ignored, nor can it be relegated solely to the sciences and its technical and functional imperatives.

Youth Culture and Sport: Identity, Power, and Politics draws together a range of chapters which take on a host of sporting practices and texts. This includes: the Little League World Series and the rise of the New Right in the United States; the racial politics of films such as *He Got Game* and *Hoop Dreams*; the politics of the "iconic suburban girl athlete"; the corporate branding of "action sport"; extreme sports and masculinity; the rise of the "skater girl" as an oppositional identity; television and the representation of girl's and women's skateboarding and snowboarding; anti-Indian imagery in youth sport; the contestation of aboriginal identity through sport in the Canadian North; and the ideology of motherhood in the United States and girl's basketball. In each of these cases, sport is treated as a deeply political space, one that can only be understood through a deep appreciation of its social contexts.

This volume, thus, does the important work of bringing a critical, cultural studies perspective to sport. Yet, the editors and authors go beyond this important intervention, looking toward sports as a site for a radical performative pedagogy. Indeed, the book is framed with a foreword by Norman Denzin and a coda by Michael Giardina, both of which discuss the importance of taking this work out into the world, intervening in our historical present as we look toward a utopian future. As Giardina quotes from Arundhati Roy, "We must create links. Join the dots. Tell politics like a story. Communicate it. Make it *real*. Present impassioned polemics. And refuse to create barriers that prevent ordinary people from understanding what is happening to them." Again, that the editors and authors look to the oft-ignored terrain of sport, only makes this intervention all-the-more pressing and necessary.

GREG DIMITRIADIS
Buffalo University

Foreword
A Critical Youth Studies for the Historical Present

NORMAN K. DENZIN

A critical youth studies program that matters must speak to and from the historical present. The terrorist attacks of September 11, 2001, on the World Trade Center in New York and the Pentagon in Washington, DC, and the now four-year old war against and occupation of Iraq have changed the shape of global capitalist relations. Consider the facts. We live in a state of perpetual terror. A "Global War on Terror" has morphed into a war on persons of color. This war, in turn, has morphed into a war on illegal immigrants, a war on aliens, and a war on insurgents and global citizens who cross national borders. Inherent within this new paradigm is that the targets of such war are all too often children.

The Bush administration has perpetuated a cycle of state-sponsored terrorism. It has created a network of secret prisons and gulags. It has repeatedly violated the Geneva Conventions. It has abridged basic rights of the Constitution, including those ensured by the First, Fifth and Sixth Amendments; that is, the right to freedom of speech, to due process, and to the right to a speedy public trial. The list of legal abuses is endless. The need for public discourse on the nature of politics, power, knowledge, citizenship, freedom, privacy, patriotism, justice, and democracy in this time of war has never been greater.

. The context that confronts scholars of youth culture is complex and, at times, unyielding, A critical youth studies of the historical present speaks from and to these spaces of violence and injury, of global terror, the spaces of nation, neo-liberal regimes, identity, self, gender, freedom, justice, equality, and hope. Conceptually and theoretically, as Michael Giardina, Michele

Donnelly, and their collected colleagues acknowledge in their crucial new volume, is how surprising and disappointing it is that "contemporary youth sporting culture—and its location to the broader spectrum of popular media and politics—has not garnered…widespread attention within the pages of most academic texts," especially with respect to the fields of cultural studies and critical theory. Countering this deficiency, this group of critical scholars offers the field new narratives and new methodologies, new ways of being in the present, new ways of looking inward and outward at the same time. We need a new language and a new way of representing life under violent, global postmodernism. Michael, Michele, and their colleagues give us the terms and tools of this new language.

A New Language/A New Direction

Here is a sample of themes covered in the chapters that follow: racial pedagogies, identity work, transgression, American empire, colonialism, youthful innocence, cultural branding, Disneyfication of security, cyberculture, indigenous rights, neoconservatism, neoliberalism, the politics of whiteness, social motherhood, and the politics of representation. This language helps us to theorize about critical youth studies in the historical present. These key terms and ideas allow us to speak of disempowered youth, marginalized native peoples, and white power. To contest a violent politics of neoliberal capitalism, the co-optation of youth culture for profit, and cinematic representations that perpetuate racial stereotypes. And to celebrate politically savvy young girls, the performance of flexible and malleable identities, and the promise of radical, progressive democracy.

More broadly put, Giardina, Donnelly, and their colleagues give us a language for policing the current global crisis (see Denzin, 2007). They help us locate, interpret, perform, contest, deconstruct, and represent the lives of a youthful global citizenry on the move. They help us craft a morally centered, critically informed dialogue focused on human rights, history, and politics at the confluence of great uncertainty. They help us imagine a critical youth studies that will interrupt history; a critical theory that will not stand silent when a nation rushes to war or sells out its children. A morally centered discourse that challenges official versions of political reality. An ethical project that challenges the ways political administrations manipulate information and produce regimes of fear and terror, whether with respect to security narratives or health concerns such as smoking. Theirs is a morally centered, politically interventionist project that argues for a politics of truth that answers to enduring issues concerning what is ethical and just.

A Cultural Studies That Matters

A cultural studies project that matters must take up *at least* four topics at the same time: First, following the lead of the chapters in book, we must start with the personal and the biographical and our own location within the world around us. We need a critical, humane discourse that creates sacred and spiritual spaces for persons and their moral communities—spaces where people can express and give meaning to the tragedy of this war and its aftermath. This project will work back and forth, connecting the personal, the political, and the cultural. It will reject terrorism and the claim that peace comes at any cost. It will help persons think critically, historically, and sociologically. It will move to expose the pedagogies of oppression that produce and reproduce oppression and injustice. It will contribute to an ethical self-consciousness that is critical and reflexive, empowering people with a language and a set of pedagogical practices that turn oppression into freedom, despair into hope, hatred into love, doubt into trust. And it will engender a critical racial self-awareness that contributes to utopian dreams of racial equality and racial justice.

Second, critical discourse must be launched at the level of the media and the ideological, including discourses on war, America, patriotism, democracy, globalization, neoliberalism, and the silences surrounding peace, human rights, and nonviolence. This discourse will call for justice without war. It will ask for calm deliberations. It will plead against rash actions that could erode human rights and civil liberties.

Third, we need to foster a critical (inter)national conversation on what is happening, a coalition of voices across the political, cultural, and religious spectra; the socialist left, green, peace, women's, gay, lesbian, African American, Asian American, and Latino movements; libertarians, young, old, students, workers, the clergy, and persons from all religions; and intellectuals. Every era must develop its own theory of radical politics and social democracy; a place where citizenship is an argument, not a sing-along. This dialogue is one that must stay alive in our conversations, mutterings, and dialogues about peace, justice, war, and the shrinking of civil liberties and social justice in America and abroad, and must get louder and continue until a progressive president and Congress is in office. We cannot let democratic dialogue be eviscerated in a time of crisis. We cannot allow discussions of immigration policy become a justification for attacks on persons of color. Or women. Or gays and lesbians. Or kids. Or Muslims, Iraqis, Palestinians, and those subjected to genocide in Africa. We cannot let the political discourse be shaped by the needs and voices of multinational corporations.

Fourth, there has never been a greater need for critical, interpretive methodologies that can help us make sense of life in an age of the hyper-real, the simulacra, TV wars, staged media events, *Top Gun* escapades by an illegally selected leader who avoided the draft during the Vietnam War. These critical methodologies must exhibit interpretive sufficiency; be free of racial, class, gender, or sexual stereotyping; rely on multiple voices; enhance moral discernment; and promote social transformation and critical consciousness. They must help informed citizens to consensually develop rock-solid, baseline definitions of political reality, enabling us to judge a political regime by its actions, not its carefully crafted, focus-group-tested buzzwords and phrases.

To Conclude

In this age of global uncertainty, we have a moral obligation to police this crisis, to confront the current situation, to speak to the death of lives, culture, and truth, to undo the official pedagogies that circulate in the media. We need testimonials, autoethnographies, performance texts, new stories, plays, and dramas about real people with real lives, the horror of it all. We need stories about what it is like to hate and feel despair, anger, and alienation in a world bursting at the seams as it struggles to reinvent its dominant mythology. We need pedagogical discourses that make these feelings visible, palpable—stories and performances that connect these emotions to wild utopian dreams of freedom and peace. We need to bring about the collapse of the corporate, neoliberal globalization project, the death of old-fashioned imperialism, the death of the new empire before it is too late.

This is what a cultural studies that matters will do, what a critical youth studies for the historical present will look like. We thank the authors and editors of *Youth Culture and Sport* for showing us how to do this.

References

Alterman, E. (2007, January 29). Iraq and the sin of good judgment. *The Nation, 284*(4), 10.

Denzin, N. K. (2007). *Flags in the window: Dispatches from the American war front.* New York: Peter Lang.

Acknowledgments

We thank our Series Editor, Greg Dimitriadis, for his generous support of this project from the very start. His help and guidance throughout the process were instrumental in bringing this volume to fruition. We also thank Catherine Bernard and Heather Jarrow at Taylor & Francis for their extraordinary patience and understanding of the bumps and bruises we encountered along the way.

Special thanks to our colleagues in the Department of Advertising and the Institute of Communications Research at the University of Illinois, and the Department of Sociology at McMaster University, as well as in the North American Society for the Sociology of Sport and the International Association for Qualitative Inquiry, for their keen insights and discussions related to youth culture and sport in the global arena. Extra special thanks to our contributors for privileging us with their thoughtful—and thought provoking—contributions.

MICHAEL D. GIARDINA
MICHELE K. DONNELLY

Introduction

MICHAEL D. GIARDINA AND MICHELE K. DONNELLY

> Culture is the primary terrain in which adults exercise power over children both ideologically and institutionally.
>
> —Henry A. Giroux, 2000, p. 4

Proem

An idyllic Saturday afternoon in Anytown, USA. The sun shines brightly. Birds chirp. Late-model black SUVs line the parking lot. Pigtailed young girls play soccer on a crisp patch of green grass at the local park. Parents shout encouragement from the sidelines. A goal is scored. Cheering erupts. Fans clap. Kids celebrate. And then one of the young soccer players is blown apart in a thunderous clap and cloud of dust. Chaos ensues. Thoughts of terrorism are ignited. Danger. Danger. Everywhere.

Shocking? To say the least. Reality? Closer to truth than fiction. The above description is from a controversial Public Service Announcement (PSA) titled "Kick Off," produced by Brooklyn Bros. advertising agency for the United Nations Mine Action Service landmine eradication program, titled "Stop Landmines." Unveiled in late 2004 under the tagline "If there were landmines here, would you stand for them anywhere?" and aimed directly at the U.S. public, the PSA was immediately banned by CNN for (allegedly) being "too violent" and "graphic," especially "in the wake of 9/11"; other U.S. networks and local affiliates quickly followed suit.[1] Premised on attacking the hypocrisy of the U.S. *sarkar* for not joining the international mine-ban treaty by shifting the realities of negotiating mine-laden backyards from "Other" (i.e., marginalized, Third World) countries to the living rooms and playgrounds of

1

everyday America, the viewer is hailed to look him- or herself in the mirror and stand in someone else's shoes in the hopes of generating action, awareness, and sympathy to a cause unknown to many Americans.

This televisual articulation of youthful innocence, sport, and the fetishization of terrorism/security narratives should come as no surprise to us. Nor should the over-wrought censorship levied against the PSA by many news outlets, for we do not have a strong, independent, morally critical press in the United States, one that is committed to the ideals of a democratic imagination, to Deweyan notions of democracy as a participatory practice. Nor do we have a media complex that sees itself as guardians of free speech or purveyors of progressive ideals. What we do have, however, is a media that can instantly produce a sea of violent, racist, and sexist images, a media with a memory but no critical history (Baudrillard, 1988, p. 126; Denzin & Giardina, 2006). A media that has usurped and refracted discourses of (neo)nationalism, faux patriotism, and pseudo-multiculturalism for the sake of its corporate masters: expanding market share, profit, and the appeasement of government regulatory bodies (such as the FCC).

Yet we must acknowledge that the extent to which contemporary youth culture is shaped and influenced does not stop at the doors of corporate empires (though it does happen to go along for the ride). That is to say, the last 20 years of rapidly expanding commercial forays into youth culture have been paralleled by a concomitant, government-sanctioned slashing of educational funding by federal agencies, the increased surveillance and restriction of the civil liberties of youth in schools and public venues, the rise in disciplinary mechanisms of control, and the rapidly expanding psychotropic medicalization of youth who are deemed to be "different" or "at risk" because of their association with particular forms of popular cultural attitudes or expressions (see Grossberg, 2005). At the same time, right-wing conservative essayists (e.g., William Bennett, Ann Coulter, and the like) and cable news pundits (e.g., Joe Scarborough, Sean Hannity, Bill O'Reilly, Glenn Beck, Michelle Malkin, and the like) continually frame young people (especially those of color) as violent, over-the-edge sociopaths who are to blame for the collapse of urban—and occasionally suburban—environments into pseudo war-zones reminiscent of the Hughes Brothers' *Menace II Society* or John Singleton's *Boyz n the Hood* (Giardina & McCarthy, this volume). And, not to be left out, the schoolhouse educational environment itself has made a hard turn backward to the Stone Age as it has been forced to implement such faulty measures as biased rewards-based standardized testing, dictated under the Bush administration's disastrous No Child Left Behind Act of 2001 (Public Law 1007–110) (see Darder & Miron, 2006).[2]

Thus, over the last few decades, scholars and critics alike have rightly begun to critically examine the multi-layered articulations of identity, power, and cultural politics germane to the mediated popular experiences of young people, the very battlefield where childhood is constructed, contested, and experienced. Such scholars have likewise charted the shifting understandings ascribed to youth culture, from the progressive oppositionality of youthful expression in the 1960s, to the so-called time of "innocence lost" in the 1980s, to, more recently, kids as the 1990s avatar of violence and risk to democratic public life. They have also been instrumental in unmasking the often-unseen links between consumer capitalism, neoliberalism, and notions of freedom and personal agency (see Cook, 2004). And, dedicated to the pursuit of social justice and the ideals of a democratic imagination, they have sought to unmask the unequal power relations at play that are concerned with the regulation, management, and manipulation of youthful populations in general via technologies of containment, surveillance, and subjectification.

However, it is both surprising and disappointing that contemporary youth sporting culture—and its location to the broader spectrum of popular media and politics—has not garnered similar widespread attention within the pages of most academic texts (sporting or otherwise). This is curious, for sport as a cultural practice occupies a crucial space in the everyday life of kids,[3] especially when we consider that more than 35 million children and young people in North America participate in organized sport (whether as part of club sport teams, community recreation programs, interscholastic and intercollegiate athletic programs, or youth sport organizations such as Little League baseball or Pop Warner football), and many millions more "consume" cultural sporting artifacts such as video games, televised events, advertisements, and officially licensed merchandise on a daily basis. Not only that, but the wider sporting arena is every bit a part of our trans/national landscape—a place inhabited by heroes and villains, an open book of storylines bold and beautiful, a history of the present told through box scores and movie scripts, *SportsCenter* highlight reels and games of catch played on the Elysian Fields of our youth. And it similarly serves as one of the strongest ties that bind us to previous and future generations, like a lyrical, ongoing conversation, ripped from the idealized frames of *City Slickers* and *The Sandlot* (see Giardina, 2005).

At the same time, contemporary sporting culture represents a damning tale of racism, sexism, homophobia, class struggles, global capitalism, media conglomeration, intense commodification, and the re/formation and perpetuation of national identity, fantasy, and mythology. Specific to a post-9/11 context, for example, the present Bush administration is currently in the process of carrying out mind-numbing assaults on Title IX (the federal legislation in the United States that has become most recognized in the popular consciousness for guaranteeing, among other things, equal opportunities in sport for both girls and boys in school settings) and steroid-testing drug policy, while likewise using the master trope of baseball as a myopic rallying cry to foster nationalist sentiments that ring hollow the patronage of "freedom" and "democracy." Not to be outdone, popular sporting institutions continue to remain beholden to a politics of representation that reverberated throughout much of the 1980s and 1990s inasmuch as perpetuating a status quo premised on sport as part and parcel of the (idealized) meritocratic American dream; that is, for example, perpetuating the much-hailed fiction that basketball is the only socially accepted and viable avenue of success or possibility for African American youth, or promoting the offensively absurd argument that the use of Native imagery as sports mascots in high schools and universities serves only to "honor" rather than exploit a group of people who were systematically exterminated by white colonial settlers (and who continue to be socially, cultural, politically, economically, and technologically discriminated against in the current moment).

This productive relationship of sport—youth, professional, or otherwise—to the context of popular culture turns on the axis of what Meaghan Morris (2004) might call its "mattering force," which here resides along the fault lines of the dominant globalizing cultural pedagogies of our time: neoliberalism, conservative cultural politics, and global consumer capitalism. It is at this intersection within the historical present that this volume interrogates and challenges contemporary articulations of youthful sporting narratives circulating throughout popular iterations of "youth" culture. Sifting through a variety of sites, contributors from the United States and Canada examine such varied topics as Little League baseball, corporate branding of extreme/action sports, the politics of whiteness, Indigenous sporting experiences, and other dis/locations of culture that reveal the tensions and contradictions at play in the ebb and flow of life in a global popular that is continually trying to revise its dominant mythology. They approach these cultural shadows from the position of (self)-reflection on literal and metaphorical border crossing—borders of ages, genders, religious and political affiliations, agreement and disagreement, and racial and class-based logics (see Alexander, 2006). In so doing, the authors collectively enquire into and reveal what philosopher Judith Butler (2004) refers to as the "conditions of emergence" that constitute, signify, and re-signify (popular forms of) cultural re/production within a globalizing system of neoliberal capitalism. Additionally, and aside from shedding a much-needed critical light on an arena of youth culture that is all-too-frequently overlooked by a majority of scholars and critics alike, the authors further challenge those working within cultural studies/critical theory to reflexively re-evaluate their theoretical and methodological approaches to engaging with popular culture in general and popular forms of youth sporting culture in specific.

The Chapters

Organizationally, *Youth Culture and Sport* is comprised of three sections that in unique but interrelated ways interrogate the articulation of youth sport to culture through a critical cultural studies lens. Section I focuses on the interplay of the politics of culture/culture of politics on youth and youth sport figurations. Section II discusses extreme/action sports as it relates to discourses of cultural branding, video games, and the flexibility of identity practices among its youth participants. And, in Section III, attention is turned to racialized pedagogies operative within youth culture, concerning both Native/Indigenous and African American populations. The three sections are linked by the understanding that "the cultural is always performative and pedagogical, and hence always political, and too frequently racist and sexist" (Denzin, 2003, p. 230), see also Diawara, 1996; Giroux, 2001).[4]

To start, Ryan White, Michael L. Silk, and David L. Andrews ("The Little League World Series") map out the current trajectory of U.S. political culture (read: neoliberalism) as read over and against the mediated production of childhood innocence in the Little League World Series (LLWS). Drawing from ethnographic field research at the 2003 LLWS, White and colleagues interrogate what they refer to as the "(ab)use" of LLWS participants—primarily 11- and 12-year-olds—by the American Broadcasting Company (ABC) [and by extension, the Walt Disney Co.] to "promote a proto-fascist, white, upper-class American agenda" via its production and televisualization of the event, particularly in the context of post-9/11 inter/national relations. Their scathing critique—which includes interviews with Little League officials, ABC broadcast personnel, and on-air talent that reveal the almost insidious (if not borderline pedophilic) governance of kids—stands as a rousing polemic against the commercial and political exploitation of America's youthful sporting participants.

Next, Michael D. Giardina and Cameron McCarthy ("Screening Race in America") critically interrogate the prevailing contemporary figurations of so-called "urban" popular culture as suggested within and against filmic narratives of youth sport and the racial logics of late-capitalism. Attempting to forge a contextual understanding of the conflicting representations of (urban) youth subjectivity, the authors locate "urban" America within broader conjunctural developments that have given rise to its mainstream appellation. They then focus on how urban popular culture is currently represented within broader pop culture formations, especially Hollywood cinema, before concluding with a close read of the Spike Lee's coming-of-age, urban basketball drama, *He Got Game*, which, they argue, is both an example and a symptom of popular racial representation that is compatible with the politics of a conservative (Black) middle class.

C. L. Cole's chapter ("Bounding American Empire") closes Section I, and deconstructs the long-standing historical intersection of sport, sex, and American imperial fantasies that, taken together and in isolation, operate as technologies of enchantment. More specifically, Cole focuses on the cultural history of U.S. Cold War body politics in relation to the production of heteronormative (sporting) figures representative of suburban American femininity (as read through "American girlhood") in opposition to the so-called gender-deviant Communist athlete. She then articulates this narrative to contemporary issues surrounding "race," drug-testing policy, and global social relations, particularly as located within U.S. fantasies about itself and its place in the global sporting community.

Section II opens with Robert E. Rinehart's chapter ("Exploiting a New Generation") on the exploitative mechanisms of cultural branding associated with extreme or action sports. He begins by reviewing the conditions of emergence that led to such breakthrough moments as ESPN's promotion of the first eXtreme Games in 1995, as well as the cultural manifestations informing such a discourse. Then, centering his attention on the so-called Generation Y (or "Millennial") demographic and the way in which the "extreme" or "action sport" label has since been co-opted by corporate interests who covet these young consumers, Rinehart offers a trenchant reading of "corporatization as we watch"—the saturation of product placement, the explosion of sponsorship agreements, and the branding of "hip" and "cool" as markers of consumerist identification. He concludes by offering some possible strategies in so order that young consumers can "mobilize against a steadily encroaching and disempowering corporate presence" in there lives.

David J. Leonard's chapter ("To the White Extreme in the Mainstream") follows, and takes up the topic of extreme/action sport video games as organized around a discourse of whiteness. Critically interrogating such popular video games as *Tony Hawk: Underground* and *BMX: XXX*, Leonard argues that video games—in particular, extreme sports video games—function pedagogically to "recreate a space of youth culture that imagines white masculinity as oppositional, cutting-edge, aggressive, physically powerful, sexually dominant, and transgressive." More specifically, he examines the popularity of such games, the extent to which rule-breaking is celebrated, and the location of white "athletes" within such a racialized space. Rather than accepting that the alternative/extreme genre challenges the status quo (as many have suggested), Leonard instead concludes that games of this nature ultimately reproduce dominant understandings of race, gender, and social relations.

Continuing the focus on extreme/action sports, Deirdre M. Kelly, Shauna Pomerantz, and Dawn H. Currie ("You Can Break So Many More Rules") turn our attention to so-called "Skaters Girls" and their multiple and complex performances of gender identity. Drawing from ethnographic field research at "skate parks" and interviews conducted with twenty skater girls between the ages of 13- and 16-years-old, Kelly and colleagues explore how the girls came to understand and make meaning from their participation in a culturally transgressive sporting activity that, for many, resulted in or allowed them to construct an "alternative identity" in opposition to mainstream/normative views of gender and sexuality. Here the performance of such an alternative identity, they argue, enabled their research participants "to maneuver within and against conventional notions of how girls should be and act, opening up a space where none previously existed."

Michele K. Donnelly's chapter ("Take the Slam and Get Back Up") concludes Section II by directing our attention to the Canadian television program, *Hardcore Candy*, which centered on a wide variety of "action" sports and consisted of stories about (North American) athletes, "learn to" ride surf, ski, or motocross programs for girls and women, and women's competitions and events. After first detailing the production elements and providing a contextual analysis of the program's dominant themes, Donnelly examines the relationship between maleness or masculinity as read through the politics of representation governing female skateboarders and snowboarders in *Hardcore Candy*. What she finds is that, despite *Hardcore Candy's* claims of promoting and encouraging women and girls to participate in such sports, the program's continual focus on injury and risk reinforces the masculine associations of skateboarding and snowboarding, and reaffirms male skateboarders and snowboarders as the only legitimate participants. That is to say, rather than offering an alternative space for female athletic participation, *Hardcore Candy* instead reinforces the messages about female skateboarders and snowboarders (and female athletes in general) that are produced by mainstream and subcultural media sources, and reminds us that girls and women continue to be "Other" to "real" skateboarders and snowboarders.

In Section III, attention is turned to the play of racialized pedagogies in relationship to youth sporting experiences and environments. C. Richard King's chapter ("Hostile Environments") discusses anti-Indian imagery and its wider location to and institutionalization within popular culture, particularly as related to sport team mascots and their effects on young people. King begins by exploring the pedagogical function by which such pseudo-Indian imagery acts to "teach" students and citizens about (a preferred, dominant reading of) race, culture, and history. He then turns a critical eye to the hostile learning environments that are created in educational institutions and on teams that continue to utilize such imagery, engaging in the process recent struggles being waged against their commercialized usage (e.g., against "Chief Illiniwek" at the University of Illinois). He concludes by offering suggestions for how we as teachers can contest the "popular pedagogy" of anti-Indian imagery in the hopes, as he puts it, of refashioning education as a site of anti-racist intervention.

Relatedly, Audrey R. Giles and Ava C. Baker ("Culture, Colonialism, and Competition") turn our attention to Canada's Northwest Territories and Nanuvut, and the way in which Northern youths' sporting participation is informed by their Northern Aboriginal identities. Arguing that sport in Canada's North needs to be understood within the larger context of colonial relations, Giles and Baker first offer a brief historical look back as a way of preparing us to look forward. Then, drawing from interviews, participant-observation, and archival research gathered over a three-year period, they discuss the Dene Games (and the way in which they have been used to build and reinforce Dene identity) and the Northwest Territories Aquatics Program (and the negotiations of identity engaged in by its participants). In so doing, they reveal the numerous ways in which (Northern) (youth) sport participation is inherently political and always in flux.

Section III concludes with Jennifer L. Metz's empirically grounded chapter ("From Babies to Ballers") on the articulation of race, gender, and mother-hood in professional women's sports. Interviewing 13 mother-athletes from the Women's National Basketball Association and Women's United Soccer Association about their childhood socialization into youth sport, the barriers of entry they faced (whether racial, gendered, or otherwise), and the role they see women's sport playing in the construction of identity, Metz addresses the underlying ramifications of socially making and marking mothers and families through youth sport (and its attendant discourses of empowerment), especially through the lens of commodified women's sport at the professional level. She concludes her chapter by addressing both progressive possibilities as well as concerns for the future-present of girls' youth sport participation.

The volume concludes with Michael D. Giardina's coda ("Youth Sport in the Shadows of American Vertigo"), which lyrically engages with the operations of identity, power, and politics in youth sporting culture in an age of global uncertainty.

By Way of a Conclusion

We live in, as the French philosopher Bernard-Henri Lévy observes, a curious sort of empire. An empire of contradiction. An empire of confusion. An empire gasping for its last shards of breath at the same time it strengthens its grasp on cultural politics. Whether in the form of racially charged collegiate mascots, the demonization of Black sporting bodies, or the militarization of public spaces, contemporary youth sporting culture is inextricably linked to neoliberal discourses of privatization, surveillance, and consumption that drive just such an empire—discourses that actively work to "transform concrete individuals into mass cultural citizens whose lines of loyalty and affiliation now exceed the territory and social geography of the nation-state" as they become aligned with global corporations such as Nike, Disney, and News Corporation, as well as imperialistic governmental regimes of truth (McCarthy, 2002, pp. 5–6). What results from such maneuvers is the depoliticization of the public sphere, the evacuation of discussion and dissent, and the erasure of political and ethical considerations that mark history as a site of struggle (producing what Giroux has called a "filmic version of popular culture").

Inserting young people and their shifting, malleable, contested identities into this equation makes for a doubly-troubling contextual plane, for "youth make visible the ethical consequences and social costs of losing a language of political and social responsibility, not to mention real spaces informed by the discourse and practices of civic engagement, critical dialogue, and social activism" (Giroux, 2003, p. 119). In traversing the fractured and often conflicting narrative collages assembled throughout this volume, we hope that it becomes evermore clear that the reiterative discursive practices and mediated moral panics pedagogically working to sustain our curious empire are, to use Larry Grossberg's phrase, succeeding in waging a war on kids. A war whose ultimate goal is the redefinition of modernity; in fact, the wholesale production of a *new* modernity that "would seem to negate the very reality, and even the possibility, of the social or, more accurately, of social agency...of many forms of individual and collective agency" (2005, pp. 365–366). Like the formal school curriculum or the world of cinema, youth sporting culture has become a fertile site for the exposition of these oppositions, a veritable battleground of social combatants struggling over the boundary lines of group identity and affiliation, over the very definition of citizenship and belonging (McCarthy, 2003). It is up to the poets, writers, artists, and scholars in critical youth studies to try and make sense of what is happening to our young people, to seek nonviolent regimes of truth that honor culture, universal human rights, and the sacred, and to seek critical methodologies that protest, resist, and help us represent and imagine radically free utopian spaces that will allow our "kids" to flourish as free moral agents.

Notes

1. In fact, the PSA aired only once, late at night, on the basic cable station The History Channel.
2. This is not to say, however, that youthful cultural practices do not serve as active sites of negotiation and contestation, providing a space in which kids can express themselves, create alternative spaces of meaning, and contest the very notion of a fixed or essentialized identity. Or that many kids take joyful pleasure consuming and experiencing pop culture products without necessarily accepting and/or adopting the intended marketed meanings. As we are well aware, kids have a seemingly innate ability to subvert and disrupt from within the outward forces operating against them that seek to produce docile bodies in the public sphere.

3. Here and henceforth, we use the term "kids" as it is generally deployed in the United States and Canada; that is, to refer to individuals under 18 years of age.
4. A note to instructors: although we have carved out three thematic sections, many of the chapters are ultimately interchangeable, able to be reordered around particular course sections not explicitly marked by our section headings. For example, the chapters by White et al., Leonard, and King can be linked together in a discussion of whiteness, the chapters by Cole, Kelly et al., and Metz can be linked in a discussion of gender identity, etc.

References

Baudrillard, J. (1988). *America* (Chris Turner, Trans.). London: Verso

Butler, J. (2004). *Precarious life*. London: Verso.

Cook, D. T. (2004). *The commodification of childhood: The children's clothing industry and the rise of the child consumer*. Durham, NC: Duke University Press.

Darder, A., & Mirón, L. F. (2006). Critical pedagogy in a time of uncertainty: A call to action. In N. K. Denzin & M. D. Giardina (Eds.), *Contesting empire/globalizing dissent: Cultural studies after 9/11* (pp. 136–151). Boulder, CO: Paradigm.

Denzin, N. K., & Giardina, M. D. (Eds.) (2006). *Contesting empire/globalizing dissent: Cultural studies after 9/11*. Boulder, CO: Paradigm.

Giardina, M. D. (2005). *Sporting pedagogies: Performing culture & identity in the global arena*. New York: Peter Lang.

Giroux, H. A. (2003). *The abandoned generation: Democracy beyond the culture of fear*. New York: PalgraveMacmillan.

Grossberg, L. (2005). *Caught in the crossfire: Kids, politics, and America's future*. Boulder, CO: Paradigm.

Levy, B. (2006). *American vertigo: Traveling America in the footstep of Tocqueville*. New York: Random House.

McCarthy, C. (2002). Understanding the work of aesthetics in modern life: Thinking about the cultural studies of education in a time of recession. Unpublished manuscript. Institute of Communications Research, University of Illinois, Urbana-Champaign.

Morris, M. (2004). *Heroes: Geopolitics, community, and the uses of aesthetics*. Keynote address at the 5th International Biannual Crossroads in Cultural Studies Conference. Urbana: University of Illinois, Urbana-Champaign.

SECTION **I**

Politics of Culture/Culture of Politics

CHAPTER 1

The Little League World Series
Spectacle of Youthful Innocence or
Spectre of the New Right?

RYAN WHITE, MICHAEL L. SILK, AND DAVID L. ANDREWS

Each year in August, as the U.S. summer draws to a close, and children are looking to enjoy their last minutes of (relative) freedom from the near-police state of mandatory drug testing, metal detectors, and myriad forms of surveillance that has become the American schooling experience (Giroux, 2003; Grossberg, 2005), a celebrated enclave of spectacularized youthful innocence is played out over the radio, television, and the Internet—The Little League World Series (LLWS). The event, annually held in Williamsport, Pennsylvania, is a particularly complex affair that serves as a mass-mediated vehicle for the performance of many of the axioms and anxieties that characterize the contemporary (young) American condition. Following Williams (1981), and given that any cultural production is rooted in particular historical, social, material, and symbolic relations (Andrews, 2006), we assert that popular mediated sport events, such as the LLWS, are both constituted by and a constituent of the discursive fields that combine to form what are necessarily contextual understandings of American (sporting) youth. Further, through its relative level of popularity, it could certainly be argued that the accumulated local (in this case, national) resonance of the LLWS is mobilized by its representation as a network television spectacle (Debord, 1994; Tomlinson, 2002).

Hence, within this chapter, and, following McDonald and Birrell (1999, p. 295), we read the media production of the 2003 LLWS critically, through the adoption of a methodology that aids our "uncovering, foregrounding, and producing counter-narratives" that allow us to unearth, and "make visible," the contemporaneous politics of popular representation through which the viewing public formulates normalized understandings of youthful innocence in response to the efforts of the American Broadcast Company's cultural intermediaries. Before proceeding, we note that the viewing public's receptive understanding of youthful innocence through spectacular (multi)mediated representations is complex, and necessarily incomplete in that this spectacle is part of an "increasing cultural complexity which forces viewers to make difficult intellectual and affective decisions" (Collins, 1994, p. 61) about the meaning(s) of popular programming. Thus, despite reservations about being able to delineate a singular message produced by televisual producers, throughout the following we will argue that the dominant narratives seen within the LLWS works in concert with other mass mediated spectacles to reinforce dominant and hegemonic truths (Denzin & Lincoln, 2005) about the contemporary sociopolitical condition regarding youth/nation/globe— thereby helping to legitimate, through populist advocacy, the innocence/ criminalization of youth at the local level, and American jingoism, militarism, and geo-political expansionism more broadly (McLaren, 1994).

Media Spectacle, Sport, and Youth Culture

Building upon the growing number of critical investigations into the labor practices and processes associated with televised sport production (see Gruneau, 1989; MacNeill, 1996; Silk, 1999, 2002; Silk, Slack, & Amis, 2000; Silk & Amis, 2000), this study offers an ethnographically oriented account of both the labor, and indeed, the laborers, responsible for the production of 2003 LLWS television broadcasts. More specifically, this study focuses on the micropolitics of production (the power and ability to represent the televised event emphasizing certain elements while downplaying, or even ignoring, others), and the ways in which they related to the macropolitics of the contemporary American moment (the discursive modes through which America has come to understand itself).

A review of production craft, and the economic and political dimensions of sporting texts,[1] is therefore essential to understanding the sport media as a powerful public pedagogy, through which various discourses are mobilized in regard to the organizing and disciplining of everyday life and popular consciousness in the service and support of particular social and political agendas (Andrews, 1995; Giroux, 2001; Grossberg, 1992, 1997, 2005). Within the United States, recent work has tended to see contemporary sporting economies as deep-seated and insidious components of the highly charged neo-conservative political trajectory of the Bush administration (see e.g., Falcous & Silk, 2005; Giardina, 2005; King, 2005; McDonald, 2005;

Silk & Falcous, 2005). In this formulation, and perhaps intensified after the rupture in imperial management (Cocco & Lazzarato, 2002) (at least in the United States), media sport has been thrust into the contemporary lexicon of consensus within which America's rightward shift (Giroux, 2005; Grossberg, 2005) is largely unacknowledged and uncontested. Thus we will argue that through the LLWS, like other forms of the corporate media, "the American public has been proferred a vision of democracy that is a mixture of Sunday barbecue banality, American Gladiators jocksniffery, AMWAY enterprise consciousness, and the ominous rhetoric of 'New World Order' jingoism" (McLaren, 1994, p. 193). In particular, and following McLaren, the sport media has become an emotive forum for the reaffirmation of conservative, right-leaning politics, specifically through the deification of normative white, heterosexual, male, Christian (sporting) bodies that matter (Butler, 1993; Zylinska, 2004).

Such imperial aims that speak to a (resurgent) nation-state sovereignty, often simultaneously, working with and against, neoliberal visions of a market economy characterized by accelerated economic momentum, free flows of capital without borders, international cooperation, and, global democracy, all policed and supervised by corporate imperial (as opposed to national sovereign) rule (Grossberg, 2005; Wang, 2002). Delineated at length within Hardt and Negri's (2000) provocative tome *Empire*, we appear to be in a new age characterized by the apparent displacement of national sovereignty by global structures and circuits of capital production/accumulation best described as, "an array of national and supranational organizations operating under a single logic of rule . . . a decentered and deterritoralizing apparatus of rule that progressively incorporates the entire global realm within its open expanding frontiers" (p. xii). This new form of sovereignty emphasizes an ideology of dispersed economic liberalism that seemingly lacks a definite, centralized, locus of power; rather, one that roams free with the drift of benign capital, supported by markets, free trade, transnational organizations, and, supranational juridical structures in which politics and morality are usurped by economics and management (Brown & Szeman, 2002; Wang, 2002).

In other words, most sporting spectacles are amongst the ever-growing mass of ideologically-like spectacles that have been used to serve the decidedly regressive cultural politics of the contemporary moment. Politics that:

> invoke patriotism as a cloak for carrying out a reactionary economic and political agenda on the domestic front while simultaneously cultivating an arrogant self-righteousness in foreign affairs in which the United States portrays itself as the epitome of purity, goodness, and freedom, while its opposition is equated with the forces of absolute evil. (Giroux, 2003, p. 2)

Thus, in one sense, we will argue that the production of the 2003 LLWS was no different than the haunting way in which it has become normal for mediated spectacles to represent the United States in ridiculous and blindly celebratory manners.[2] That this type of programming has become entrenched within the machinations of the Bush administration's "violent politics of truth concerning America and the so-called threats by terrorists to democracy and freedom" (Denzin, 2004a, p. 137) is a potentially devastating movement in popular culture. Perhaps, most dangerously, sport has thus been internally mobilized within the United States as a central symbolic tool in the contemporary totalitarian regime as an Orwellian theater of misrepresentation and propaganda (Denzin, 2004b).

"The creation and cultivation of a culture of fear has had both an impact on youth while creating a crisis that attacks the very heart of democracy in the United States" (Giroux, 2003, p. xxi). As such, and following Steinberg and Kincheloe (1997, 2004), Giroux (2003) and Grossberg (2005), it can be argued quite literally that the United States is waging a war on its own youth. In other words, sporting spectacles, Fox News, and other mass media productions continually espouse the inherent greatness of the American way, and take part in an unstructured, yet collective, forgetfulness which leaves out the real struggles that minorities from multifarious identity formations (class/ethnicity/gender/age/ability to name a few) must endure in the United States (Baudrillard, 2002; Giroux, 1996). This leaves the representation of children through media spectacles in an oppositional and tenuous position where:

> On the one hand, it [youth] is something to be cherished. Kids are the embodiment of America's future, the fulfillment not only of the American dream but also of its promise as a nation. Kids' innocence not only means that they need our protection but even more, that they define a kind of ideal of love and openness. When there is trouble, it cannot be their fault; it must always be outside forces-society-that have produced "kids in trouble." On the other hand, childhood/youth is dangerous and alien. Kids are then seen as troublesome and threatening, and when they are in trouble, it is their own fault; it is because they are trouble. How these two views are balanced determines how the country treats its kids at any particular moment. (Grossberg, 2005, p. 3)

Unfortunately, more often than not children are being increasingly (mis)represented through various forms of media as murderous, dangerous, and uncontrollable—despite overwhelming empirical evidence to the contrary (Giroux, 2003; Grossberg, 2005).

Given this intensified two-fold attack on otherness, both to outside nations/nationalities/ways of being and inside on (American) youth, our response in the form of this exercise is part of a political agenda that endeavors to foster a more progressive future where the utopian ideals of justice, empowerment, freedom, and love (Denzin, 2004a) are the most important values in American/worldwide society. Importantly in regard to this chapter, while we be looking at the (ab)use of children by the American Broadcast Company (ABC) (and, given its connection as a subsidiary, by the Walt Disney Co.), to promote a proto-fascist white, upper-class American agenda, there will be a distinct focus on the war on youth (Giroux, 2003). While focusing on the place of children within the contemporary socio-political moment, care will be taken to not degrade the many other highly interconnected subject-position identities that are being taken advantage of during this regressive moment. Thus, following Grossberg (2005, p. 113):

> By talking about children and youth, I don't mean to sound like I am privileging this axis over other—racial, ethnic, gendered, or sexual—axes of difference. And while, on each of these axes we are witnessing rearticulated and reinvigorated attacks, I do believe that there is something new about the attack on children, and that it is so little addressed either in public or intellectual life, suggests that it may provide some kind of key to understanding the larger revolution.

Finally, in attending to the larger revolution, we will attempt to expose the regressive acts nurtured and expressed in and through, the affective realm of popular culture, and these commercial cannibalizations of the mind-numbing nationalist assaults and war cries of the American Right (which, of course, co-articulate race, gender, sexual, and class identities within and against local, national, and [especially] transnational contexts, [Giardina, 2005]) provide the context for our ethnographic-oriented interrogation[3] of America's national pastime.

The Little League World Series

Within the present climate of national and global uncertainty characterized by ubiquitous violence, endless attacks on democracy, a seemingly perpetual state of war on an endless supply of evil like drugs/terrorism/global warming/Iraq/youth (Denzin, 2004a, 2004b; Giroux, 2005; Hardt & Negri, 2005; Roy, 2001), the very institution of the LLWS—as embodied in the corporeal performance of children playing baseball—has come to represent a cathartic paean to a simpler, more peaceful, stable, and inveterately mythic vision of America as utopia. The affectivity of youthful innocence at the LLWS is so pervasive in its programming that it has created the context for one ABC producer to mention that it:

is about appointment family television in a lot of ways. The goals are
so right for what goes on elsewhere in the world where there's violence
and drugs and everything else. This is what's good about a lot of things
in life, not just sport. (ABC Production Crew, 2003)

More importantly, ABC's ability to (mythically) represent a time of sim-
plicity, peace, harmony, and baseball has become wildly popular for such
a seemingly marginal event. As a product of the Little League Corporation
(LLCo), the LLWS draws well over 300,000 spectators yearly, and is televised
by the American Broadcast Corporation and the Entertainment & Sport
Programming Networks (ESPN & ESPN2). Founded in 1947 as a four-team,
single-elimination, event featuring four sides from within the United States,
by 2003 the tournament had grown to incorporate teams from 105 countries,
who compete in 16,000 games, over 45 days for the privilege of reaching the
LLWS tournament in Williamsport.

From the outset, and perhaps not unexpectedly given the moral right and
superior status historically bestowed upon it through proximal contamina-
tion by the seeping doctrine of American Exceptionalism (cf. Ferguson,
2004; Hardt & Negri, 2005; Sennet, 1999), the Little League World Series
has historically been about inculcating young Americans and their foreign
counterparts with hyper-conservative ideals. These ideals, characterized by
family values, traditional gender roles, youthful innocence, in addition to a
love of God, country, and capitalism (see Van Auken & Van Auken, 2001),
run distinctly against a Communist-inspired "Godless ideology" of equality, social justice and welfare (Herbert Brownell Jr., Attorney General of the
United States, 1954 Little League World Series program, in Van Auken & Van
Auken, 2001, p. 64). As such, and under the mandate of appointment family
television, the LLWS has become an important space for the deification of a
White, upper-middle-class, belief system that assigns blame for the inability
to adhere to/become successful in the neoliberal economic system on the
individual (Harvey, 2005).

Partly as a result of its overt pandering to White, upper-middle-class
consciousness over the past half century, the tournament has achieved a
cult-like following in the United States—particularly in suburban American
homes (ABC, personal communication, 2004). It is important to note here
that as the official *World* Championship of Little League Baseball (Musburger,
2001; Van Auken & Van Auken, 2001), the LLWS is set in a context through
which the understanding of the world is prefigured on the centrality and
preeminence of the United States and things American.[4] Further, in purely
economic terms, ABC's success at (re)creating this context over the past
45 years[5] has driven market-value of the LLWS upward. For example, the
LLWS was first aired live in 1989, and just over a decade later coverage has

expanded to include game coverage from both the *United States* and *International* brackets on ABC, ESPN, and ESPN2, and forms a central part of ABC's mid-August ratings. Interestingly, and somewhat disturbingly (given that the athletes are generally 11- and 12-year-old boys), the ratings have become so high that the LLWS final outdrew game seven of the National Hockey League's Stanley Cup Final in 2002 (ABC, personal communication, 2003). By 2003, 26 of the 32 games held in Williamsport were aired live; the six games not covered being preliminary games from the International bracket. Following Debord's (1994) broader polemic of a spectacular society in which the spectacle serves, this chapter focuses on the production of the 2003 LLWS media spectacle, offering analysis of the relationships between the singular spectacular event (Tomlinson, 2002)—the LLWS—that cannot be divorced from the society of the spectacle of which it is a constituent and constituting element. Therefore, the balance of this chapter will delineate the spectacular use of youth to help underpin the dominant socio-cultural ideologies normalized by the dominant political movement of the times—the New Right's neoliberal agenda.

The Production of a Spectacle

At present, a strong argument could be made that the LLWS is an event that has always been deeply embedded with dominant American sociopolitical sentiment, and, given its rise in popularity, that there is a need to critically unpack the creation of its spectacular embodiment. To best understand the event we will describe how the 2003 LLWS spectacle was formulated and executed. Then, given this context, in conjunction with our understanding of the post-9/11 sociopolitical moment, we will be able to delve deeper into the actual narrative storyline the production workers attempted to formulate.

Prior to the LLWS, both in-game producers and features producers (as well as their teams that consisted of announcers, researchers, graphics creators, and camera-operators) were instructed "to put (their) ears to the ground" (ABC, personal communication, 2004) to give the viewers "what they wanted" (ABC, personal communication, 2004) through the creation of pre-game 'teases', in-game stories and information about the teams, players, and Williamsport (field notes, 2003; Gowdy Jr., 2003). Based on post-production research from the 2002 LLWS and pre-production meetings before the event, the producers of the 2003 LLWS decided that what the viewer wanted to see were four interrelated narrative storylines: "'[great] moments', 'kids having fun', 'a day in the life of a Little Leaguer', and the tournament as the 'international pastime'" (ABC, personal communication, 2003).

In addition to pre-tournament commercials seeking to contextualize the LLWS as multi-ethnic, all-inclusive, and innocent, the manufacture of affectively anchoring segments—referred to as features—designed to connect the broadcast and the audience, are perhaps the most integral part in forwarding specific narrative stories during sporting spectacles (Andrews, 1998; Gruneau, 1989; Silk, 1999, 2001, 2002). Through features segments the producers played a large role in creating meaning (Hall, 1980; Tomlinson, 2002) for the event. During our interview and observation period, we could discern that it was through the use of oft-repeated, professional strategies like: scripting a storyline that was read during each opening *tease*,[6] creating several short transition elements to be shown prior to, or during, innings, and, forming short baseball fundamental teaching pieces, that the features producers felt they were able to forward the four interconnected intended narratives (ABC, personal communication, 2003). As with most other spectacular arrangements, most feature clips at the 2003 LLWS were underscored by emotive music, and highlights from previous games, to "inform the viewer about the game's participants, and excite them about the impending contest" (ABC, personal communication, 2003; field notes 2003). Thus the ultimate goal of the features crew was to get viewers to invest themselves enough to watch the event by making the "contest itself . . . the climax which resolves the curiosity and excitement built up over the day" (Gruneau, Whitson, & Cantelon, 1988, p. 272), thereby creating a televisual product that will gather the largest amount of viewers (ABC, personal communication, 2004).

Given their mandate by the in-game producers to "treat each game differently" (ABC, personal communication, 2003), and provide a different script with a different angle "on a game-by-game basis" (ABC, personal communication, 2003), the features team had near-total control over whom, or what, they were and were not taping which allowed for more directed meaningful segments of the 2003 LLWS televisual narrative. The smaller, six-person features team followed the same narrative themes throughout the duration of the 2003 LLWS. For example, one of the features producers informed us that their

> main goal is basically [to] tell great stories about the kids who come from all over the world to [the] Little League World Series. You know you can have these great transitions and great flashes but if you don't have a story, which you can tell throughout Little League, you pretty much have nothing. (personal interview, 2003)

In their efforts to construct and maintain a coherent narrative with the features producers, the in-game production crew—through filming, interviewing, and editing techniques—attempted to build an "instant relationship" (field notes, 2003) between the home-viewer and the athletes. To gather information on the domestic and international players, coaches, and participant's immediate family-members, ABC production workers asked the same set of 20 to 25 questions of each player, while probing for "unique and engaging stories" (ABC, personal communication, 2004) that would capture their intended audience in "team-by-team" fashion during the days leading up to the 2003 LLWS broadcast (ABC, personal communication, 2003). Additionally, the in-game graphics creators built visual effects for use on game-specific information,[7] and several on-field camera workers set up their locations around both the fields at the LLWS in such a way as to give a "professional," yet "youthful," feel to the spectacle (field notes 2003; ABC, personal communication, 2003). Finally, the in-game production team was in charge of providing the announcers information that they had gathered throughout the week, and conducted meetings helping to ensure that in conjunction with pre-production strategies like feature editing, advertisements, camera-use and positioning, and formulaic research questioning, a consistent *preferred narrative* would be presented to the consumer: one that celebrated the 2003 LLWS as a youthful yet *international* pastime (field notes 2003; ABC, personal communication, 2003; italics ours).

Executing International Innocence

At the outset of this project, the shaky and ironic relationship between the spectacularized narrative of wide-eyed youthful innocence, cultural diversity, and the corporate agenda of the United States—through which American law dictates that capital accumulation at all costs is the prime directive (Kelly, 2001)—became quite apparent. To illustrate, ABC's choice to celebrate the LLWS through the innocent eyes of youth that had yet to be jaded by world events such as 9/11, and the wars on Iraq and Afghanistan, would seem to be a progressive turn in the popular narrative strategies used by mainstream media companies. However, and following Giroux, this is a typical strategy employed by Disney and its subsidiaries that often creates affective renderings of "childhood innocence," and through its (multi)mediated products "produce identifications that define the United States as white, suburban, middle class, and heterosexual" (2001, p. 127).

Given Disney's propensity for producing multi-mediated accounts that serve to erase historical inequities by creating myriad utopian visions of youth, the production crew's effort to employ the first three narratives ([great] moments, kids having fun, a day in the life of a Little Leaguer) should come as no surprise. However, while in one sense the international pastime narrative logically fits into the Disney schematic, the choice to (re)present the tournament as all-inclusive seemed to run counter to American national popular opinion at the time, which, given the hyper-militaristic support of America, was characterized by (now dated) popular culture artefacts like Toby Keith's top-selling album *Shock n' Y'all* (2003), a schmaltzy revisiting of the 1980

United States *Miracle on Ice* hockey team through both the 2002 Salt Lake City Olympics and the Disney film *Miracle* (Silk & Falcous, 2005), and even from the unreported choice for the team from the *Transatlantic* (made up mostly of American expatriates) to refuse to recite the Little League Pledge which suggests they represent Saudi Arabia (field notes, 2003). Moreover, despite governmental calls for spectacular arrangements of American superiority (Silk, Bracey, & Falcous, 2007), the pre-production of the 2003 LLWS explicitly set out to distance itself from any form of U.S.-centric narrative. One of the marketing personnel for ABC explained the reasoning behind the choice to represent the 2003 LLWS as the International Pastime:

> Aside from it being an angle we've never taken, we figured that since it's the Little League World Series, we could highlight that in the promotion. More often than not, a "World" championship in any major sport is actually just a U.S. championship. This one is different, and since it's a U.S. team vs. a team from another country in the finals, we wanted to bring that element to the fore. Furthermore, since there are so many Spanish-speakers in the U.S., we thought we'd have fun with "Take Me Out to the Ballgame" (Sung in Spanish) in one of our executions. (personal interview, 2003)

He further reasoned that "in light of the patriotism and the 'things American angle', we really never let that enter our thinking. We're simply trying to make engaging, unique, likeable promotion(s) for our properties. We thought this would be something new and fresh" (personal communication 2003).

It was from this point of view that ABC/Disney tried to carve a niche of youthful innocence and togetherness in a world that, as a partial result of 9/11, had gone terribly wrong (Kellner, 2004). Though, in the past, ABC and LLCo have had a few issues maintaining the assumed innocence of the event,[8] as mentioned previously, their success in creating the popular belief that the LLWS is an idyllic utopia for children has blossomed into a lucrative commercial product. During the 2003 LLWS, the cultivation of cultural diversity and youthful innocence narratives were quite often the focus of both the production crew and announcers. For example, while observing their efforts we often found that the production crew would overtly stage and film scenes with the children—ranging from the seemingly benign team-wide first-look at *Lamade Field*, the exuberance on display when the teams initially encountered their living quarters, various team cheers and superstitions, to the questionable choice to tape and broadcast a boy's first experience meeting his newborn baby sister (a meeting that was delayed initially by his participation in the tournament and later added by ABC for dramatic effect) (field notes, 2003; Gowdy Jr., 2003).

Interestingly, the coverage of the *US* bracket tended to focus more on the seemingly innocent and youthful narrative of having fun—depicted as the ultimate goal for each team. On the contrary, however, the production crew found it easier to weave the cultural diversity narrative into games involving the *International* bracket, where less pre-game footage was available,[9] and less was known about the participants. Oftentimes the proclamation of the event as the international pastime was followed by shots of obvious *others* who were dressed in ethnic garb, and eating culturally specific food that was not sold at the event (Gowdy Jr., 2003). On the surface, this would seem to be an unabashed celebration of difference, but upon deeper inspection however, this could also be seen as contributing to the American sociopolitical trajectory in the post-9/11 moment which suggested that converse to rogue nations like Iraq, Afghanistan, Cuba, and/or Venezuela, individuals in the United States are treated in a fair, just, and equitable manner (Giroux, 2005).

More to the point, in the following section, we outline how, as a "spectacular" media event, the LLWS was related to the broader society which it serves, and of which it is an extension (Debord 1994), and was centered on a populist platform that positioned the United States as "hallowed," "moral," "indispensable"; a "vast inaccessible reality that can never be questioned" (Debord, 1994, #12[10]). In this sense, we point to the particular slippages, and outright fissures, in the (faux)progressive notions of internationalism, suggesting that the production of the 2003 LLWS was deeply embedded in the reproduction of an ever-growing and dangerous ideology fueled by the American government and that has seeped into the public sphere (Grossberg, 2005; Kelly, 2001), thus necessarily eschewing a world promoting democracy, human rights, and the international rule of law (Hardt & Negri, 2005). As one of the production crew explicitly explained: "why would Americans [viewers] be excited about sharing its culture? People hate America. We're a selfish country. We have what everybody wants, and it doesn't seem like we'd share. We think our shit doesn't stink. We don't share." Yet, despite this portrayal of innocence, of distance from the aggressive appropriation, mobilization, and substantiation of commercialized sport within the geo-political trajectories of the current Bush administration (and thereby resistive Anti-Americanisms [see e.g., Giroux, 2005; Harvey, 2003; Sardar & Wyn-Davies, 2002, 2004]), the international narrative straddled the imperialist aims of the current administration, espousing one very clear and superior unilateral hegemon (Hardt & Negri, 2000) that dictated this cartographic, if not, epistemological, space of the LLWS spectacle—the United States.

(Sporting) Superiority

Embedded within a sense of internationalism and youthful innocence, we argue that the LLWS stands as an exemplar of the supposedly ethically and morally based historical destiny that the United States should lead the world (Hardt & Negri, 2005). Further, we assert that the LLWS contributes to a discourse that is at the center of what David Harvey (2003) terms the shift, although not outright replacement, in the dominant U.S. political regime from a neoliberal state to neoconservative imperialism. In other words, the LLWS spectacle was bound with a society which has been urged by the current administration to recognize the "inherent greatness" (Ferguson, 2004, pp. 43–44) of U.S.-led corporate capitalism in the instantiation of an imperialist empire in which the "sovereign must stand above the law and take control" (Hardt & Negri, 2004, p. 9). The new role of the United States in this world is thus not simply about nationalisms or internationalisms, but about how, in the space of a mediated sporting spectacle focusing on innocent children, sovereign nation-state politics intersect and interact with emergent modes of power, religiosity, moral tyranny, and sovereignty. In the case of the LLWS, and despite claims of cultural diversity, we argue that these processes were evident in the placing of the United States at the center of international relations and in the language of Empire.

Through this understanding of the *foreign* policy of the present-day U.S. neo-conservatism (embodied in the 'election' of George W. Bush, and predicated on moral principles based in Christian fundamentalism) 9/11 has become framed within this logic as a sign of God's anger at the so-called permissiveness of a society that allows abortion and homosexuality. This form of rhetoric has filtered through the mechanisms of what Henry Giroux (2005) has termed the *proto* fascism of the Bush administration: the cult of traditionalism, the corporatization of civil society, a culture of fear and patriotic correctness, the collapse of the separation between church and state, a language of official newspeak, and the ownership and control of the media. Moreover, following Hardt and Negri (2004), we view the perpetual state of war located within U.S. neoconservatism as a regime of biopower for which the 2003 LLWS spectacle both served and extended the neoconservative agenda in place at that particular time.

As a spectacle fulfilling the needs of the new-Right agenda, a secondary narrative proffered by ABC was that the LLWS was the *field of dreams* (quite clearly an updated take on the national pastime mythologizing machine known as *Field of Dreams* [1989]) for international competitors. As was announced prior to the *International* Bracket final, the United States was the place on earth in which dreams (the American Dream) could be realized:

> Across spacious oceans and desert lands, they have traveled to *their field of dreams*. Stories these twelve year olds bring back to their countries of great lessons learned. It's a story of a Russian team that won their first game ever, or a Venezuelan fisherman who sent his son with 4 dol-

lars to play, or maybe even a story of love… We've all come to expect dominance from the *Far East*. When Japan defeated Mexico City, they *earned* their seventh consecutive trip to the International championship. So why has Japan been so successful? Maybe it is been the long practice sections, or *their* ideals of perfection, or maybe the answer is they love, and dream, baseball as much as anyone…anywhere. Like the *Far East*, Curaçao's heart also beats for baseball. Free willing *spirits* enjoying the warmth of Williamsport, and a passion of a great game … But no matter what the outcome, they will return to their countries with stories to tell. But what makes *us* different is what brings the opposite ends of the world together. (Gowdy Jr. 2003; italics added)

Through a critical reading of the narrative produced by ABC, it is quite easy to see that this passage is instructive in many ways. Not only is this particular game the culmination of the *International* bracket and allows the winner to earn the right to get to the game that matters (the World Series Championship game against the U.S. representative), but it serves to position America as the hub, the special place, in which others can achieve their dreams.

It should come as no surprise that ABC would discursively construct *us* (U.S.) as a special place for which other cultures can visit, learn, be free, succeed—realize a dream—and, at the same time, continue to mark off the United States as different and clearly superior. Indeed, this narrative formed a consistent theme for the ABC production crew and LLCo workers who, in more personal moments, often essentialized, and in some cases demonized, the success of the "foreign" and "New York" teams[11] from past years as some sort of natural (dare we say: genetic/moral) differences between the 'invaders' and the teams of mostly white, upper-middle class, suburban children that have success in the United States (field notes, 2003). Unfortunately, this ultimately serves to cloud the extreme socioeconomic differences between the teams competing in the LLWS, which in many cases, is American affluence versus third-world dependency that clearly problematizes claims that this tournament is at all innocent.

For example, according to Stephen D. Mosher (2001), many of the children representing teams from the Caribbean and Latin America come to the tournament extremely underfed, and gain several pounds during their ten-day stay, a hunger that is compounded by extreme jet-lag that many experience after the long trip to Williamsport (field notes, 2003). Seeing that "many of these children from South of the U.S. look drawn, tired, and withered" (field notes, 2003), it was surprising to us that rather than question the socio-political reasons why these children live in the devastating conditions that they do, through the lens of "superiority," ABC "really played up" (ABC, personal communication, 2003) acts of "charity" to other nations. Using this strategy, ABC superficially celebrated teams from Moscow, Russia; Altagracia, Venezuela; Dharan, Saudi Arabia; and Mexico City, Mexico coming to the utopian baseball fields of the U.S., while at the same time doing nothing to question the domination of South American, Middle Eastern, and Eastern nation states (Butler, 2002; Giroux, 2005; Klein, 1988, 1991, 1995; Zinn, 2003).

In fact, much to the contrary, the features crew produced a series of vignettes to highlight, despite inequalities, that the 2003 LLWS was contested on a "level playing field" (Little League, personal communication, 2003). One such feature focused on Magglio Ordoñez, a native Venezuelan and an All-Star left fielder for Major League Baseball's Chicago White Sox, who learned that the team from Altagracia, Venezuela, came to the United States without shoes, gloves, or uniforms, and a single bat made out of a wood post (field notes, 2003; Gowdy Jr., 2003; Little League, personal communication, 2003). Upon notification of the team's economic disparity Ordoñez cut the team a blank check, and told the players "to buy whatever they want with it" (field notes, 2003; ABC, personal communication, 2003). Of course, that Ordoñez, a native Venezuelan who was *living* the American Dream, was placed on a pedestal, further reinforced the special place of the U.S. as a *field of dreams*—yet says nothing of the incessant race/class-ism endured by *foreigners* at the hands of official immigration policies, the directives of the Department of Homeland (In)Security, racial profiling on highways and at airports, or the physical and psychological abuse on the bodies and minds of the abject American (see e.g., Ahmed, 2002; Giroux, 2005; Harvey, 2003; McLaren, 2002; McLaren & Martin, 2004; Merskin, 2004). Indeed, that the executive producer would claim the LLWS as "a piece of Americana" hawked through satellite to 105 countries (Gowdy Jr., 2003)—then have his employees joke on the side that the 16-year-old assistant coach from Venezuela was constantly in trouble for "hitting on American girls" (field notes, 2003)—further emphasizes the somewhat messier juxtapositions and intersections between nation-state sovereignty and emergent modes of power, religiosity, and (racialized) moral tyranny within the neo-conservatism of the Bush regime.

Taking account of the aforementioned, we assert that the LLWS has deployed empty metaphors, manipulated (if not replicated) discourse in the service of the Bush regime, and generally, through language, conflated war, religiosity, militarization, hyper-conservative morals, and sport. Using Henry Giroux's (2005) belief that in the United States through this type of programming we are experiencing a "real" version of Orwellian Newspeak that when coupled with Umberto Eco's (1995, p. 15) concept of "eternal fascism" works to produce an impoverished vocabulary, and an elementary syntax [that limits] the instruments for complex and critical reasoning." Giroux (2005) further suggests that the tools of language, sound, and image are being "increasingly appropriated in an effort to diminish the capacity of the American public to think critically . . . to engage in critical debates, translate private considerations into public concerns, and recognize the distortion and lies that underlie many of the current government politics" (pp. 22–23).

The stage for such action, fully bound with the seemingly daily collapse of the separation between church and state, was set at the 2001 LLWS[12] when President Bush visited Williamsport following his induction into the Little League Hall of Excellence:

> You know years ago when I was playing on those dusty little league fields in west Texas I never dreamed I'd be president of the United States, and I can assure you I never dreamt I'd be admitted into the Little League Hall of Excellence . . . one of the things I did dream about was making it to Williamsport, PA, for the LLWS. Little League is a family sport, I can remember my mother sitting behind the backstop in Midland Texas, telling me what to do . . . she still tells me what to do, and my advice to all the players is listen to your mother. But for all the moms and dads who take special time out of their lives are able to play the great sport of baseball thank you from the bottom of our hearts. You prioritized your family and that's crucial for a *healthy world* to make sure our families remain strong . . . On behalf of the presidency thank you for what you do, may God bless the teams that play here, may god bless the families represented here, and may God bless the great United States of America. Thank you very much.

Herein, Bush evoked strong family and religious values—although we are careful to note here that not all religions are equal in Bushworld, since he is of course referring to Christianity—utilizing the LLWS as another space in which to parade religious rhetoric as political identity and in which to direct the leadership and policies of a "healthy" world. Unchallenged Christian (moral-familial) authority at the LLWS is not exclusive to Bush's rhetorical speeches. Prior to *every* sanctioned Little League Baseball game—no matter where it is played throughout the world—the young participants are expected to recite the Little League Pledge which states: "I trust in God/I love my Country, and will respect its laws/I will play fair, and strive to win/but win or lose, I will always do my best" (Van Auken & Van Auken, 2001, p. 42).

Further, during the portion of the LLWS tournament played in Williamsport, awards are given out to the Little League Parents and Mom of the year which celebrates the good deeds of wed—and by U.S. law, heterosexual—parents of U.S. Little Leaguers[13]. While these awards, and specifically the use of God in the recitation of the Little League Pledge, have been questioned in the recent past (see Kemsley, 2003), the complaints have been viewed as nothing more than the liberal attack on right-wing Christianity, morality, and tradition. Suffice to say this "tradition is steeped in the demonization of youth as well as unequal relations of race, class, gender, and sexuality" (Giroux, 2003; Grossberg, 2005). Given the recent (mis)treatment of athletes like Carlos Delgado, Toni Smith, and Steve Nash who refused to recognize renditions of the U.S. national anthem or "God Bless America" (see Giardina, 2005), the reaction by those in power to the questioning of their "superior"morality hardly comes as a shock. Even at the 2003 LLWS this came to the fore in the stands as we heard one of the parents from Michigan comment that, in regard to the 5′11″ superstar pitcher from Curacao (Tharick Martines), "they don't start counting their age until they're two down there" (field notes, 2003). Sentiments such as these (which were pervasive throughout the event) only further serve to position the United States as a morally innocent entity in the face of "attacks from foreigners," both symbolic and literal, that must be prevented at all costs.

Through this context then, the public space of the LLWS was an important cultural location for deploying the values of militarism, in the form of the 2003 LLWS, which among almost all forms of popular life, has become increasingly organized around values supporting a highly militarized, patriarchal, and jingoistic culture that is undermining "centuries of democratic gains" (Giroux, 2004). For instance, despite ABC's conscious attempts to promote intercultural goodwill during the World Championship game (with repeated shots and announcer narrative of the Japanese and Floridian players congratulating one another after hitting homeruns), advancing the notion of innocence at the event by parading Mickey Mouse around the field during the fourth inning, and downplaying the significance of the United States playing another country,[14] the growing culture of militarism was played out by children on the diamonds of the LLWS.

More to the point, through an early discussion with a Little League official, we were told that Little League had taken steps to join the heightened counter-terrorist police state of post-9/11 "America" by implementing a simulated post-attack exercise in June (personal interview, 2003), and installing metal detectors that all people entering the Little League premises had to pass through (field notes, 2003). Further, immediately prior to the final game and following a rendition of the "Star-Spangeled Banner" by a local State Policeman (another site that is increasingly indistinguishable from the military), there was a four-fighter-jet flyover before the final game while a group of local Air Force and Marine Corps servicemen held a flag that took up over one-third of the outfield during which Dugout (the official Little League mascot) could be seen standing at attention—an act not seen during a rendition of the abbreviated Japanese national anthem. Coupling the latter with the fact that LLCo and ABC both vehemently defended the tradition of having local fourth graders paint trash cans representing the different countries participating in the event in an effort to teach students about other cultures—which, for example, led to the somewhat telling juxtaposition of having the Jewish Star of David (representing Israel) prominently displayed on a trash can while players evoked God in their pre-game rituals (ABC personal communication, 2004; field notes, 2003; LLCo personal communication, 2004)—the power and dominance of the United States was undeniably apparent.

In this sense, and as Gilroy (2001) has contended—somewhat bolstered by the Bush administration's frequent use of sporting metaphors (see King, 2005)—that war, in language, has become sport, highlighting the important role of the U.S. sporting media in foreclosing the possibility for critique and vibrant democracy, instead deteriorating into a combination of commercialism, propaganda and entertainment while shrouding the (domineering) realities of the event (Giroux, 2005). At the LLWS, and as discussed above, not only did the crew reify the neo-conservativism of Bush by downplaying the overt police state of this new America, but language, national superiority, and, imperialist ambitions fused together to (re)assert the language(s) and success of the colossus (Ferguson, 2004).

Coda: Conducting Children Through Children

> We really wanted to bring it back to the kids . . . *integrated with the stories we set out to tell.* (ABC, personal interview, 2003; italics ours)

To this point, the 2003 LLWS has been discussed as a spectacular media event that was framed as a highly scripted, controlled, conscious effort by media production workers to, however, superficially, represent the event as a celebration of a truly international youth pastime. Through the seemingly 'innocent' eyes of youth a narrative was constructed that served to erase an historic moment in which the world was far from naïve, idyllic, and safe from the damning effects of neoliberal capitalism, emergent modes of power, religiosity, moral tyranny and sovereignty. Further, the information uncovered by our research ethnography, and presented in the context of this chapter, endeavors to extend the small, yet growing, work on the U.S. (sport) media. In so doing, we have hoped to draw attention to the often unquestioned and insidious place of sport as part of the powerful economy of affect that serves particular geo-political trajectories (see, for example, Falcous & Silk, 2005; King, 2005; McDonald, 2005; Silk & Falcous, 2005). More chillingly, given that its focus is the seemingly benign realm of children's baseball, the LLWS broadcast is able to disguise itself and evade critical consciousness and critique.

In an effort to combat this line of thinking we vehemently implore that the LLWS has become another space in which our society needs to contest Disneyfied innocence (Giroux, 1995, 2002). Thus, far from the sanitized world that Disney's youth seem to live in, we would also argue that the 2003 LLWS production not only provides a space for a perverse form of public pedagogy that conditions—if not trains—American youth in the doctrines of Bush's fanatical, fascist, neo-conservative, visions of geo-political domination, it also does so just as the same administration is waging an internal, domestic war against the poor, youth, women, people of color, and the elderly (Giroux, 2003, 2004, 2005; Grossberg, 2005). In this sense, the LLWS becomes vehicle for commercial and political exploitation of children in the service of the New Right Bush agenda that simultaneously punishes children through the seemingly endless removal of multiple social benefits for kids (Giroux, 2003; Grossberg, 2005).

The LLWS thus provides a seemingly innocent space that sneaks into the collective (un)conscious of a captive audience through a powerful pedagogical discourse of geo-political domination, a discourse "sculpted from the spare rib of a world laid waste by America's foreign policy" (Butler, 2002, p. 183). Children, then, become the focus for the most perverse (maybe pedophilic) reaches of the Bush administration. As such, along with an array of other practices for shaping identities and forms of life—advertising, marketing, the proliferation of goods, the multiple stylizations of the act of purchasing, cinemas, videos, pop music, lifestyle magazines, television soap operas, advice programs, and talk shows—the LLWS spectacle contributes toward a "civilizing project very different from the 19th-century attempts to form moral, sober, responsible, and obedient individuals, and from 20th-century projects for the shaping of civility, social solidarity, and social responsibility" (Rose, 1999, p. 1399). Operating on, and targeting, the troops assembled in the *Bush Youth*, ethopolitics (Rose, 1999) forms moral, sober, responsible, and obedient individuals, boundaries preserved through design, consumer practices, and more explicitly, through regulative and normative codes of conduct—the LLWS being a prime (time) space for celebrating (and thereby governing) such behavior.

Notes

1. In addition to observations, semi-structured interviews (Fetterman, 1989) were conducted with LLCo's volunteer "uncles," security members, media, and publications departments, ABC's entire features production crew, researchers, the *Lamade* Stadium graphics team, the "A" announcing team, as well as the *Lamade* Stadium game director, producer, and co-ordinator. Further, formal, semi-structured interviews (Amis, 2005), were conducted with key actors (Fetterman, 1989) of LLCo and ABC that centred on the dominant meanings ABC wished to advance through the production of the LLWS. Finally, following the event, and to supplement the interview and observation data, the to-air broadcast of the entire 2003 LLWS tournament was analysed using a semiotic methodology advocated by Gruneau et al. (1988).

2. For instance, it is now normal for ABC's representations of Super Bowl XXXVII to be hosted, in part, on the USS *Midway*, and on numerous other warships at 'undisclosed Gulf locations'; for the kick off of the 2003–04 National Football League to be presented live from the Washington monument in Washington, DC (prefaced by President Bush's announcement that it was "time to play some football"); for ESPN to present *Sportscenter* live from Camp Arifjan, Kuwait; for the Olympic coverage of Iraq's first soccer game to be framed by NBC as America freeing Iraq and making it possible for the team to compete; for the delayed 2002 Super Bowl and the 2002 Salt Lake City Opening Ceremony to provide the space for the revision of history (see Cole & Cate, 2004; Falcous & Silk, 2005; King, 2005; Silk & Andrews, in press, Silk & Falcous, 2005; Silk, Falcous, & Bracey, 2007).

3. The micro-ethnographic (Wollcott, 1995) approach was employed in an effort to better grasp and analyze the economic, political, and cultural intricacies underpinning the production of an international sporting event in an attempt to "demystif[y] [some of] the images that parade before our lives and through which we conceptualize the world and our role within it" (Jhally, 1995, p. 86). Entrance to the LLWS was acquired through the Director of Media Relations at LLCo, late in March 2003 who supplied access to ABC's production, editing, and graphics trucks. Throughout the build up and the event itself, access was granted to observe, ask questions, and collect whatever other data were available (such as press releases, production guidelines) (Hammersley & Atkinson, 1995) with the ABC/ESPN research team and production labor force that included producers, directors, and, features crew, in addition to LLCo's entire labour force.

4. For example, the LLWS has sought to guard its masculinist, hegemonic vision of America by protecting its sporting space from female intrusion (LLWS had to back down after several court decisions based on Title IX in 1974, allowing girls to compete); police non-American successes and (international teams were banned for one year in 1974 for, of all things, emphasizing winning, while at the time of our initial research, all 141 award winners found in the Little League Hall of Excellence were U.S. citizens); ban all national anthems except the "Star Spangled Banner" until 2002 (and still only play abbreviated versions of the anthems of international teams); and, alter LLWS rules to ensure a team representing the United States would always appear in the final (following an all International final in 1985) (Van Auken & Van Auken, 2001). The last rule change was strongly suggested by ABC (personal communication, LLCo, 2003) and speaks to the notion that any hope for cultural diversity and respect will necessarily be set aside when market-value comes in direct contradistinction to it.

5. ABC has owned the rights to broadcast the LLWS in some capacity since the early 1960s. This is the longest standing relationship between a sporting event and a broadcaster in United States history.

6. A tease at the LLWS could be defined as the short 1–3 minute, highly emotive, introduction to each game aired on ABC.

7. The current game's score, inning, base runners, outs, and speed at which the last pitch was thrown.

8. In 1992 a team from the Philippines was found to have children who were over age, and, more famously, in 2001 Little League superstar, Danny Almonte, was also found to be too old to participate in the event.

9. Prior to the LLWS the regional championship games played in each of the eight United States Bracket regions aired on ESPN and ESPN2. There was no broadcast of any International Bracket regional finals.

10. In accordance with Kellner (2001), due to the differences in the many translations of *The Society of the Spectacle*, when referencing Debord, we will use numbered paragraphs from the text.

11. It was interesting that the workers at LLCo (a large majority of whom were White, upper-middle class) would include the New York teams from 2001/2002 in with the "others" from International competition since the New York City teams were mostly comprised of Dominican and Puerto Rican children.

12. The importance of Bush being at the 2001 LLWS just days before the 9/11 attacks, and during the event at which Danny Almonte was celebrated as a hero only to be found out for cheating is not lost on the authors here. His statement later that "he was disappointed that Almonte would cheat, but that he wasn't disappointed in his fastball" is exactly the type of two-faced

response that often emanates from the mostly white visitors, and producers of the LLWS spectacle.

13. Interestingly, former major league baseball player Ken Caminiti's (who publicly admitted to steroid use during his time in Major League Baseball, which contributed to a dangerous drug addiction and his eventual death) parents won the award in 1997.

14. This was partially achieved by lowering the volume of its in-crowd microphone feed when the throng of 45,000 people began chanting "U.S.A., U.S.A." or, somewhat more arrogantly, "America, America." The chanting was deafening at the event and only referred to the U.S. champion as the "team from Florida."

References

Ahmed, M. (2002). Homeland insecurities: Racial violence the day after September 11. *Social Text*, *20*(3), 101–115.

Andrews, D. L. (1995). Excavating Michael Jordan: Notes on a critical pedagogy of sporting representation. In G. Rail & J. Harvey (Eds.), *Sport and postmodern times: Culture, gender, sexuality, the body and sport*. Albany: State University of New York Press.

Andrews, D. L. (1998). Feminizing Olympic reality: Preliminary dispatches from Baudrillard's Atlanta. *International Review for the Sociology of Sport*, *33*(1), 5–18.

Andrews, D. L. (2006, November). Toward a physical cultural studies. Alan Ingham Memorial Address, *North American Society for the Sociology of Sport Conference*: Vancouver, B.C.

Baudrillard, J. (2002). *Screened out*. London: Verso.

Brown, M., & Szeman, I. (2002). The global coliseum: On empire. *Cultural Studies*, *16*(2), 177–192.

Butler, J. (1993). *Gender trouble: Feminism and the subversion of identity*. New York: Routledge.

Butler, J. (2002). Explanation and exoneration, or what we can hear. *Social Text*, *20*(3), 177–188.

Cocco, G., & Lazzarato, M. (2002). Ruptures within empire, the power of Exodus: Interview with Toni Negri. *Theory, Culture & Society*, *19*(4), 187–194.

Collins, A. (1994). Intellectuals, power, and quality television. In H. Giroux and P. McLaren (Eds.), *Between borders: Pedagogy and the politics of cultural studies* (pp. 56–73). New York: Routledge.

Debord, G. (1994). *The society of the spectacle*. (Donald Nicholson-Smith, Trans.). New York: Zone Books.

Denzin, N. K. (2004a). The war on culture, the war on truth. *Cultural Studies/Critical Methodologies*, *4*(2), 137–142.

Denzin, N. K. (2004b). Crossroads in Cultural Studies 2004 Mandate. http://www.crossroads2004.org/cfp.html. Accessed July 24, 2004.

Denzin, N. K., & Lincoln, Y. S. (2005). *The Sage handbook for qualitative research*. London: Sage.

Eco, H. (1995). Eternal fascism: Fourteen ways of looking at a black shirt. *New York Review of Books*, November-December, 15.

Falcous, M., & Silk, M. (2005). Manufacturing consent: Mediated sporting spectacle and the cultural politics of the war on terror. *International Journal of Media & Cultural Politics*, *1*(1), 59–65.

Ferguson, N. (2004). *Colossus: The price of America's empire*. New York: Penguin Press.

Field of Dreams [Motion picture] (1989). United States: Universal Pictures.

Giardina, M. D. (2005). *Sporting pedagogies: Performing culture & identity in the global arena*. New York: Peter Lang.

Gilroy, P. (2001). Foreword. In B. Carrington & I. McDonald (Eds.), *Race, sport and British society* (pp. xi–xvii). London: Routledge.

Giroux, H. (1995). Animating youth: The Disneyfication of children's culture, *Socialist Review*, *24*(3), 23–55.

Giroux, H. (1996). *Fugitive cultures*. London: Routledge.

Giroux, H. (2001). *The mouse that roared: Disney and the end of innocence*. Lanham, MD: Rowman and Littlefield.

Giroux, H. (2002). Terrorism and the fate of democracy after September 11th. *Cultural Studies/Critical Methodologies*, *2*(1), 9–14.

Giroux, H. (2003). *The abandoned generation: Democracy beyond the culture of fear*. New York: PalgraveMacmillan

Giroux, H. (2004). War talk, the death of the social, and the disappearing children: Remembering the other war. *Cultural Studies/Critical Methodologies, 4*(2), 206–211.

Giroux, H. (2005). *The terror of neoliberalism.* Boulder, CO: Paradigm.

Gowdy Jr., C. (Executive Producer). (2003, August 11–25). *Little league baseball world series* [Television Broadcast]. New York: American Broadcasting Company.

Grossberg, L. (1992). *We gotta get out of this place: Popular conservatism and postmodern culture.* London: Routledge.

Grossberg, L. (1997). *Bringing it all back home: Essays on cultural studies.* Durham, NC: Duke University Press.

Grossberg, L. (2001). *Caught in the crossfire: Kids, politics and America's future.* Boulder, CO: Paradigm.

Gruneau, R. (1989). *Making spectacle: A case study in television sports production.* In L. A. Wenner (Eds.), *Media, sports, and society* (pp. 134–156). Newbury Park, CA: Sage.

Gruneau, R., Whitson, D., & Cantelon, H. (1988). Methods and media: Studying the sports/television discourse. *Society and Leisure, 11*(2), 265–281.

Hall, S. (1980). Encoding/Decoding. In S. Hall (Ed.), *Culture, media, language: Working papers in cultural studies, 1972–1979.* London: Hitchinson.

Hardt, M., & Negri, A. (2000). *Empire.* Cambridge: MA: Harvard University Press.

Hardt, M., & Negri, A. (2005). *Multitude.* New York: Penguin Press.

Harvey, D. (2003). *The new imperialism.* Oxford: Oxford University Press.

Harvey, D. (2005). *A brief history of neoliberalism.* Oxford: Oxford University Press.

Keith, T. (2003). *Shock 'N Y'all.* Sony Dreamworks.

Kellner, D. (2002). September 11, social theory and democratic politics. *Theory, Culture & Society, 19*(4), 147–159.

Kellner, D. (2004). Media propaganda and spectacle in the war in Iraq: A critique of U.S. broadcasting networks. *Cultural Studies—Critical Methodologies, 4*(3), 329–338.

Kelly, M. (2001). *The divine right of capital.* Minneapolis, MN: Berrett-Koeler Publishers.

Kemsley, J. (April 16, 2003). Godless little league?: Coach objects to 'Trust in God' pledge. *Santa Cruz Sentinel.* Retrieved December 12, 2003, from http://www.santacruzsentinel.com/archive/2003/April/16/local/stories/01local.htm

King, S. (2005). War games: The culture of sport and militarization of everyday life. Spotlight paper presented at the 5th Biannual International Crossroads in Cultural Studies Conference. Urbana: University of Illinois, Urbana-Champaign.

Klein, A. (1988). American hegemony, Dominican resistance and baseball. *Dialectical Anthropology, 13*(1), 301–312.

Klein, A. (1991). *Sugarball: The American game, the Dominican dream.* New Haven, CT: Yale University Press.

Klein, A. (1995). Culture, politics and baseball in the Dominican Republic. *Latin American Perspectives, 22*(3), 111–130.

MacNeill, M. (1996). Networks: Producing Olympic ice hockey for a national television audience. *Sociology of Sport Journal, 13*(1), 103–124.

McDonald, M., & Birrell, S. (1999). Reading sport critically: A method for interrogating power. *Sociology of Sport Journal, 16*(2), 283–300.

McDonald, M. (2005). Imagining benevolence, masculinity and nation: Tragedy, sport and the transnational marketplace. In M. Silk, D. Andrews, & C. Cole (Eds.), *Sport and corporate nationalisms* (pp. 127–142). Oxford: Berg.

McLaren, P. (1994). Multiculturalism and the postmodern critique: Toward a pedagogy of resistance and transformation. In H. Giroux and P. McLaren (Eds.), *Between borders: Pedagogy and the politics of cultural studies* (pp. 192–224). New York: Routledge.

McLaren, P. (2002). George Bush, apocalypse sometime soon, and the American imperium. *Cultural Studies/Critical Methodologies, 3*(2), 327–333.

McLaren, P., & Martin, M. (2004). The legend of the Bush gang: Imperialism, war and propaganda. *Cultural Studies/Critical Methodologies, 4*(2), 281–303.

Merskin, D. (2004). The construction of Arabs as enemies: Post September 11 discourse of George W. Bush. *Mass Communication and Society, 7*(2), 157–175.

Mosher, S. D. (August 15, 2001). A hotbed of talent, but not for little league. Retrieved March 1, 2003, from http://espn.go.com/moresports/llws01/s/2001/0815/1239786.html.

Musburger, B. (2001). Bronx team bedazzling the crowds. Retrieved March 1, 2003, from http://espn. go.com/abcsports/columns/musburger_brent/2001/0822/1242568.html.

Rose, N. (1999). Community, citizenship, and the third way. *American Behavioral Scientist, 43*(9), 1395–1411.

Roy, A. (2001). *Power politics.* Cambridge, MA: Sound End Press.

Sardar Z., & Wyn-Davies, M. W. (2002). *Why do people hate America?* New York: Disinformation.

Sardar Z., & Wyn-Davies, M. W. (2004). *American terminator: Myths, movies and global power.* New York: Disinformation.

Sennet, R. (1999). Growth and failure: The new political economy and its culture. In M. Featherstone & S. Lash (Eds.), *Spaces of culture: City-nation-world* (pp. 14–26) London: Sage.

Silk, M. (1999). Local/global flows and altered production practices: Narrative constructions at the 1995 Canada Cup of Soccer. *International Review for the Sociology of Sport, 34*(2), 113–123.

Silk, M. (2001). Together we're one? The "place" of the nation in media representations of the 1998 Kuala Lumpur Commonwealth games. *Sociology of Sport Journal, 18*(3), 277–301.

Silk, M. (2002). Bangsa Malaysia: Global sport, the city & the refurbishment of local identities. *Media, Culture & Society, 24*(6), 775–794.

Silk, M., & Amis, J. (2000). Institutionalized Production Practices: The Case of Kuala Lumpur 98. *Journal of Sport Management, 14*(4), 267–293.

Silk, M., Slack, T., & Amis, J. (2000). An Institutional Approach to Televised Sport Production. *Culture, Sport & Society, 3*(1), 1–21.

Silk, M., & Falcous, M. (2005). One day in September/one week in February: Mobilizing American (sporting) nationalisms. *Sociology of Sport Journal, 22*(4), 447–441.

Silk, M., Bracey, B., & Falcous, M. (2007). Performing America's past: Cold war fantasies in a perpetual state of war. In S. Wagg, & D. Andrews (Eds.), *The new cold war.* London: Routledge

Steinberg, S., & Kincheloe, J. (1997). *Kinderculture: The corporate construction of childhood.* Boulder, CO: Westview Press.

Steinberg, S., & Kincheloe, J. (2004) *Kinderculture: The corporate construction of childhood, 2nd ed.* Boulder, Co: Westview Press.

Tomlinson, A. (2002). Theorizing spectacle: Beyond Debord. In J. Sugden & A. Tomlinson (Eds.), *Power games: A critical sociology of sport.* London: Routledge.

Van Auken, L., & Van Auken, R. (2001). *Play ball!: The story of little league baseball.* University Park: The Pennsylvania State University Press.

Wang, B. (2002). The cold war, imperial aesthetics, and area studies. *Social Text, 20*(3), 46–65.

Williams, R. (1981). *The sociology of culture.* Chicago: Schocken Books.

Zinn, H. (2003). *A people's history of the United States 1492–present.* New York: HarperCollins.

Zylinska, J. (2004). The universal acts: Judith Butler and the biopolitics of immigration. *Cultural Studies, 18*(4), 523–537.

CHAPTER 2

Screening Race in America
Sport, Cinema, and the Politics of Urban Youth Culture

MICHAEL D. GIARDINA AND CAMERON R. MCCARTHY

Proem[1]

The popular negotiation and representation of race and racialized identities has long been a favored instrument within popular sporting figurations for perpetuating a White capitalist patriarchal hegemony. This is revealed most notably in relation to a slew of recent cinematic endeavors such as *He Got Game* (Lee, 1998), *Hoop Dreams* (S. James & Marx, 1994), *Remember the Titans* (Howard, 2000), and *Love & Basketball* (Prince-Bythewood, 2000); the rising prominence of a new class of Black entrepreneurs as signified by former National Basketball Association (NBA) star Earvin "Magic" Johnson and Black Entertainment Television (BET) founder and current Charlotte Bobcats (NBA expansion team) owner Robert Johnson (see Giardina & Cole, 2003); and the public-private investment in the future of (White, middle-class) American girlhood as located within the alleged pro-family, pro-empowerment, pro-girl rhetoric of both the Women's National Basketball Association (WNBA) and the Women's United Soccer Association (WUSA; see Metz, this volume).

Given the power of trans/national (cultural) sporting agents, intermediaries, and institutions to actively work as pedagogical sites hegemonically reinscribing and representing neoliberal discourses on sport, culture, nation, and democracy, it is imperative for cultural critics to excavate and theorize the "contingent relations, structures, and effects that link sport forms with prevailing determinate forces" (Andrews, 2001, p. 116). To this end, we critically interrogate the prevailing contemporary figurations of urban popular culture as suggested within and against filmic narratives of youth-oriented sport, attempting in the process to forge a contextual understanding of the conflictual representations of (urban youth) subjectivity within American popular culture. We begin by locating urban America within broader conjunctural developments that have given rise to its mainstream appellation. We then move on to focus on how urban popular culture is currently represented within broader pop culture formations, especially Hollywood cinema. We conclude by examining the Spike Lee film *He Got Game* (1998), which we view as both an example and a symptom of popular racial representation that is compatible with the politics of a conservative (Black) middle class. In doing so, we adhere to Denzin's (2002) call of challenging the popular racial order by advocating for a radical, progressive democracy that adheres to a (post)performative moral ethic of interpretation, care, and social change.

The Politics of Race in Clinton's America

In 1992, Stuart Hall's essay, "What is This 'Black' in Black Popular Culture," offered a preliminary response to the conjunctural specificities out of which the overarching narrative of Black popular culture was being shaped and defined. Some 15 years later, with the legacy of the Clinton years still to be imagined and the phantasmagoric mediacracy of postmodern America at center stage, it is perhaps appropriate to begin by rephrasing the question, asking instead, "What is this 'popular' in urban popular culture?" However, to spin Hall's original question is more a rhetorical observation than a specific theoretical strategy deployed in attempting to enter into a discussion of such a polysemous formation as urban popular culture. Furthermore, to do so would wrongly suggest that this formation, and those various groups that identify with it, could ever be unproblematically subsumed under one umbrella term. Rather, for purposes here, neither the urban nor the popular need necessarily be divorced from its whole: the (re)iterative discursivity of the formation itself.

As witnessed throughout the decade of the 1990s, discourses centering on race and diversity became increasingly prevalent in mainstream popular discussions. In the case of what has routinely been referred to as the overarching sphere of urban popular culture, a seemingly progressive but transparently conservative shift has occurred over the last decade whereby the faux, color-blind all-Americanness of such 1980s luminaries as Michael Jordan and Bill Cosby has been replaced by a multiplicity of representations depicting so-called authentic urban cultural emissaries. Located within the sociopolitical milieu of the Clinton administration (see below), the (multi)cultural landscape has coalesced into a mélange of images and representations that *appear* to shift toward a more diverse and oppositional version of urban cultural signification. But, in the process of (re)defining acceptable boundaries of diversified social relations (just as we had nefariously seen in the Reagan era), tropes such as *multiculturalism, hybridity*, and *diaspora* became renarrated "through a proliferation of images and practices into a normalized, non-politically charged discourse that assumed that ethnic minority communities were homogenous and somehow representative of an authentic and unified culture" (Giardina & Metz, 2001, p. 210).

For example, we witnessed the emergence of hip hop culture in the mid- to late 1970s originally staking out a position as a progressive social movement that cut across racial and ethnic geographies in the face of eroding urban infrastructures (Watkins, 1998). However, as Watkins (1998) reminded us, it was not until hip hop became intensely commodified—for better or worse—that it began to receive any widespread attention and become an economically viable outlet for the expression of Black culture. But this commodified expression of the self became screened through the lens of profitability, not one's culture; narratives of resistance, revolution, and militancy were diluted and/or tailored to meet an ever-growing (White) audience. Farai Chideya (1997) cogently explicated this phenomenon:

> Who's pushing the rawest rhymes to No. 1 on the charts? For years now, the largest volume of hip hop albums has been sold to white kids who've deposed heavy metal and elevated hip hop to the crown of Music Most Likely to Infuriate My Parents. The suburban rebellion—its record buying tastes, its voyeurism of what too often it views as "authentic black culture"—has contributed to the primacy of the gangsta-rap genre. (p. 47)

Given the hearty consumption of hip hop by White youth, it is no surprise that other facets of urban or street culture—from the militant to the mundane—have been similarly appropriated and repositioned to meet with the demands of a specific target audience.

Chief among these other facets of stylized cultural signification, the popular resonance generated by and through the NBA and its players during the 1990s and the National Football League (NFL) in the early years of the twenty-first century stands as a practical exemplar of the renarration of Blackness as rearticulated through the urban center during the Clinton era. Previously, the War on Drugs narrative of the Reagan era (circa 1986) privileged basketball as a solution to inner-city problems defined by gangs, violence, and out-of-control consumption (Cole, 1996). As Cole (2001) argued, "Sport and gangs [became] represented not only as channels for what [was] understood to be corporeal predispositions of African-American youth but as the available substitutes for the 'failed black family'" (p. 69). In the parlance of modern identities, gang members, whose deviance was coded through notions of laziness, unemployment, and violence, thus "produce[d] what/who are normal and acceptable: the urban African-American athlete" (Cole, 2001, p. 70). Over time, as witnessed in the early to mid-1990s, the dialogues surrounding the so-called Crime Bill debates of 1994 and the Gingrich Revolution moved to articulate basketball with criminality (Cole & Giardina, 2003) by criticizing endeavors such as "Midnight Basketball" (see Hartmann, 2001) as a waste of public resources.

But now, it seems, there has been yet another shift in the popular accep-tance—one might say, celebration—of the commercialized and commodified urban style. Aside from NBA players and their mediatized representations of the streetball lifestyle, we similarly witness video games such as the *NBA Street* series,[2] becoming widely profitable commercial successes on high-end video game consoles such as PS3 and xbox360; ESPN, the premier cable sports channel, recently featuring an ongoing documentary of a traveling streetball barnstorming group that regularly sells out local arenas playing a sort of Harlem-Globetrotters-meets-Rucker-Park style of basketball; MTV hosting a Big Brother-like reality show called *Who Got Game?* in which streetball players are voted off the show on a weekly basis; and basketball-themed movies organized around African American basketball players reeling in rave reviews.[3]

The particularity of Hollywood cinema has a long-standing relationship with popular discourses on sport, especially as related to the representation of childhood or narratives dealing with sport as part and parcel of "growing up." The Walt Disney Co., for one, has been a key player in this arena, with theatrical releases of late including, among others, *Air Bud* (1997), *Angels in the Outfield* (1994), *Miracle* (2004), and the much-ballyhooed *Mighty Ducks* trilogy (1992, 1994, 1996), as well as numerous sport-themed shows airing on cable television's Disney Channel (e.g., *The Jersey, Totally Hoops*, etc.). Com-bine this with such coming-of-age films as *Field of Dreams* (1989), *Hoosiers*, *The Natural* (1984). *Rocky* (1976), *Annapolis* (2005), *The Rookie* (2002), *Rookie of the Year* (1993), and even *Seabiscuit* (2003) and *Cinderella Man* (2005), and you have an impressive corpus of texts performing a mediated, pedagogical function (see also Giardina, forthcoming). In so order to better understand the context within which cinematic endeavors are located, it is necessary to briefly examine the filmic language governing such texts in the 1990s.

Cinematic Revelations

Throughout the late 1980s and into the early 1990s, Hollywood cinema saw an influx of and was then dominated by a series of hood/barrio films that adhered to the realist code of filmmaking (Denzin, 2002). That is to say, these films presume a near-perfect relationship between a thing and its representation as can exist, and because of this, the images and narratives depicted should be taken as if they were factual. In the process, these films reinscribed a racial order that privileged White over Other—the assimilation of Black/Brown culture to White, middle-class narratives of nation, family, and law. However, if these images are taken as the Durkheimian *facts of life* (a constructed and negotiated term bearing little resemblance to lived textuality) they proclaim to be, then unproblematic representations of—for instance, the surveillance narrative in hood films—sets in motion a schema whereby to question such a representation would be to question the larger state apparatus that supports the status quo. Contextually speaking, movies in this vein, such as *Menace II Society* (Hughes, Hughes, Williams, & Bennett, 1993) and *Boyz n the Hood* (Singleton, 1991), fueled conservative discourses about race and family relations by allegedly professing to present their narrative representations as true-to-life glimpses into the lives of African American and Latino/Latina youth, which, at the time of their release, was not a glimpse most middle-class White Americans had been familiar with. In doing so, cinematic representations of graphic gun and drug violence in the Black hood and the sexual violence within the Latino prison system served to further demonize each group (Denzin, 2002).

Up until 1995 or so, this genre remained relatively unreflexive, leaving larger sociopolitical and socioeconomic factors untouched and explicitly grounding the source of such violence and moral decadence in the rhetorically tenacious claims of the dysfunctional urban family structure, absent male role models, and instances of personal failure. By representing a community seemingly out of control, on the verge of implosion (be it the hood/gang or prison/gang representations), and on the brink of spilling over into White America, the hood/barrio films acted in accordance not with a political interventionist agenda but, rather, a neoconservative agenda to inscribe on and mark the body —in typical Reaganite fashion—as the root cause of national problems. However, as the Clintonite project began to fully take shape, such filmic narratives slowly began to react and change. Whereas the late 1980s/early 1990s were overrun with cinematic racial allegories of the Black and Brown hood that "celebrate[d] a violent, mysoginistic masculinity" and "turn[ed] women into crack addicts, ho's, bitches, and lazy welfare mothers" (Denzin, 2002, p. 113), the latter half of the 1990s saw filmmakers, especially African American filmmakers, purporting to reverse such a trend (Denzin, 2003). No longer was the assimilation model explicitly promoted in films that took up issues of urban American culture; rather, it was subtly written into the underlying fabric of the narrative. Films ranging from *What's Cooking?* (Berges & Chadha, 2000) and *How Stella Got Her Groove Back* (McMillan & Sullivan, 1998) to *Soul Food* (Tillman, 1997) and *Bamboozled* (Lee, 2000) marked a new paradigm of representing minority groups and characters in a positive, multicultural light. That is to say, movies such as these publicly endeavored to create a new space for what Manthia Diawara has referred to as a "New Black Planet" by putting forth examples of a progressive, feminist, neo-Black aesthetic that screened race not through a White lens but, rather, through a critically informed, race conscious, female-centric point of view.

And yet, while moving away from blatant violence and rampant sexism in favor of opportunity, community, and responsibility, the narrative arcs remained locked in a liminal space between progressive and conservative insights. This follows the argument set out by bell hooks (1990, 1995) who, although envisioning a politics of radical Black subjectivity as a liberatory site of transformation from the margins of society where counterhegemonic narratives and constructions of the self can be fully realized, contended that much of what passes today for counterhegemonic discursive practices are anything but. Rather, as hooks wrote, they are a reinscription of the very same hegemonic structures that such practices allege to disrupt or challenge. Put another way, despite progressive *moments* of liberation found in films in the mid- to late 1990s (e.g., the explicit and proud ownership of their own sexuality by the two lead female characters in *How Stella Got Her Groove Back*, the positive representation of a lesbian relationship in *What's Cooking?*, or the strong, family-centered narrative of *Soul Food*, a majority of these films ultimately fall back on rather conservative positioning by locating their leading characters in a deeper ideological narrative that sees them as almost within reach of breaking free from the bonds of social entrapment but ultimately unable to fully overcome the powerful constraints generated by such conservative representations.

Enter Sport

So, how does sport fit into this highly contestable and contradictory discursive space? What is the role of sport in this historical moment of the rising popular saliency of urban cultural forms? Related to the place of sport within the 1990s, Hollywood cinema's, for instance, wildly successful (pseudo-)documentary films such as *Hoop Dreams* were to bring (White) middle-class America face to face with urban American sporting narratives as framed through the realist lens of its independent filmmakers (see Cole & King, 1998). Shocking White audiences around the country with its real-life depiction of daily life in urban America—specifically, the Cabrini Green Housing Project in Chicago, Illinois—and receiving near-unanimous praise within the mainstream press (cf. Ebert, 1998), the film was stitched into the ideologically represented fabric of the 'hood as constructed in early-1990s films such as *Boyz n the Hood* and *Menace II Society*. That is, viewers were presented with a narrative reinforcing the idea that "the postindustrial ghetto suffocates the lives and opportunities of poor African American youths" (Watkins, 1998, p. 222), and that those who live in such a place are there of their own lifestyle choice and not larger systemic problems: Poverty, welfare dependency, and a struggling economy was thus articulated to individual shortcomings and the breakdown of the (mythic) family among minority segments of the population (Cole & King, 1998; Jeffords, 1994).

Correlatively, as Cole and King (1998) write with regard to the representation of the film's two main characters, African American high school basketball players William Gates and Arthur Agee,

> The figure of the basketball player, defined over and against the criminal (gang member that governs America's representation of African-American men in the mid-1980s to the mid-1990s)...functions as a means of displacement that reconciles middle-class America's sense of itself as compassionate as it calls for and endorses increasingly vengeful punitive programs. (p. 78)

Success among young Black youth had thus been coded with escaping from the inner-city "jungle" through the most (allegedly) viable of avenues: (the prospect of playing) professional sport (specifically basketball). Although indicative of the politics of representation governing the first half of the 1990s, *Hoop Dreams* does not resonate quite so well with the latter half of the decade. Or does it? Enter Spike Lee. Already highly regarded as one of America's most important filmmakers, and a self-avowed avid sports fan (of the New York Knicks and New York Yankees), Lee took his turn in narrating the urban condition through sport with his 1998 release *He Got Game*, a coming-of-age drama about a top-ranked high school basketball star from Coney Island, New York, and his turbulent relationship with his (incarcerated) father. In the next section, we take up this film and argue that its narrative structure succinctly captures the (urban) cultural milieu of the Clinton era as represented in popular culture—that is, a milieu that embodies a "black postnationalist essentialism" (Wallace, 1992, p. 125) that is "compatible with the politics of a conservative black middle class" (Denzin, 2002, p. 154). Furthermore, although not to over-generalize about contemporary Hollywood cinema, we believe the film to be indicative of the larger racist infrastructure governing the current conjunctural moment in American history.

Screening Race in America

Lee's (1998) urban basketball drama, *He Got Game*, is sutured into the prevailing sociopolitical landscape of (urban) America in the mid- to late 1990s. Generally speaking, both public and popular disposition toward U.S. urban centers has, over the years, followed a contradictory hypermoral impulse. At various times emphasizing cold disinterest, at other times seen as the object of almost laboratory-like social experimentation and intervention, urban

America hangs in a liminal state between all-out decay and the possibility of social and economic renewal. This pendulum of neglect and intervention swings, sometimes frenetically, one way or another, as the urban context continues to be viewed by bureaucratic and cultural elites through a paradigm of cultural deficit and moral underdevelopment. Since the high point of the civil rights era and its culminating fruition in the ameliorative programs of the Great Society/War on Poverty initiated under the Lyndon Johnson administration in the late 1960s (e.g., Head Start), the urban centers of the United States have been the target of revisionary strategies of both policy makers and policy intellectuals. This revisionary disposition has been, to give but one example, operationalized in the policies of benign neglect found during the Nixon/Carter years and the aggressive disinvestment of the Reagan/Bush era. At the same time, the urban centers, despite their profound marginalization in terms of the uneven allocation of public and private resources, have attained a surplus status in popular media and public policy discourses as the site of the most profound problems affecting the country and as, in fact, the tragic ballast weighing down the ship of state.

It could be said that up until the 1990s, the dominant framework around which both public policy and the surplus popular social meanings were generated was the Keynesian formula of (more or less) social welfarism. In the early 1990s, this overwhelming paradigm of Keynesianism was both rhetorically and practically overturned as the newly ordained Clinton administration sought to connect urban centers to its broad-scale global neoliberal initiatives vis-à-vis universalizing entrepreneurship. As the administration sought to spread the gospel of unfettered capital around the world through the North American Free Trade Agreement (NAFTA), General Agreements on Tariffs and Trades (GATT), and the World Trade Organization (WTO), it simultaneously turned its brassy new corporatist gaze on the inner city by speaking the language of enterprise zones, self-help, and community voluntarism. The urban center was/is thus a piece of a much larger puzzle of the proliferation of new social meanings that translate the capitalist enterprise form of modern conduct to the conduct of organizations (e.g., charter schools, corporate partnerships, and voucher programs in education) and the conduct of individuals; the problems of inner-city life have become the new targets of self-management, regulation, the restraint of individual appetites, and the moral purposive voluntaristic investment of the inner-city dweller himself or herself.

Such was the language of the 1993 *Building Communities, Together: Guidebook for Community-Based Strategic Planning for Empowerment Zones and Enterprise Communities*, authored by the President's [Clinton] Community Enterprise Board, which stated in part:

If this program is to stabilize and reinvigorate neighborhoods, residents must be free from the fear of crime and violence. Job creation, improved housing, and enhanced service delivery are crucial in most potential empowerment zones and enterprise communities, but a commitment to the reduction of crime and violence through coordinated law enforcement is necessary to community stability, the delivery of health education, and other social services and economic development...Unchecked violence, gun and drug trafficking, drug use, and other serious felonies will stifle investment, development and community building emphasis of the initiative. (pp. 45–46)

Yet, upon close inspection of such lofty rhetoric, as Cole and Giardina (2005) point out in their case-study analysis of the New York City/Upper Manhattan Empowerment Zone project, such (de)moralizing jingoism is eerily reminiscent of something that President Reagan said in 1982;

We must make America safe again, especially for women and elderly who face so many moments of fear...Study after study shows that most serious crimes are the work of a relatively small group of hardened criminals. Let me give you an example—subway crime in New York City. Transit police estimate that only 500 habitual criminal offenders are responsible for nearly half of the crimes in New York's subways last year...It's time to get these hardened criminals off the street and into jail...We can and must make improvements in the way our courts deal with crime...These include revising the bail system so that dangerous offenders, and especially big-time drug pushers, can be kept off our streets. (*Public Papers of the Presidents of the United States 1982*, 1983, p. 2)

Though writing in response to Reagan's quote above, Andrews' (1993) words remain applicable to the 1993 guidebook: "Without ever referring to race or ethnicity, it is manifest that the threat to American society he vocalized was a black male inhabitant of American's anarchic urban jungles" (pp. 114–115). The outcome is that security becomes mobilized around economic stability and corporate investment opportunities: incarcerating or evicting young Black (or Latino) men becomes the naturalized, and accepted, outcome of "cleaning up" the so-called inner city and paving the way for corporate expansionary measure (a fate we have seen repeated in empowerment zones from New York and Cleveland to Memphis and Los Angeles).

However, as we have also seen, these so-called "problems" have also become highly marketable images for which mainstream American youth culture has become heavily invested in consuming. As we have increasingly witnessed, the marketing armatures of corporate America have aided in turning the urban condition into one of exploding profitability as they rewrite the historical conventions associated with urban culture primarily in terms of the "stylized elements of cool" (Carrington, 2001; N. Klein, 2002) it has come to signify to a primarily White youth consumerist market. As part of this containment and redirection of racial antagonism—seen within a historical context of the rapid changes taking place in the material reality and fortunes of people, their environments, and the institutional apparatuses that govern and affect their lives—Clinton would prove himself a master craftsman, a silver fox speaking in forked tongues to both the African American poor and the White professional middle classes.

What appeared to be smoke and mirrors were actually highly calculated tactics in which representational politics assumed a pivotal role. The State, corporate interest and private individuals/groups now operate in tandem in a vigorous effort aimed at reorienting the urban centers in the United States from a Keynesian, welfarist ethos toward a post-civil rights, post-Keynesian, post-welfarist future. This trend is seen most concretely in the creation of empowerment zone initiatives that have heightened public-private investment in historically low-income urban centers. But, as Cole (2001) is keen to point out,

> such investment amounts to little more than rewriting the urban communal landscape—organized around the systematic displacement of the "aesthetically disenchanting"—and embedding in the "rebuilt" urban center "highly marketable, sanitized styles and signs of subversion, antiauthoritarianism, and experimentation that designate it as an 'alternative space.'" (p. 117)

Although *He Got Game* is a direct response to these changing material conditions reflective in and of the urban center, and although it acts in concert with popular representations of race and racialized identity as deployed throughout various forms of popular culture, it is also a response to three specific sporting tropes surrounding African American athletes that acquired significant media attention as Lee was producing his film.

The first is that of high school basketball players foregoing college to enter the NBA draft. In 1995, Kevin Garnett, a high school player from Chicago who was generally considered the top prep prospect in the country, declared that he would enter the NBA draft instead of playing at the collegiate level. He was subsequently drafted fifth overall (by the Minnesota Timberwolves) and signed a then-record contract for rookies in the NBA. Although the story itself received a fair amount of attention, nominally framed in terms of getting out of the projects in favor of financial security, it was not until the 1996 draft that the trend became an issue. In this draft, two more high school players were drafted in the first round—Kobe Bryant (13th overall) and

Jermaine O'Neal (17th overall). Coupled with Georgetown University's Allen Iverson leaving school early to enter the draft (selected first overall)—the first time a player under head coach John Thompson had left the school early for the NBA—the mainstream press took up the issue as one of crisis, as yet another example of African American youth choosing the fast money (i.e., NBA contract, endorsement deals) over education. This became tied to the second trope—that of minority athletes as criminals. In particular during this time, the NBA saw a rash of players arrested for marijuana possession (e.g., Isaiah Rider, Allen Iverson, Marcus Camby), and other African American athletes such as Leon Lett (football) and Dwight Gooden and Darryl Strawberry (both baseball) also made headlines for their brushes with the law vis-à-vis drug use.

The third trope Lee picked up on was that of the absent (Black) male father as articulated to sport. At roughly the same time as the film was released, an issue of *Sports Illustrated* featured a cover shot with the headline "Where's Daddy?" and included an article titled "Paternity Ward" (Whal, Whertheim, Munson, & Yaeger, 1998). Capitalizing on the general conservative discourse on absentee fatherhood popular at the time, the article went on to discuss absent athlete-fathers but saved its harshest rhetoric for condemning African American fathers within the NBA. Although acknowledging that paternity suits were prevalent in all sports, the article went out of its way to single out NBA players. Although offering several reasons for the high propensity of paternity suits against NBA players, including road trips, money, and visibility, the article problematically settled on one's race as the most likely answer by stating that "the NBA has a higher proportion of black players (80%) than football (67%) or baseball (17%)... and that out of wedlock births are a persistent problem in the African-American community" (p. 68).

Spike's (New?) Urban Ghetto

And so, entrenched within this discursive space, we get Lee's ode to basketball, fatherhood, and urban America. *He Got Game* opens with a series of stereotypical images that speak to and are readily identifiable to most people in the United States—fair-haired White youth a la *Hoosiers* (Pizzo & Anspaugh, 1986) shooting baskets amid pastoral scenes of Middle America juxtaposed with images of young Black youth engaged in raucous games of playground ball within the projects of inner-city America. Open-spaced farmlands versus fenced-in urbanscapes. Freedom versus restraint. Suburbia versus the Cabrini Green Housing Project. As the opening montage fades, complete with the obligatory gesture to Michael Jordan by way of his statue outside the United Center in Chicago, we are left with Jesus Shuttlesworth (played by photogenic NBA star Ray Allen) and his cousin, Booger, shooting jump-shots on a fenced-in basketball court dramatically shadowed by their towering project development. Whereas we have just been inundated with rolling countrysides, clean outdoor parks, and stunning visuals of Middle America, the only thing visually appealing to the camera in the Coney Island project is the chained-in courts—newly resurfaced—with an expensive professional-style plexiglass backboard. As Jesus takes his shots, the camera switches back and forth to his father (played by Denzel Washington), an inmate at Attica prison, who shoots jump-shots from the top of the key in the prison recreation yard under the watchful eye of a machine-gun-carrying White prison security guard. In these initial minutes of the film, we are presented with a spin on what Cole (1996) has called the sport-gang dyad—that is, the idea that sport and gangs are represented not only as channels for what are understood to be corporeal predispositions of African American youth but as the available substitutes for the "failed black family"...splitting black youth into forces of good and evil (pp. 370–371).

The storyline of *He Got Game* is straightforward, if not overly melodramatic. Jesus is the top-ranked prep player in the country, drawing scholarship offers from leading collegiate powerhouses such as Duke and Arizona as well as the prospect of jumping straight into the NBA. Concurrently, his father, Jake, is serving a 15-year prison sentence for the manslaughter of Jesus's mother. A week before the deadline for prep players to sign letters of intent as to which college they will attend, the prison warden at Attica informs Jake that the governor of New York is an alumnus of Big State University and would be grateful if Jake can convince Jesus to sign a letter of intent to play for the school. In return, the governor offers to commute Jake's sentence. In the course of their conversation, the question of basketball operating in the life of African Americans is brought to light by the warden:

[Jake is seated in the desk chair opposite a White prison warden in his mid-50s]

Warden: As you already know, you've picked the perfect recreation. Dr. James Naismith [basketball's acknowledged inventor] knew what he was doing. It's a great game, isn't it?

Jake: Basketball, yes.

Warden: You played some?

Jake: Uh, yes, sir, when I was younger. You know, uh, I put in a little work.

Warden: I coach my son's team.

Jake: I ran a neighborhood center [flashback to coaching his son at night].

Warden: You coached?

Jake: Nah, nothing like that there. Just, you know, I see somebody out there, a little kid who needs some help [flashback to son], I work with you, you know, give him a few tips [flashback to son]. But nowadays, uh, Warden, they—these kids ain't gonna listen to nothin' you say, you know. They think they know it all. All they wanna do is dunk and—you know, everything like that. Their fundamentals is, uh—is, like, sorely lacking.

Warden: That's strange. I haven't had that problem yet.

Jake: Yeah, well, your kids—they smart. They know they don't listen to you, they end up in here with me.

Warden: I never thought about it like that.

It is crucial to understand this scene not only in terms of pointing out the disparities found between the life experiences of the warden and Jake insofar as involvement in sport (i.e., *of course* the warden had never thought about sport in those terms), but it also serves as an indictment of basketball—pro or otherwise—and the much-propagated theme of the day that the fundamentals (i.e., shooting and passing the basketball) of many younger players were weaker than in times past as the dunk had become a major preoccupation of the time, especially with slam dunk contests trickling down to the collegiate and high school levels. Moreover, the NBA was at the time (and continues to be) experiencing an influx of highly skilled and fundamentally-sound European players that threatened to take jobs away from American-born (read: African American) players. Their conversation also moves to equate being in prison as having to do with personal choices made free from any larger institutional constraints: the narrative was clear—disobey the rules-based social order and you end up in prison with Black felons.

In one of the very next scenes, Lee reinforces the overdetermined belief that sport is the only way out of the ghetto for young African Americans when he introduces the starting five on Jesus's high school basketball team, the Lincoln Railsplitters:

[each player speaks directly to the camera, one on one, breaking the fourth wall as if being interviewed, and states his reason for playing basketball]

Lonnie "Dub" Dukes: The game brings me love, peace, and happiness.

Sip Rodgers: My name is Sip Rodgers. I go to Abraham Lincoln High School. I play the two-spot. We're the Railsplitters, and nobody's fuckin' with us.

Jesus Shuttelsworth: Basketball is like poetry in motion. Just comin' down the court, you got a defender in your way. You take him to the left, take him back to the right, and he's fallin' back, and you just "J" right in his face. And then you look at him, and then you say "What?"

Mance Littles: Basketball's the birthplace of all of my dreams, of everything

that I wanna be, of everything I wanna accomplish, and what it is
that I wanna do in life.

Booger Sykes: I feel handsome when I'm on the court. I feel like I'm somebody.

Unlike in, for example, *Menace II Society*, Jesus and his friends are not scary,
young, nihilistic Black males driving the film; instead, theirs is a world full
of (possible) hope organized not around drugs or gang violence (though it
does exist in the background outside of their immediate sporting lives, as
Lee shows) but around sport and the much-hailed fiction of basketball as the
only socially accepted avenue of success for African American youth (Cole,
1996; Cole & Andrews, 1996).[4]

Thus do we see Lee integrating his environment in such a way that previous
hood/barrio films had not overtly done: The urban landscape of Jesus and
his friends is harmoniously interracial, a pastiche of ethnicities all coexisting
without incident. The race-related violence that existed in Lee's early work
such as *Do the Right Thing*, a film inspired by the Howard Beach killings in
Queens, New York, in December of 1985, is nowhere to be found. Nor is
the Black-on-Black violence of *Menace II Society*. Like an edgier version of
a Gurinder Chadha film filled with commercialized multicultural longings,
the utopian vision Lee strives for is hamstrung by its ideological position.
Although it is undeniable that Lee deserves praise within this film for starting the work of challenging long-standing colonial and patriarchal narratives
of dominance and subordination—both within the urban center and with
regard to African American athletes—it is no longer sufficient, as Denzin
(2002) reminded us, "to offer examples of good and bad films, including
inventories of negative images. It is time to move away from the search for
an essentialist (and good) black or brown subject" (p. 185).

As the build-up surrounding Jesus and his choice of college continues
to grow, we see him tempted with the allure of easy money associated with
signing with a (stereotypically sleazy) agent and declaring himself eligible for
the NBA draft (a la Garnett, Bryant, O'Neal, and Iverson), offered a brand
new Lexus from his abusive uncle who is explicit in his desire to get a kick-
back from having raised Jesus, offered $10,000 from his high school coach
for inside information as to where he will attend college, offered a $36,000
platinum and diamond-encrusted watch from the sports agent, and, on a
recruiting visit to Tech University, hears about the benefits of attending the
school insofar as generous alumni and other such accoutrements of big-time
college basketball. However, Jesus is immune to such (monetary) pressures
and is instead always framed as the hard-working, individualistic young man
taking care of his younger sister and being socially and culturally aware of
the larger world around him.

But back to Jesus and his father. After the two have several tense meet-ings—in which Jesus claims that he "doesn't have a father anymore"—the stage is set for the anticlimactic final scene. As Lee moves toward this eventual resolution, we see, via flashback, Jesus's childhood vis-à-vis interactions with his (present) father. On the last night of Jake's freedom, the two play a game of one-on-one. Jesus, by now the better player, easily defeats his father, and the two police officers assigned to follow Jake come and take him away in handcuffs. However, Jesus decides to attend Big State University anyway thus setting up a two-fold resolution. First, Jesus has gotten out of the projects via basketball. In doing so, he has also lived up to and in accordance with traditional notions of the (Reaganite) meritocratic American dream—hard work, moral values, and commitment to family irrespective of socioeconomic status or larger systemic barriers.

Second, his father is forever fated to his life in prison, as we see Jake back in prison—perhaps a bit wiser, but certainly no better off, the governor having reneged on his promise of freedom. Where Lee fails in his moralizing tale is in reducing the solution to the problems of the inner city to simply getting out, as Jesus leaves Coney Island for the greener pastures of big-time college basketball. As Denzin (2002) remarked, "Lee's Afrocentric aesthetic is not the radical or militant aesthetic of the Black Arts Movement of the 1960s and 1970s" (p. 156). Rather, Lee's Afrocentricism "is a conservative aesthetic that *appears* [italics added] radical" (Denzin, 2002, p. 156). Although Lee clearly has on his agenda the positive representation of African American men, no space is created within the film that allows for the community to be revitalized on its own (i.e., empowerment zones aside); Lee chooses to make it the site of a glossy, pop culture, Urban Decay *Lite*. Because of this move, as Hall (2000) pointed out, such a strategy depoliticizes the transgres-sive potentiality of the message by leaving us (only) with a commercialized multicultural vision that "assumes that if the diversity of individuals from different communities is recognized in the marketplace, then the problems of cultural differences will be (dis)solved through private consumption, without any need for a redistribution of power and resources" (p. 210).

Despite the, at times, gritty realism of *He Got Game*, the film saw its mainstream success precisely because of its explicitly conservative message, couched as it is against a backdrop of urban slang and ghettoized popular references. As famed film critic Roger Ebert (1998) opined in his glowing review of the film for the *Chicago Sun-Times*, "The father and son win, *but so does the system*" (para. 10, emphasis ours). The system, of course, consists of a double fiction—one that endorses the police state and the White capitalist order it protects while at the same time offering itself as the authoritative answer to the very societal ills it (re)produces and (re)generates: young

Jesus leaves his community, Jake goes back to prison, and everyone (and everything) is safe and secure.

The popular appeal and reception of movies such as *He Got Game* (and others in this vein) thus

> remains intricately bound within an historical context that has shaped and has been shaped by America's fascination with and acquired literacy of "urban problems," particularly as those problems have been rendered visible through coming of age narratives of African American male youth. (Cole & King, 1998, p. 51)

And, likewise, as Denzin (2002) writes, "The contemporary history of race relations in America is, in large part, a history of the representation of violent, youthful minority group members in mainstream Hollywood cinema and in commercial television" (p. 1). Thus, we are left with a film whose originary narrative erases political and ethical considerations that mark history as a site of struggle by producing what Giroux (1995, p. 51) has called "a filmic version of popular culture" (p. 57)—one that effaces the everyday hardships and ground-level struggles of daily life in favor of a faux progressive vision of hope. Through it all, though, we are led to believe that this is just another (tragically hip) day in America's urban centers.

Coda

The location of sporting narratives within mainstream Hollywood cinema finesses—some might say, obfuscates—the violent historicity of race relations throughout the whole of American sporting endeavors, and leaves us only with a popularly conceived view that sport is always and only a bastion of (hetero)-normativity and (fictionalized) All-American values. Such a simplistic, mainstreamed view of sport as a colorblind, value-neutral institution is found in an article written by S. L. Price (1997) for *Sports Illustrated*, ironically titled "Whatever Happened to the White Athlete?" we quote at length:

> [Jackie] Robinson ushered American sports into an era of significance beyond the playing field. During the next two generations, the once monochromatic world of team sports became a paradigm of, and some a spur to, racial equality. One milestone followed another: Larry Doby broke into the American League several months after Robinson's debut; the NBA and NFL were completely integrated; a Texas Western basketball team with an all-black starting lineup beat Adolph Rupp's all-white Kentucky squad in the 1956 NCAA final; the same year the Boston Celtics named the first black head coach of a professional team; the Washington Redskins' Doug Williams in 1988 became the first

black quarterback to win a Super Bowl. Management was still firmly white—and, regrettably remains so today—but one could argue that the playing field has become the nation's common ground, the one highly visible stage on which blacks and whites acted out the process of learning to live, play, and fight together as peers. (p. 33)

The story remains much the same today. As David J. Leonard (2004) is keen to write, "The [current] success of black athletes and the supposed adoration America has for MJ [Michael Jordan], Shaq [Shaquille O'Neal], Tiger [Woods] and LeBron [James] is [still] posited as evidence of racial progress and colorblindness." Unlike Tommie Smith, John Carlos, and Harry Edwards who, "rather than celebrating the suggestion that sports were at the forefront of racial advance…increasingly came to assert that sports were tied to a racist, oppressive system" (D. Thomas, 2004, n.p.), the aforementioned stars of today continue to be firmly ensconced in a depoliticized narrative about the racial politics of contemporary sporting culture. The truth is, sport is colorblind only fantasyland, not in actual practice.[5]

Given the above, it is imperative that we as progressive scholars must engage with a critical eye the mediated pedagogies working to produce such a racialized discursive space within youth-oriented sporting narratives and offer alternative readings and interpretation on the all-too-commonly accepted Master narratives that are popularly promoted within the cultural mainstream. Confronting such disquieting developments head on, doing everything we can to unmask unequal power relations at play that are concerned with the regulation, management, and manipulation of population in general via technologies of containment, surveillance, and subjectification is our charge. For, as one of us has previously written:

We are knotted together in the brave new world of out of place modern subjects, fettered as we are by particularism and combustible resentment, a world in which power located in the center and built upon rule at a distance and strategies of divide and conquer, now seems peculiarly fragile, vulnerable, and distracted. Now the managers of the metropolis must reckon with the horrors that have been systematically perpetrated upon the world's dispossessed beneath the gaze of the US suburban popular … in a world that's oh so topsy-turvy. (McCarthy, 2007, pp. 288-289)

Notes

1. This chapter draws in part from and updates arguments in Giardina & McCarthy (2003) and Giardina (2005, ch. 5).
2. The *NBA Street* series is one of Electronic Arts' most popular and profitable sport game series. It includes *NBA Street Vol. 1, NBA Street Vol. 2, NBA Street Vol. 3, NBA Street Homecourt,*

and *NBA Street Showdown*. Other "street ball" oriented console or PC games include *Street Hoops* (Activision), *Freestyle Street Basketball* (Vivendi Universal), and *AND 1 Streetball* (Ubisoft),

3. At the same time, it should be noted, NBA commissioner, David Stern, has since implemented a dress code policy to curb what he considered to be a gang-influenced dress amongst the league's younger players.

4. One particularly graphic scene later in the film continues this theme wherein Jesus is both dissuaded by a local Puerto Rican gang leader named Big Time Willie against drugs, gambling, and the possibility of HIV/AIDS (in what would be Lee's 5-minute public service announcement to the audience, because Jesus has already clearly experienced and rejected most of these temptations anyway) all the while being reminded that he is being looked after and should be grateful. See Giardina and McCarthy (2005) for an extended discussion of this particular scene and its racial politics.

5. Consider, if only briefly: in the United States today, more than 4,500 high schools, colleges and universities, and dozens of professional and semi-professional sports teams use pseudo-Native American symbols as mascots to represent themselves on the playing field (see King, this volume); sport (especially basketball) remains a much-hailed fiction of being the only socially accepted avenue of success or possibility for African American youth (Cole, 2001); racial stacking—that is, the allocation of a player to a certain position based on stereotyped racialized perceptions of the abilities of the athlete—remains a common practice of coaches in both youth sport and high school athletics programs; and out of the Division 1A collegiate football programs, only a paltry four (or 3.41%) had Black head coaches in 2002 (as compared to the 41% of college football players who are Black).

References

Andrews, D. L. (1993). *Deconstructing Michael Jordan: Popular culture, politics, and postmodern America*. PhD dissertation. Urbana: University of Illinois, Urbana-Champaign.

Andrews, D. L. (2001). Coming to terms with cultural studies. *Journal of Sport and Social Issues*, 26(1), 110–117.

Berges, P. M. (Writer), & Chadha, G. (Writer/Director). (2000). *What's cooking?* [Motion picture]. United Kingdom/United States: Trimark Pictures.

Carrington, B. (2001). Postmodern Blackness and the celebrity sports star: Ian Wright, "race" and English identity. In D. L. Andrews & S. J. Jackson (Eds.), *Sports stars: The cultural politics of sporting celebrity* (pp. 102–123). London: Routledge.

Chideya, F. (1997, March 24). All eyez on us. *Time*, p. 47.

Cole, C. L. (1996). American Jordan: P.L.A.Y., consensus, and punishment. *Sociology of Sport Journal*, 13(4), 366–397.

Cole, C. L. (1998). Addiction, exercise, and cyborgs: Technologies of deviant bodies. In G. Rail (Ed.), *Sport and postmodern times* (pp. 261–276). Albany: State University of New York Press.

Cole, C. L. (2001). Nike goes toBroadway. *Journal of Sport & Social Issues*, 25(2), 115–117.

Cole, C. L., & Andrews, D. L. (1996). "Look—it's NBA showtime!": Visions of race in the popular imaginary. In N. K. Denzin (Ed.), *Cultural studies: A research annual, vol. 1* (pp. 141–181). Stamford, CT: JAI.

Cole, C. L., & Giardina, M. D. (2005). Magic Johnson's urban renewal: Empowerment zones and the national fantasy of HarlemUSA. In C. McCarthy, W. Crichlow, G. Dimitriadis, & N. Dolby (Eds.), *Race, identity, and representation in education* (2nd ed., pp. 379–392). London: Routledge.

Cole, C. L., & King, S. J. (1998). Representing Black masculinity and urban possibilities: Racism, realism, and hoop dreams. In G. Rail (Ed.), *Sport and postmodern times* (pp. 49–86). Albany: State University of New York Press.

Denzin, N. K. (2002). *Reading race: Hollywood and the cinema of racial violence*. London: Sage.

Ebert, R. (1998). *He got game*. Retrieved May 8, 2000 fromhttp:// www.suntimes.com/ebert/ebert_reviews/1998/05/050104.html

Giardina, M. D. (2005). *Sporting pedagogies: Performing culture & identity in the global arena*. New York: Peter Lang.

Giardina, M. D. (forthcoming) *From soccer moms to NASCAR dads: Sport, culture, & politics in a nation divided.* Boulder, CO: Paradigm.

Giardina, M. D., & Cole, C. L. (2003, April). The national fantasy of HarlemUSA: Empowerment zones, Clintonian neoliberalism, and racialized consumption in urban America. Paper presented at the annual meetings of the British Sociological Association, York, UK.

Giardina, M. D., & McCarthy, C. R. (2005). The popular racial order of urban America: Sport, identity, and the politics of culture. *Cultural Studies/Critical Methodologies, 5*(2), 145–173.

Giardina, M. D., & Metz, J. L. (2001). Celebrating humanity: Olympic marketing and the homogenization of multiculturalism. *International Journal of Sports Marketing and Sponsorship, 3*(2), 203–223.

Giroux, H. A. (1995). Innocence and pedagogy in Disney's world. In E. Bell, L. Haas, & L. Sells (Eds.), *From mouse to mermaid: The politics of film, gender, and culture,* (pp. 43–61). Bloomington: Indiana University Press.

Hall, S. (1992). What is this "Black" in Black popular culture. In G. Dent (Ed.), *Black popular culture* (pp. 21–33). Seattle, WA: Bay Press.

Hall, S. (2000). The multi-cultural question. In B. Hesse (Ed.), *Un/settled multiculturalisms: Diasporas, entanglements, transruptions* (pp. 209–241). London: Zed Books.

Hartmann, D. (2001). Notes on midnight basketball and the cultural politics of recreation, race and at-risk urban. *Journal of Sport and Social Issues, 25*(4), 339–372.

hooks, b. (1990). *Yearning: Race, gender, and cultural politics.* Boston: South End.

hooks, b. (1995).*Teaching to transgress: Education as the practice of freedom.* London: Routledge.

Howard, G. (Writer) (2000). *Remember the Titans* [Motion picture]. United States: Walt Disney Pictures.

Hughes, A. (Writer/Director/Producer), Hughes, A. (Writer/Director/Producer), Williams,T. (Writer), & Bennett, M. (Producer). (1993). *Menace II society* [Motion picture]. United States: New Line Cinema.

James, S. (Writer/Director), & Marx, F. (Writer). (1994). *Hoop dreams* [Motion picture].United States: New Line Features.

Jeffords, S. (1994). *Hard bodies: Hollywood masculinity in the Reagan era.* New Brunswick, NJ: Rutgers University Press.

Klein, N. (2002). *No logo: No space, no choice, no jobs.* New York: Picador.

Lee, S. (Writer/Director). (1989). *Do the right thing* [Motion picture].United States: MCA/Universal Pictures.

Lee, S. (Writer/Director). (1998). *He got game* [Motion picture]. United States: Touchstone Pictures.

Lee, S. (Writer/Director). (2000). *Bamboozled* [Motion picture]. United States: New Line Cinema.

Leonard, D. J. (2004). The next M.J. or the next O.J.? Kobe Bryant, race, and the absurdity of color-blind race rhetoric. *Journal of Sport & Social Issues, 28*(3), 284–313.

McCarthy, C. (2007). After 9/11: Thinking about the Global, Thinking about Empathy, Thinking about the Postcolonial. In N. K .Denzin and M. D. Giardina (eds.), *Contesting Empire/Globalizing Dissent: Cultural Studies after 9/11* (pp. 280-289). Boulder, CO: Paradigm

McMillan, T. (Writer), & Sullivan, K. R. (Director). (1998). *How Stella got her groove back* [Motion picture]. United States: 20th Century Fox.

Pizzo, A. (Writer), & Anspaugh, D. (Producer). (1986). *Hoosiers* [Motion picture]. United States: MGM.

President's Community Enterprise Board (1993). *Building communities, together: Guidebook for community-based strategic planning for empowerment zones and enterprise communities.* Washington, DC: U.S. Government Printing Office.

Price, S. L. (1997, December 8). Whatever happened to the White athlete? *Sports Illustrated,* 30–51.

Prince-Bythewood, G. (Writer/Director). (2000). *Love & basketball* [Motion picture].United States: New Line Cinema.

Reagan, R. (1983). *Public papers of the presidents of the United States: Ronald Reagan, 1982.* Washington, DC: U.S. Government Printing Office.

Singleton, J. (Writer/Director). (1991). *Boyz n the hood* [Motion picture]. United States: Columbia Pictures.

Thomas, D. (2004). The cold war roots of the Mexico City Olympic protest. Paper presented at the

5th International Biannual Crossroads in Cultural Studies Conference, Urbana, IL: University of Illinois, Urbana-Champaign.

Tillman, G., Jr. (Writer/Director). (1997). *Soul food* [Motion picture]. United States: 20th Century Fox.

Wallace, M. (1992). Boyz n the hood and jungle fever. In G. Dent (Ed.), *Black popular culture: A project by Michelle Wallace* (pp. 123–131). Seattle, WA: Bay Press.

Watkins, S. C. (1998). *Representing: Hip hop culture and the production of Black cinema.* Chicago: University of Chicago Press.

Whal, G, Wertheim, L. J., Munson, L., & Yaeger, D. (1998, May 4). Paternity ward: Fathering out-of-wedlock kids has become commonplace among athletes, many of whom seem oblivious to the legal, financial, and emotional consequences. *Sports Illustrated*, p. 62.

CHAPTER **3**

Bounding American Empire
Sport, Sex, and Politics

C. L. COLE

In his 2004 State of the Union address, George W. Bush offered an interpretation of an America dedicated to what he characterized as "great works of compassion and reform," an America rising to meet what he called "great responsibilities." His optimism wavered momentarily when he took up the theme of America's children, invoking age-old threats to education and health. He simultaneously proclaimed declining drug use among teens while blaming some professional athletes for falling short of their representational role, for the third-party effect of their steroid use. Invoking the imaginary special bond between athletes and children, Bush declared that "The use of performance enhancing drugs like steroids … is dangerous, and it sends the wrong message: that there are shortcuts to accomplishment, and that performance is more important than character." He then called on "team owners, union representatives, coaches and players to … send the right signal. To get tough and to get rid of steroids now."

As if on cue, the next week's *New York Times*' sports section featured a long, front-page article about steroids and sport. But the article was not about the U.S. scandal that had been unfolding for months. Instead, the article, melodramatically titled "East German Steroids' Toll: They Killed Heidi," attempted to affectively consolidate the East German sport drug scandal as the most notorious in sporting history, conveniently obscuring the then present-day U.S. scandal. In general, the article depicted former East German athletes seeking compensatory justice for damages they experienced under the hand of state-sport officials who administered, allegedly without the athletes' consent, performance-enhancing drugs. The *New York Times*

55

represented their victimization—coded in terms of *childhood*—as violated trust that led to corrupt athletic performances and a wide range of health problems like liver tumors, heart disease, infertility, and eating disorders. But most specifically the article concentrated on the "gender death" of Heidi Kreiger, now Andreas, a female-to-male-transsexual, who, for the *New York Times*'s U.S. audience, could stand in for the most horrific violences and perverse transformations of an over-rationalized sport system.

The article organized Heidi's experience of the world and self almost exclusively in terms of steroid-induced pain, suffering, and isolation. Heidi's apparent unreadability as female—as well as her shame and humiliation for being seen as gay, a pimp, or a drag queen—serves as the narrative's pivotal atrocity. Isolated from all but the world of sports, where she excelled—she was the 1986 European shot put champion—Heidi's suffering is resolved not after becoming Andreas (her new male identity), but only after he enters into a heteronormative relationship with another (female) victim of the East German sport system and renounces his former sporting victories as fraudulent. Theirs, as the author put it, "began as a desperate kind of love": Two victims, betrayed by adults they trusted, psyches and bodies damaged, both suicidal, who met at the criminal trials of their abusers and are now building a "normal" life together (Longman, 2004).

Against the backdrop of the developing World Anti-Doping Agency (WADA)—an international police force dedicated to "clean [that is drug-free] sport" through the constant monitoring of athletes and their urine archive—and an unfolding U.S.-based sport-related drug scandal, one might expect the article to expose the hypocrisy of U.S. accusations against Communist sport. But that is not the case. Instead, "they killed Heidi" reinforces American Cold War stereotypes and a preoccupation with violations of femininity that have long enchanted "America." Indeed. Heidi/Andreas is the literal embodiment of the fantastic figures that have long propelled America's anti-Communist sport narratives, narratives themselves driven by diagnostic tools like drug and sex testing. That is to say, "Heidi" is an expression of a governing narrative about nation constituted at the crossroads of sport, sex, and American democracy. As systems that, together and in isolation, activate, confirm, and extend a sense of natural bodies, all three bracket the body's technological condition. In their press for the natural and, relatedly, the original, the three systems cultivate, classify, and mark bodies in parallel and divergent ways as deviant, foreign, morally inferior, unproductive, imitations, and hybrids. As such, the three practices operate as technologies of enchantment.

Sport's ethical ground relies on an ontology and epistemology of the human. Thus, while sport draws together and then sorts out bodies, the sorting process is not reducible to athletic performance but, crucially, requires attending to the parameters and performances of the human. Given sport's interpretive ground, remarkable performances—although the ostensible goals of high-performance sport—are never simply celebrated as breakthroughs. Instead, they are suspected to be evidence of potential breakdowns—breakdowns that facilitate nightmare fantasies of what and who is responsible for, the origin of, the accomplishment: the hidden hand of drugs? Science? An enemy state? And, rather than provoking debates about the boundaries of the supposed natural (e.g., self/other; free will/compulsion; human/machine; man/woman), such performances are domesticated by visualizing strategies (e.g., sex and drug testing) that manage and sort the alien and the natural and, by extension, sport's idealized coding.

"Gender verification" is one strategy of making that elusive natural body visible in sport. Between 1966 and 1992 gender verification took the form, first, of visual inspection, then, a more probing gynecological exam, and increasingly, high-tech chromosomal analyses. Not incidentally, the justification for gender verification quickly moved beyond screening for men impersonating women to rationales that rhetorically confused and implicated non-normative sex and performance-enhancing drug use. The result? Narratives of international sport, at least in the United States, populated by a wide range of boundary creatures (i.e., drug-crafted athletes, steroid men/women, intersexed, transsexed, hypermasculine, and hypermuscular females) imagined as Communist athletes.

In 1990, one international governing body, the International Amateur Athletic Federation (IAAF) revoked its sex-testing requirement, claiming that the test was invasive, humiliating, potentially psychologically damaging, and even resulted in the disqualifications of females who had no physical advantage. But, despite these claims, the organization transformed drug testing—a space where genitals are seen because urination must been done under observation—into the official unofficial site for sex testing. Ten years later, the International Olympic Committee (IOC) conditionally suspended sex testing while maintaining their right to subject "suspect" female athletes to further examination. And, following the IAAF, they, too, gave gender verification refuge in drug testing.

With this background in mind, I want to illuminate the cultural history in which "Heidi" is enmeshed. To this end, I begin by tracing the events and anxieties that first fixed America's attention on the Soviet athlete and then more narrowly on Soviet track and field athletes, particularly on a creature known as "Tamara Press and her sister." I argue that Tamara Press and sex-testing were mutually constitutive: gender verification brought an aura of scientific authority to America's claims about Tamara Press's female masculinity, and Tamara Press (the collectively forged images and history) was the ironic proof of gender verification's necessity. Although Tamara Press and her sister never underwent sex testing, they became America's most fantastic and enduring emblems of the Communist athlete and failed sex (at least until 1976 when America's gaze was directed to East German athletes). In fact, for America it was the *absence* of the Press sisters from the first sex-testing competition that confirmed their guilt. I consider the production of gender-deviant figures at the intersection of two cults—the cult of sportsmanship and the cult of true suburban womanhood—as they are articulated within two related contexts: the American Cold War and the post–civil rights era.

When considered in this historical-cultural context, the biography and bodily habitus of contemporary America's iconic suburban girl athlete can be seen to be born out of an earlier performance of U.S. democracy over and against an imagined gender-deviant Communist athlete. Given this history, Bush's 2004 appeal to end steroid use cannot simply be dismissed, as some have suggested, as a distraction from more pressing political issues. Instead, the deployment of America's sport-drug narrative—a narrative whose meaning is supposedly obvious and nonpartisan—is inseparable from the actual making of Bush's political agenda and the production of his image as a quintessential American leader promoting a transparently American Way of Life.

What the Other Superpower Looks Like

I begin my investigation the year after the Soviets announced that they had an atomic bomb. In 1950, in the midst of a military stalemate, the USSR announced that after a 40-year absence, they would participate in the upcoming Olympic Games. America's response was predictable. Prominent U.S. accounts depicted the Soviets as boasting about their athletic prowess; the U.S. media provided semi-detailed reports of the Soviet's supposed systematic violations of fair play; and they documented what they claimed were the Soviet's shameless claims to false victories. The U.S. media self-righteously ridiculed the Soviets for using international sport for propaganda purposes, for advancing *their* political, economic, and moral war in violation of sport's mythic ideals. These violations were framed as symptoms of Soviet character—their excessive competitiveness, deceptiveness, and disregard for rules.

Indeed, for America, anxieties about Soviet sport were inseparable neither from fears of Soviet imperialism nor from anxieties about America's moral superiority, which was marked especially by its so-called truth-telling project. In 1951, Richard B. Walsh (of America's International Information and Education Program) declared America's widespread commitment: "To meet and beat down these [Soviet] lies, the U.S. Government, assisted by private groups, has greatly stepped up its truth-telling programs. ... Through press, radio, motion pictures, overseas information centers, and the exchange of persons, we are telling the truth on an unprecedented scale. We have done well as far as we have gone" (p. 1007).

I imagine that Walsh's aim, given his position, was to recruit American athletes for the U.S. State Department's "Campaign for Truth." To this end, Walsh flattered the athletes: "We can expect nothing finer than American sportsmanship, for sportsmanship is *democracy at work* [my emphasis]." Territorializing global sport for the United States, Walsh concluded that, "sportsmanship is deeply rooted in our country's heritage." In this context, America's truth-claims rested on two beliefs: a belief in the cult of sportsmanship and a belief in the absolute polarity of Soviet and American characters. Thus, for America, sportsmanship was an instrument for embodying political culture and for linking conduct, performance, and moral superiority to America. In so doing, and in this context, sportsmanship would—and did—yield America's favorite sporting Other: a being recognized as the Communist athlete. As a product of democracy at work, the Communist athlete, in its negative space, prominently functioned to enchant America's athletic embodiment and America's imagination.

In 1952, *Life Magazine* depicted the Soviet's appearance at the Olympics in terms of "muscles pop[ping] through the iron curtain," and they did so against a background of the "American cult of sportsmanship" and America's desire to see signs of visible transgressions. Comparatively, *U.S. News & World Report* provided a narrative of Soviet sport, under the headline, "Stalin's 'Iron Curtain' for Athletes," built around key codes of corruption: isolation and secrecy, state-sanctioned interactions, violations of the amateur code, political indoctrination, heavy scrutiny and regulation, and their policing of their athletes' susceptibility to the pleasures offered by the Western way of life. Although sex deviance apparently plays no part in the account provided by *U.S. News & World Report*, the caption of one photograph is symptomatic of the terms that would define America's sporting encounter of the Soviets. The photograph is of Soviet discus thrower Nina Dumbradze and is simply, without any explanation, captioned "A Russian specialty: Soviet Amazons."

Life seemingly approached the Soviet athlete from a different angle. The article's opening image of U.S. athlete Jim Fuchs gazing in lustful admiration of "the Amazon" herself intimates that even international politics are not powerful enough to overcome the natural order of things. While heteronormative sexual difference renders visible a "common humanity," American anxieties about the need to see difference are apparent as *Life*'s visual images repeatedly direct attention to and from sameness.

Life concretized the image of the Soviet as outsider through a moral geography that measured the Soviet's literal and figurative distance from the Olympic Village. In a photograph of several seemingly "ordinary" Soviet athletes, it is this lack of difference that is problematized. This very "ordinariness" is represented as a nefarious impersonation—a state-sanctioned performance of the ideal (American) body. In this case, the American body is represented as the original site of vibrancy and spontaneity, the register of life itself. Yet, *Life* (the magazine), like *U.S. News & World Report*, offers representations of the sort of mutants that the Soviets would produce, if they went uncontrolled. The photograph is of Soviet athlete Tamara Press, cropped to accentuate her musculature, or in *Life*'s words, her "tank-shape." As a sign of Soviet militarism and excess, the image calls into question the integrity of the Soviet body.

Certainly the evocation of cyborgs through images of unnatural tank-shaped bodies was not unique to sport—it dominated American depictions of Soviet women. However, the scope of international sport—its competitiveness and regulation of nation and sex and its display of the effects of "democracy at work"—facilitated deep, affective attachments. International sport functioned as a dramatic enactment of the moral and physical chaos associated with the Soviets and its innocent American victims. This drama was most vividly played out in what were imagined to be grossly unfair competitions of Communist gender hybrids—the product of a perverse, overrationalized, and inhuman sporting system—versus America's natural girls. For at least the next 20 years, albeit alternating in intensity and appearance, Tamara Press and her sister became visual shorthand for threats to American women, the American family, and the American way of life. These dramatic stagings of U.S. sportsmanship were key to mobilizing extraordinary states of indignation and national fervor and negotiating the contradictions of American democracy and, relatedly, America's shame and pride.

Our (White) Girls/Their Deviants

In 1964, *Life Magazine* prominently featured America's female athletes in a 10-page celebratory photo essay entitled "The Grace of Our Olympic Girls." Arizona diver Barbara Talmage appears on the cover and signifies the angelic and suburban girl next door. The possessive pronoun *our* positions women as part of national culture and points to their bodies as signs of community, nation, gender, and American identity. In short, the bodies are depicted as independent, autonomous, and free of constraints, devoid of mixed signifiers and boundary violations. Quintessential signifiers of masculinity—strength and muscle—are concealed through gesture, clothing, camera angle, distance, and setting. Individualism is asserted in relation to a collective symmetry and proportion established through poses connoting grace, pleasure, and effortlessness. A series of artistic poses, repeated fluid and rhythmic lines and forms, suggest that sameness, unity, and coherence are what matter.

Two years later, and coincidently the same year that the United States would announce that winning was now a national priority, *Life* published an article explaining the need for sex-testing in the Olympics. Asking if girl athletes are really girls, *Life* brought tales of suspicion, impersonators, and sex-change surgery to the foreground. *Life Magazine* offers a tutorial in what transsexuals might look like by presenting before and after photographs of what they claim are transsexual athletes. The accompanying photographs are shot from distorting angles that make the athletes appear unnaturally proportioned. Tamara Press and her sister are two of the featured monstrosities. Noticeably missing from this account is America's claim to these girls. Yet this defined the context on which the United States awkwardly and ambivalently reflected and even attempted to legislate the relationship between *its* girls and women and sport.

On June 27, 1970, CBS aired a celebratory news clip ostensibly devoted to women's liberation's gains in girls' sports. Yet, CBS actually takes its cue from an unacknowledged dynamic: a strong yet unstable sense of American masculinity marked by a tension between male privilege and women's liberation, the civil rights movement, and Black and Soviet accomplishments in sport. For CBS, its magical resolution comes through America's White suburban girl who successfully negotiates several national burdens, including the gender-deviant Communist athlete. A patronizing tone governs much, but significantly not all, of the narrative. Indeed, the main shift in tone is racially motivated.

> A slightly out of focus still image of a White man with USA on his chest going over a hurdle is shown under a voiceover: *For years the image of track has been of graceful, slender, and, of course, swift men. Whenever women competed they rarely seemed quite feminine.* Under continuing commentary, there appears an image of Soviet athlete Tamara Press, in an open and aggressive stance. *But as our society goes through the swirl of women's liberation, so does the world of sport. And the revolution is beginning in the grade schools, as Heywood Halebourne reports from California.*
>
> The viewer's perspective is adjusted by Halebourne who appears not at an elementary school but in the private space of a suburban home: *This looks like one of these TV families which speak of dry cereal as if were pate de foie. But the subject of conversation is not the crispness of the flakes, but the competitive prospects of the family's nine-year-old candidate for stardom.*
>
> Voiceover: *Little girls used to set off for school with no thought other than speculation as to which attractive boy would dip one's pigtails in the inkwell. Now, for nine-year-old Jill Boyd there is the bracing prospect of*

medals and applause for feats of track and field. The girls to whom the recess yard was a place for experimenting with social patterns are now absorbed in physical patterns, as Debbie Kind spins [image of girls in dresses spinning with petticoats] *through the orbit light years away from the pantomime tea parties of old. A couple of medium size Los Angeles suburbs have turned out these well-organized, smartly uniformed Ontario-Montclair Cheetahs. And, even the attendant matrons are pliable to discipline as visions of a medal for the mantel dance in their heads.*

Our point of entry, as Halebourne suggests, *is* immediately recognizable, but not simply because of the TV family. Three national myths are summarily invoked: the American way of life defined by the suburbs, Tamara Press, and the American melting pot. The space that opens our suburban excursion is consistent with that popularized in family sitcoms like *Leave It to Beaver* and immediately conjures up ideals about home, family, and consumer lifestyle. But, although Beaver was never affected by the 1950s Cold War, the 1970s suburban girl is both the stakes and the site of that struggle.

In a striking moment of astonishing incoherence, we are told that the monstrous Tamara Press occupies a defining place in America's psyche. And, that place is "fixed" by race, class, sex, and generation: it is, precisely, the young, White, suburban girl who bears the burden of the nightmarish figure. National forces and the complex political conditions that shaped girls' relationship to female masculinity are erased, as the psychic power of "Tamara Press" is invoked to explain the girls' profound alienation from what is represented as "playing track." We are asked, on the one hand, to applaud the suburban girls' exorcism of the demon that led them to believe that they could not control or would lose control of their muscularity (and that this could be disastrous) and to imagine their track pursuits as a significant accomplishment not just for girls, but, given the gender-deviant Communist athlete, for the nation. On the other hand, we are assured that, for these girls, track is simply an expressive vehicle for fun, a temporary, trivial pursuit that will no longer satisfy them upon arriving at adolescence. Suburban girls, unlike Tamara Press, who has, along with the Soviet state, forsaken her biological destiny, will follow their natural (feminine) development and thus their more compelling interests (marriage and motherhood).

Coach Bill Peterson: Uh, the critical stage in this is, oh, about 14 ... due to the fact that maybe they were a big star in the 12 to 13 division, uh, and then they go into 14 to 17 age group and they're overwhelmed by the competition. Uh, it's very critical at this stage. They either become very interested, or maybe get a little boy crazy and stray off.

The narrative is, in the end, not about women's liberation and a struggle waged on behalf of American girls, but one waged *against* women's liberation and on behalf of America's suburban future—a future in which White, heteronormative masculinity and its related structures, values, and behaviors are projected indefinitely.

To a great extent, the narrative's multiracial dimension—a dimension that enacts racialized corporeal norms—is instrumental in securing suburbia's mythic future. Black and White girls might occasionally run alongside one another in CBS's commentary, but America's women's track culture is hardly integrated. Black girls, visibly older, competitive, and apparently unaffected by Tamara Press (a national trauma), are represented in striking contrast to their diminutive, White counterparts. In fact, with the exception of Wilma Rudolph, Black women remain outside the scope of the narrative. Even California native Barbara Ferrell's previous performances at the Mt. SAC relays—she took first in the 100 meter for three consecutive years—remain unacknowledged. Statements of admiration are instead reserved for Chi Cheng, an Asian immigrant. CBS invites Cheng, its example of racialized productivity and competence and sign of America's women's sporting success, to offer social commentary about America's progress in women's track:

Newscaster: Those who persist think to run in the steps of such idols as Chi Cheng, three times an Olympic competitor, once an Olympic medal winner who runs anything up to 440 yards, flat out or over hurdles. Last year, a coach's poll shows her as the supergirl of track. And as one who has competed through 10 years of geometric growth, she has an historian's viewpoint.

Chi Cheng: I came here in 1963 and, and at that time was, just a few clubs around. But seven years after, now, there are so many clubs around now. It's unbelievable.

Voiceover: Vince Reel, Chi Cheng's coach, feels like the erstwhile image of the track girl as a weight-lifting wallflower has completely faded.

Vince Reel: I think women's track in the United States got off to a bad start when they brought Tamara Press and her sister over here. Most of the girls are now finding out that you have to have a good build to compete in this sport. Well, I think it's becoming a fad, actually. Little girls begin and get their friends interested because they can go on trips and get medals. And, there are hundreds of them, these little characters out there running around, warming up, and putting on track shoes, measuring their steps, and they go clear down to age five. The meet directors are finally waking up in this country to the fact that women's events are more attractive, shall we say, than men's events.

Halebourne: Trampled under all these spikes is the notion that girl athletes come from Frankenstein's laboratory stamped "second" and that a preteen's best friend is her doll. You don't have to look like your brother, or Tamara Press for that matter [close up of Tamara's face], to play his game.

Halebourne: Legend has it, Diana the Huntress raced as lightly and swiftly as the moonbeams that lit her path. For a time, her successors seemed to erase their grace with fierce awkwardness. Today's girl runners are a credit to the moonlit body with a bow.

How are we to make sense of such conspicuous erasures? Notably, the CBS report on girls' track aired just two years after Black U.S. track athletes Tommie Smith and John Carlos raised a gloved-fisted protest on the victory stand at the 1968 Mexico City Olympics. After the United States Olympic Committee (USOC) acquiesced to the IOC (International Olympic Committee), by both apologizing for Smith's and Carlos's conduct and then by expelling Smith and Carlos from the Olympic village, numerous, primarily Black, athletes engaged in various actions to express solidarity. The U.S. women's 4×100-meter relay team, made up of four Black women—Barbara Ferrell, Wyomia Tyus, Midrette Netter, and Margaret Bailes—dedicated their gold medal to the two expelled athletes.

During the 1950s and 1960s, driven by the desire to counter international criticisms of racism in the United States, the U.S. State Department had sponsored athletic tours that featured Black athletes. Given the role of Black athletes in advancing U.S. propaganda and foreign policy, Smith's and Carlos's actions—and those that followed—were seen as a betrayal of America's international image. (In fact, by the time CBS aired its track story, civil rights leaders had fallen under heightened FBI scrutiny and were suspected of being Communists themselves.) Within this context, it seems less remarkable that the only Black female athlete named named in the story was one who had not competed for 10 years but who had taken part in the U.S. State Department tours.

Moreover, in 1965, the United States abolished the last of its long-standing Asian exclusion laws. One year later, U.S. News & World Report published an article that defined Chinese Americans as the model minority over and against African Americans, who were depicted as a drag on the nation. Thus, Chi Cheng's elevation to the preeminent figure of social change and, relatedly, to that which redefines women's track as "attractive" entertainment enacted these anti-Black civil rights codes. Cheng, who actually married her White coach, Vince Reel, is a remarkable example of the sort of ideological work that the Asian female body is forced to perform in American culture. In this case, submission of a model, minority, female body—through marriage—to the regulation of the American coach serves to contain anxieties about White women's loosening sexuality and about growing Black Power. Indeed, Cheng's national appeal is inextricably bound to the role that the Asian woman's body is forced to play in sustaining the erasure of Black women as she negotiates the space where the conflicting meanings between race and sexuality engage the contradictions of democracy.

Conclusion: Re-Enchanting America

In closing, I want to return to the U.S. drug scandal that I discussed in the introduction to the chapter and the context in which George W. Bush initiated his war on drugs in sport. During the Bush presidency, numerous events threatened to make visible an administration that lacked compassion as it was implicated in deception and arbitrary deaths globally and locally (Corn, 2003). Rather than engaging in thoughtful and ethical reflection, dissent and debate were replaced by aggressive national rhetorics—America's technologies of enchantment.

The U.S. fantasies of itself and even its place in the global sports community was undermined as America's sporting order of things became increasingly vulnerable. In 1999, the IAAF not only charged the U.S. Track and Field Association with routine drug use among U.S. athletes but claimed that U.S. drug officials had been complicit in covering up the positive drug tests. Relatedly, a former USOC official had leaked evidence to the press that confirmed that U.S. officials had routinely covered up U.S. athletes' positive results. In the months before Bush's 2004 State of the Union address, Dick Pound, WADA chairman, specifically took "American sportsmanship" to task as he expressed outrage at Washington's disingenuous stance about performance-enhancing drug use. He condemned U.S. professional sports league doping policies, particularly those of Major League Baseball and the National Football League as trivializing and dismissive of the war on drugs in sport. More pointedly, Pound claimed that the United States broke its promise to support WADA, first by reducing the amount pledged and then by failing to pay its dues altogether. Pound proposed sanctions that, among other things, would preclude nonpaying members from bidding to host the Olympic Games (a direct threat to New York City's hopes for hosting the 2012 Games). And he advocated turning the United States into a sports pariah: "If [IOC President] Jacque Rogge goes around to all the federations and says don't have any events in the United States, and turns them into a pariah … hopefully that will get some attention from Pennsylvania Avenue" (WADA, n.d.).

While Pound declared White House antidrug leadership hypocritical and deceptive, the U.S. media were making BALCO (Bay Area Laboratory

Cooperative) new designer steroids, particularly THG, and slang like "the clear" and "the cream" household names. The media coverage of the 18-month federal investigation of BALCO turned into a spectacle as the bodies of African American sport stars were typically used to organize the "leaked" confidential testimony from high-profile athletes. In this context, the United States had to rise, or at least appear to rise, to the responsibility of taking drug use in sport seriously. Eight days before Bush's State of the Union address, the administration seized that opportunity. In a nationally televised press conference held on February 12, 2004, John Ashcroft, the U.S. attorney general, accompanied by the commissioners of the Food and Drug Administration and the Internal Revenue Service, announced the indictment on charges of conspiracy, money laundering, and distribution of steroids, against four individuals, none of whom were athletes. In his statement, Ashcroft said, "Nothing does more to diminish our potential—both as individuals and as a nation—than illegal drug abuse. The tragedy of so-called performance-enhancing drugs is that they foster the lie that excellence can be bought. … Illegal steroid use calls into question not only the integrity of the athletes, but the integrity of the sports they play" (quoted in Department of Justice, 2004).

Arizona Senator John McCain, who chaired the Senate Commerce Committee that investigated BALCO (and who coincidentally then sat on the Senate Armed Services Committee currently investigating the torture of Iraqi prisoners by the U.S. military), quickly clarified the urgency behind drug-testing in terms of sending a "clean team" to the Athens Olympics. In McCain's words, "It [an Olympic doping scandal] will harm our image and will contribute to our image, whether deserved or undeserved, that the United States is a bully and unethical" (quoted in Almond, 2004). Thus, as McCain made clear, the war on drugs in sport is a preemptive strike—in this case, one meant to shore up America's floundering image of exceptionalism and moral superiority—rather than address the overwhelming evidence to the contrary.

Predictably, Black bodies, popularly invoked since the 1980s to interpret U.S. illegal drug scandals in general, became the metonym for drugs. While the well-established transphobic device that I discussed in the introduction temporarily relieved anxiety about the United States' dubious claims to innocence, the unfolding drama nevertheless played out across the bodies of African American athletes, particularly African American female athletes. America's pre-Olympic purification ritual targeted African American athletes Michelle Collins, Chryste Gaines, Regina Jacobs, Kelli White, and Marion Jones. Indeed, in an eerie Catch-22, their past athletic accomplishments (Collins was the 2003 world and U.S. titlist in 200 meter; Gaines held the national title in the 1,500 meter; White was the 100 and 200 meter world champion; and Jones was a five-time Olympic gold medalist) were recast as evidence of their guilt. Thus, the imagined threat those performances posed to American sportsmanship was resolved through a triumphant narrative organized around America's ability to detect their guilt, even in the absence of positive drug tests. The United States Anti-Doping Agency featured America's favorite post–Cold War sporting icon, the suburban White girl, as a sign of the restoration of the natural order of things in its "clean sport" campaign.

The true scandal of sport in the United States is the way it is used to enchant already powerful bodies with even more authority by demonizing already vulnerable others. George W. Bush's cynical "good sport" pose is not new to politics. But perhaps it covers for what will someday be remembered as epic deception and unprecedented corruption, even by notorious American standards.

Note

1. This chapter originally appeared as "Bounding American Democracy: Sport, Sex, and Race" in *Contesting Empire, Globalizing Dissent: Cultural Studies after 9/11* (Denzin & Giardina, 2006). It is reprinted here with the kind permission of Paradigm Publishers.

Bibliography

Almond, E. (2004, May 17). Why John McCain is getting involved. Retrieved from http://www.mercurynews.com/mld/mercury news/sports/8685231.
Are girl athletes really girls? *Life*, October 7, 1966, pp. 63–66.
Corn, D. (2003). *The lies of George W. Bush: Mastering the politics of deception*. New York: Crown Publishers.
Department of Justice. (2004, February 12). Four individuals charged in Bay Area with money laundering and distribution of illegal steroids. Press release. http://www.usdoj.gov/opa/pr/2004/February/04_ag_083.htm.
The grace of our Olympic girls. *Life*, July 31, 1964, pp. 38–47.
Longman, Jere. (2004, January 26). East German steriods' toll: 'They killed Heidi'. *New York Times*. Retrieved from http://query.nytimes.com/gst/fullpage.html?sec=health&res=9C01E3D917 38F935A15752C0A9629C8B63
Muscles pop through the iron curtain. *Life*, July 28, 1952, pp. 15–16.
SI.com. (2004, January 21). *World officials welcome Bush's anti-drug plea*. Retrieved May 20, 2004, from http://www.sportsillustrated.cnn.com/2004/more/01/21/bc.eu.spt.oly.bush.doping.ap.
Smith, M. To win the Olympic war. *Life*, July 28, 1952, pp. 17–19.
Sokolove, M. (2004, January 18). The lab animal. *New York Times Magazine*, p. 28. Retrieved from http://www.nytimes,com/2004/01/18/magazine18SPORTS.html.
Success story of one minority in the U.S. *U.S. News & World Report* (December 26, 1966), p. 73.
USADA Release. (2003, December 22). *U.S. Government and WADA's continued cooperation marked by full payment of United States' 2003 dues*. Retrieved May 20, 2004, from http://www.letsrun.com/2003/usadapraise.php.
WADA mulls urging IOC to make U.S. a sports outcast. (n.d.) Retrieved from http://www.asianathletics.org/html/news/asian-news/WADA-mulls-urging-IOC-to-make-U-S-a-sports-outcast.html.

Walsh, R. B. "The Soviet athlete in international competition." Department of State Bulletin, Washington, DC (December 24, 1951).

World Anti Doping Agency. (n.d.). *WADA statement on Kelli White*. Retrieved May 23, 2004, from http://www.wada-ama.org/en/t1.asp

SECTION **II**

Branding the "Alternative"

CHAPTER **4**

Exploiting a New Generation
Corporate Branding and the Co-Optation of Action Sport

ROBERT E. RINEHART

[Brands] are commercial propaganda, much more insidious than political propaganda, which has never achieved such planetary scope.
—Emmanuelle Garnaud, 2000

. . . tell the traveling public "Get on board. Do your business around the country. Fly and enjoy America's great destination spots. Go down to Disney World in Florida, take your families and enjoy life the way we want it to be enjoyed."
—George W. Bush, September 27, 2001

The above quote is from a speech given by U.S. President George W. Bush to a group of airline employees at Chicago's O'Hare International Airport just two weeks after the U.S. airline industry virtually had come to a standstill post-9/11. It was meant to serve two major purposes: it was intended to re-assure an American public—frightened by repetitive visual traumatization through a voracious and voyeuristic media—that flying was again safe, and it was meant to tell the world that the United States would not let a terrorist attack affect "our way of life." But it also served third and fourth purposes: the statement demonstrated that the U. S. way of life insisted upon a capitalist model of spending beyond one's means, and it showed that perception and the surrounding aura of advertising—in this case advertising as exhortation to spend, spend, spend!—could be convincing and, indeed, could itself produce self-certain conviction.

Leaders have often sought to reassure their publics during times of crisis, but rarely have leaders—even of capitalist nations—sought to reassure by overtly calling upon the crass commercial resources of a nation as sites of nostalgic comfort and basic security. Thus, it is that visiting Disney World (not coincidentally in Bush's gubernatorial brother Jeb's home state of Florida) received a White House sanction as a patriotic gesture that people could perform in order to recover from the devastating trauma of 9/11. The fact that Disney is a part of a non-threatening, collusive "living brand" (Nadeau, 2007, p. 279), which translates to a continual source of what Ritzer (2005) has come to claim is consumer "enchantment," only serves to make Bush's statement more comforting to American consumers: it is as if the terror and shock of the events of 9/11, replayed over and over and over *ad nauseam*, could somehow be assuaged by the cuddly, feel-good consumption of Disney artifacts and presence. The nostalgic yearning for a yesteryear-that-never-was is a part of this mindful-less retreat from reality, and media corporations, performing what Michael Eisner termed "synergies" with one another, push and pull at the consumer. The very same ABC/Disney/CapCities venture that brought you terrorists (repeatedly) steering an airplane into the Twin Towers comforts you with a (repeated) reenactment of a safer, more "enchanted" time.

Thus, as a Disneyfication of security has occurred, so, too, has a linkage between sport, security, "traditional" values, and consumerism become naturalized. Nowhere has the use of sport as a vehicle for consumerism been more obvious than in extreme, or action, sports. While the professed values of action sports participants trace their roots from non-violent, non-traditional, oppositional, and non-consumerist ethos, the appropriation of such sport forms by commercially-driven trans-national corporations has created an uncomfortable dynamic.

Gen Xers and the Millennial Generation (or Gen Yers) are the primary targets of the dismantling of individual agency—aligned, of course, with the implicitly naturalized rhetorical assumption by Bush that Americans are their most patriotic when we are consumers. Gen X has been characterized as a whole generation of mythical slackers (Holt, 2004, pp. 51–53); the Millennial Generation ("born in or after 1982"; Howe & Strauss, 2000, p. 4) has been characterized (in contrast to Gen X) as

> . . . unlike any youth generation in living memory. They are more numerous, more affluent, better educated, and more ethnically diverse. More important, they are beginning to manifest a wide array of positive social habits that older Americans no longer associate with youth, including a new focus on teamwork, achievement, modesty, and good conduct. (Howe & Strauss, 2000, p. 4)

While Gen X still embraced a counter-culture ethos, the Millennials are demonstrating an aversion to controversy, to disagreement, to oppositional stances. On the one hand, Neil Postman (cf., 1985, 1994) characterizes current generations' troubles as fundamentally media-driven. At the same time, Grossberg (2005) points out that "the so-called millennial generation. . . are living in a society in which the government spent significantly more on their parents than it did on them" (p. 38). Giroux (2000) sees a more complex problem: an ambivalent attitude by adults, a giving up of agency, a refinement and efficient manipulation of corporate culture, all structures which serve to induce children to behave in ways antithetical to their own best interests. Is this because the Millennial Generation has already been appropriated, seduced through commercial socialization (that is, the socialization that occurs when an individual identifies *primarily* with corporate goals), to assume themselves as, most saliently, consumers? And has this sociological seduction occurred in the quiet non-struggle within and from such corporate giants as Disney, Fox, or ESPN, in such gentle venues as Disney World, the Gravity Games, or the X Games?

The claim is that Generation Y ("the Millennials") is the first generation to be totally immersed in branding, because "branding," as opposed to the mere "advertising" of a tangible product, really reached its ascendancy beginning in the 1980s (Klein, 2000). As Shank (2005) describes it, branding "allow[s] an organization to distinguish and differentiate itself from all others in the marketplace" (p. 228). But the emphasis on product and mass advertising, so prevalent televisually during the 1950s and, prior to that, from the late 1800s onward, has neatly elided with this new seamless emphasis on branding.

Concomitant to that emphasis, and, of course, resistant to it as well, stands a new consumer, one awash in branding symbology, immersed in myriad logo-identifications, who is perhaps a dupe of the complex postmodern world of advertising. While Giroux (2000), I think rightfully, points out that "popular culture is not only a site of enormous contradiction but also a site of negotiation for kids, one of the few places where they can speak for themselves, produce alternative public spheres, and represent their own interests" (p. 13), kids also own less and less power on a daily basis *vis-à-vis* transnational corporations. Their very persons have grown up with a natural-ized stance that they are consumers—few alternatives have been offered to that self-identity. Assumptions that the world is a growing capitalist endeavor, and that capitalism is somehow linked with democratic ideals, are rarely questioned. And marginalized groups are especially disempowered: Giroux (2000) points out that "Latino and black youth bear the burden of an adult society that either views them as disposable and as a threat to middle-class life, or reifies them through a commercial logic in search of a new market niche" (p. 14).

In terms of this "commercial logic," we see in the sport marketing literature, for example, cases of how sport marketers may more effectively *motivate* consumers, of how they may provide more efficient services, of how they might rate consumer satisfaction. The very *facts* of consumerism are rarely questioned in such literature. But if they are rarely questioned by adults, who presumably have more experience and more perspective, how are they viewed by children?

If that targeted consumer[1] happens to be youthful, happens to have a *tabula rasa* upon which corporate interests may imprint their messages of consumption—not just of certain products, but of consuming itself—the use of such repetitive marketing devices has evolved into a mass-marketed socialization of youth with the goal of creating over-consuming adults. In the 1990s, the tobacco industry was maligned for targeting youth for consumption of cigarettes and tobacco products, but one of the motivating forces behind that legal attack on the industry was based on health issues. Creating lifelong consumers, such as Disney and the NFL and MLB and NHL (and so on) do, is seen as an almost-exclusively positive gesture by corporations. After all, if kids aren't fawning over Donald Duck or Tiger Woods, aren't modeling Tony Hawk or Kim Possible® (whose "brands" are hegemonically constructed as positive), the thinking goes, they might be getting into trouble! As Giroux (2000) explains, the linkages between "the market and representative democracy [are seen as constituting]. . . with few exceptions, the universal values of the new global village" (p. 1). The potential for extreme sport to align itself with such a cultural myth have been, and continue to be, realized, often at the expense of spectators, athletes, and the general public. And branding provides one of the key linkages between the marketplace and this sense of democratic values. In a sense, identification with a brand has been portrayed as a substitute for representative democracy.

Branding, ubiquitous as ever, marks postmodern sport: the Nike swoosh marks professionalized collegiate teams (due to product and sponsorship deals wrought by Nike with many of the coaches—and schools—in the United States), corporate interests mark bowl games (e.g., PapaJohns.com Bowl, Allstate Sugar Bowl, Wells Fargo Sun Bowl, Outback Bowl), and corporations even mark sites like arenas and stadia (e.g., Le Centre Molson/The Molson Centre, now the Bell Centre, in Montreal; AT&T Park—formerly SBC and Pacific Bell Park—in San Francisco; TD Banknorth Garden/Fleet Center in Boston). But while it marks postmodern sport, as well as the adults who consume it, branding also marks and socializes youth consumers in unseen and often unexamined ways. As Hughes (2004) puts it, there is a "corporate aggression [by] brands" that results in "prefabricated desire" (pp. 6–7).

The inculcation of such a "prefabricated desire" is the goal of many corporate interests, but also the goal of such religious and cultural zealots like James Dobson: "The predominant value system of an entire culture can be overhauled in one generation, or certainly in two, by those with unlimited access to children" (cited in Grossberg, 2005, p. 305). Grossberg's characterization of youth today sees neither the "*tabula rasa* of the Enlightenment [nor] the noble savage of romanticism and the counter-Enlightenment" (2005, p. 304): rather, kid culture today attempts to "throw the asocial child into the position and life of adulthood" or "beat, both literally and figuratively, the wildness out of the child. . . ." (p. 304).

And of course, branding ideologies and techniques have become more and more sophisticated in their usually successful attempts at overhauling the "value system" of youth. Sport marketing types of branding, in their most recent incarnations, rely on what former-CEO Phil Knight of Nike has been credited with introducing: "the marketing of ideas" (Pelletier, 2002). This type of branding, where the actual physical product's visibility is purposely diminished in favor of the very *idea* of the product, the surrounding *aura* of the product, is very difficult to oppose. It is difficult to oppose because it is ubiquitous, because it is difficult to oppose *ideas* in a foundationally-democratic culture, and because this type of branding is about products that are, on the face of them, non-contestably benign. Ultimately, of course, the lifestyle that multinationals want consumers to align with is that of the over-consuming adult. But this process starts much earlier, for young[er] consumers.

Branding, in contemporary culture, still marginally involves a product, a tangible bit of easily-replicable something, but branding tends more toward holistic selling of lifestyle, of attitude, of ethos, of emotional or symbolic identification with that product—and, more than that, with a product's *image*. Examples abound in popular culture: the simple sizzle of a "brownish sugared water [can transform] into a commonly desired fluid called Coke" as a brand of desired soda (Katz, 1994, p. 149); the use of team names as brands, such as the Fighting Irish of Notre Dame, is meant to "ensure the name symbolizes strength and confidence" (Shank, 2005, p. 225); and Disney World is branded to be a site "where 'the fun always shines,' [as it] makes an advertising campaign out of a real utopian longing" (The Project on Disney, 1999, p. 7).

The selling of a series of ideological constructs, including individuality and an emotional product-identification, is, of course, meant to discriminate between mass-produced items, so that one type of shoe encourages healthy lifestyle; while a second merely is a shoe; a third is intended for use value, for example, for pronators or supinators, by virtue of some obscure construction; a fourth discriminates between the male and the female foot—and argues that any biological differences are significantly interladen within the brand of the shoe. Ironically, as corporate brands encourage discrimination between nearly identical fabricated objects, they simultaneously encourage mass-think in creating desire for a simulacra of a life. Nowhere is this kind of branding—this marketing of ideas—more prevalent than in the sports arena, and particularly within the new sport forms of action/lifestyle/extreme sports. These sports are relatively new; the forms of promotion, likewise, hold trendy and "cool" currency as well (the irony of marketing to mass groups is that, while the branding efforts privilege individuality and uniqueness, the massified nature of selling/consuming requires groupthink).

And yet, while this branding of youth culture cum action sports is simultaneously insidious and blatant, it is quite under-studied in sport studies literature. In this chapter, I intend to, first, provide a brief background regarding these action or extreme sports, particularly in terms of what their "sportification" has done to youth culture; second, discuss the simultaneous expansion and appropriation of so-called extreme sports by corporate America and multinational and transnational corporations; and third, illuminate what an expansion of cultural and societal trends toward consumption of action or extreme sports may mean for youth culture itself.

The Advent of Action Sports: A Model of Expansionism and Corporate Co-Optation

Action sports (sports like skateboarding, Rollerblading®, wakeboarding, snowboarding, BMX, motocross, and others)[2] have in common with each other the fact of an encompassing excitement, a sense of daring, a skew of the derring-do, that is meant to create in the consumer (in this case, the participant) a sense of disorientation, of what Caillois (1961) terms "vertigo." The thrill aspect of the sports themselves combines easily—and seemingly, naturally—with the self-proclaimed outside statuses of the participants. When the X Games broke onto the 24/7 cable television programming scene in 1995, mass audience for what was up until that time relatively esoteric and grass-roots types of activities was merely an experiment in programming. In fact, Ron Semiao, an ESPN executive, who has been credited with coming up with the idea of putting niche-type recreational activities (like snowboarding, Rollerblading®, skysurfing, street luge, wakeboarding, bungee jumping, and skateboarding) into a multi-event, Olympic-style format, said:

> . . . advertisers were trying to associate themselves with something—a lifestyle, a culture. [additionally] . . . there was no *Sports Illustrated* of extreme sports, no Olympics. (cited in Hughes, 2004, p. 129)

Semiao and ESPN were willing to jump into that breach.

As extreme sports have evolved, from grass-roots play to recreational activities to bona-fide sports, the normalization of extreme activities *as* sports has been inevitable. But originally (if there are, in fact, originals), the activities were not envisioned by their practitioners as *sports*. They were *lifestyle* choices; they were self-expression; they were artistic, and non-conformist, and campy, and decidedly a way for (usually) teenaged kids to be active, to transport themselves, to recreate, to hang out with other kids, and to grow up, independent of (for a short time) adult supervision and guidance. So, when ESPN decided to appropriate these activities, they found themselves in a dilemma: how do you sell cutting-edge to mass America? The ideas seemed oxymoronic, and yet tantalizing: how do you take something hip, and give it some sort of shelf life that will exploit a whole new generation of consumers? (Art critics have, of course, dared to speak these questions, in regard to singular, elite, non-massified art forms, and in regard to the avant-garde and mass culture dynamic, but to apply that dynamic to *sport*? Unthinkable. [cf., Rinehart, 1998b].) One possibility was to attempt to take the activities and marry their ethos—with slight tinkering—with the existing, successful, celebrated mainstream sports ethos.

Though it was a bit of a risk to attempt to change youth's attitudes about these activities, to re-create them as "sports," ESPN executives and corporate culture brought many resources to bear. They brought in young, hip announcers; they used "sport" announcing kinds of formulas, with current athletes as color commentators; they historicized the activities, gave them origination myths; they inundated the airways with MTV-type advertising for the eXtreme Games; they attempted to create "superstars" in order to increase fan identification with the sports (Rinehart, 1998a).

Additionally, the star statuses of the athletes have changed: as extreme sport athletes gain greater notoriety, the statuses of "role model" for youth consumers comes into question. Where ESPN (and various sponsors) earlier worked to attempt to get name recognition of athletes in the public eye, now the cult of celebrity flourishes quite similarly to how it works in mainstream sport (Andrews & Jackson, 2001). That is to say, there is an attraction/repulsion dynamic operating such that a public persona is lionized, scrutinized, then, inevitably, vilified for some social *faux pas*. In fact, recent identification of Evel Kneivel as the so-called grandfather of extreme works to privilege the outside statuses and the emphasis on derring-do of extreme sport practitioners: this further increases the creation of untouchable, attraction/repulsion types of celebrity statuses of the athletes, and, as a result, leads to higher elements of product viability. Thus, consumers of extreme sport have readily bought into the assumed and naturalized aspects of risk that are both inherent in and created within extreme sport discourse (see, e.g., Lyng, 2005).

During the past decade or so (from the first eXtreme Games in 1995 until now), ESPN's stance toward extreme sports has also changed. An experiment in programming in 1995, the X Games have spawned a proliferation of action sports events, modeled as multi-event extravaganzas, in the ensuing years: thus, there are local, regional, national and international competitions (competition is a key element for the activities to become naturalized as sports), from the Gravity Games to the Vans Tour to SheShreds to the Dew Tour, and so on (cf., Rinehart, 2000; Mickle, 2007). The spread of such multi-event gatherings has followed the pattern of English sports at the turn of the 20th century (cf., Guttmann, 1978, 1994): from local, to regional, to national, to international—but much more rapidly, and with much more spillage and temporal overlap between categories. Electronic media, including cable television, satellite television, and the Internet, have spawned what McLuhan (1964) termed "the global village." However, the "cutting-edge" aspect of extreme/action sports (one key aspect of "cutting-edge" is that the masses are not yet doing it) has to be continually renegotiated by ESPN and others (cf., Rinehart, 1998b). But some aspects of the actual excitement of action sports remains.

For the participant, the identification with physically-disorienting aspects within action sports is often exhilarating, like the joy one may experience when riding a thrilling roller coaster. But of course, not all human beings enjoy the vertigo of a roller coaster. The grass-roots participant, on up to the professional, totally-immersed insider, still is attracted to the "thrill" of the ride, no matter what that ride may be. Whether they are extolling how "rad" a street luge ride was, or marveling at the "perfection" of a well-executed 1080° (or three revolutions) on the snowboard slopes, participants are still excited by the way action sports provide relatively safe degrees of disorientation and thrill.

But purveyors and entrepreneurs of action sports not only require *participants* to model the thrilling aspect of the activities (the product), they also require *spectators/consumers* who identify with the brand of action sports themselves. The vertiginous aspect of action sports is fundamental, both to the enjoyment of and the selling of the actual activity, and to the branding of "extreme" or "action" or "lifestyle" sports. But it is the emotional identification with "action" sports themselves that requires less of an embodied commitment on the part of spectators and consumers.

Though marketers of action sports would have their consumers identify with hip and cool poses when attaching to their brands (c.f., Majors & Billson, 1992; Pountain & Robins, 2000), most of the ways that action sports have become commodified have followed a relatively conservative agenda. That is to say, these attempts by marketers to sell action sports to young people have utilized strategies for branding that have worked before on other generations, with other products. Selling lifestyle without commitment to the actual lifestyle, though, is a relatively new and trendy concept. To be a poser is to be anti-establishment, to retain hip without buying in to the actual lifestyle: to be a poser is to retain control. Of course, the irony of posing is that posers are criticized by insiders within the sport, and by casual observers to the lifestyle—all while simultaneously gaining cultural capital for being posers. However, marketers, realizing that ambiguity can lead to the receiving of media messages very differently by consumers, have gleaned a mass market from non-committed youth who rub against, for example, hip hop street culture—as certified by actual skaters, these wannabes are meant to be posers, but it is necessary to marketers that they are *consuming* posers. Their very *posing* has been framed by marketing departments and ad campaigns as ironic and hip.

Thus, as in most contemporary sport forms, in action sports there are those who participate and those who watch, but of course most do a little bit of both. The insiders of these activities originally (circa 1995 and earlier—that is, before ESPN attempted to co-opt leisure and lifestyle activities into a unified and homogeneous sportified brand) saw them as either aesthetic art forms or as lifestyle choices (cf. Rinehart, 1998b). Indeed, terming them "sports" was a branding attempt by ESPN in the mid-1990s to create identification with mass audiences for fairly esoteric, elite lifestyle activities.[3] This co-optation of the "sport" label to apply to skateboarding, Rollerblading®, windsurfing, and so on, fairly quickly lead to an easy acceptance of these activities *as* sports.

What Maguire (2005) has termed "an accelerated phase of corporate-media-sport alignment" (p. 24) has resulted in an "emergence of the global consumer" (p. 25). This global consumer is aware of a multiplicity of transnational corporations, aware of an abbreviated "signature" for these corporations (cf., Nike's swoosh), and culturally competent in finding her/his place within the consumer base for these newly-created transnational corporate brands. The global consumer resonates with the brand: as Katz (1994) puts it, "well-marketed products become brave or sexy" (p. 149). The meta-message for youthful consumers of extreme or action sports is that they are aligned with mainstream sporting practices while simultaneously rejecting mainstream sporting values. They can still see themselves as highly rebellious, while still consuming brands cum lifestyle.

The "consumer" of action sports may be both participant of the sport and spectator of the sport—and so the natural consumption of the sporting lifestyle easily elides into experiencing the brand that is many of these transnational sports. Some of the branding logics for action sports grass-roots participants, spectators, and elite-status action sports athletes are similar, since the overriding message is to teach these youth how to consume a new variety of sport product.

Branding, both at the macro world of action sports themselves (by, for example, ESPN and NBC and Disney), and at the received, micro level of the individual participants, reiterates the logics of sport consumerism. The individual participants, whose sponsorship offers, coupled with a current cultural climate encouraging self-scarification efforts like tattooing, piercing, and branding, often appear as an artistic statement of self, demonstrate both individual agency (and in fact, this individual agency has been effectively branded as rebellious, outlaw, and, therefore, cool) and co-optation by transnational corporations (which is sometimes an uneasy fit, but athletes emphasize that it is they who are agents of their own destiny—their rebellion continues to re-emphasize their ability to simultaneously take corporate dollars and thumb their noses at corporate ethos). It is noteworthy that the agents in charge of multinational marketing reinforce this "anti-hero" stance of the postmodern-day action sports athlete, since the only audience it is duping is the audience of youthful consumers. The front stage/back stage effects of branding lifestyle sports to youth is complex, yet it again follows a rather typical, successful formula: though the stars are corporate pawns, and may have lost much of their rebel stances by becoming sponsored in the first place, the selling point to consumers is that they have retained their ethics and integrity. They are still cutting-edge. Unfortunately, if theories about the avant-garde movement might be applied, as soon as they have become mainstreamed, they are, by definition, no longer cutting-edge.

Sportification of Daily Life

Everywhere, the formula for sport has been used to sell: in many mainstream sports, the effects of the modernist age holistically have created a baby boomer generation whose expectations for sport include a beginning, a middle, and an end; a linear flow; an emphasis on process as well as on product. In touting the so-called "new" sports, ESPN borrowed from some of those expectations, to be sure. But, a post-modernist ethos has caught on, both in the arts and architecture, and in sporting practices. Thus, in their electronic presentation, North American sports have gradually become choppier, result-oriented, and non-linear (while presenting in a linear, albeit segmented, fashion), educating North American audiences to an MTV-style of sports viewing (cf., Rinehart, 1998b). The postmodern sports viewer has learned to fill in the gaps between cause and effect while watching televised sports. This is, of course, quite a different experience from actually being there—and it allows for ESPN to create events like the X Games which work to create heightened senses of cultural and symbolic capital for television viewers and on-site spectators alike.

Other television shows have also utilized this successful sports formula: reality TV shows create MTV-style quick cuts conveyed with hand-held cameras to intensify any dramatic tension that exists between competing chefs, clothes designers, performers, and the like. This strategy of filming and editing has successfully been used for adventure racing (e.g., *Amazing Race, Eco-Challange*), *The Real World, Survivor, Project Runway*, and *Top Chef*, for example. Generations X and Y are deeply influenced by this multinational, corporate-driven, pseudo-cutting-edge style. This style of presentation has proven successful in sports programming in North America (and some say, globally; Wheaton, 2004), and it works to draw in audience with tried-and-true formulaic television.

ESPN (a myriad of extreme sport programming), NBC (primarily the Gravity Games), ABC (affiliated with ESPN, through Disney)—all of these North American-based communication multinationals have imprinted their value structures upon X and Yers. What constitutes those value structures? How have these multinationals used expansion and appropriation of extreme sports—as a vehicle—for an advancement of their own self-serving agendas?

Primarily the value structures are marketing efforts. For example, in the early days of both the televised Summer and Winter X Games, sponsorships were in the form of advertising—canned 30-second ads, sometimes tying into the extreme sport phenomenon, sometimes not. In 2007, branding is the dominant motif: in a recent telecast, Men's Superpipe contestant Tanner Hall was interviewed. His "uniform" consisted of a Red Bull-stickered safety helmet, an X Games windbreaker over his jacket, which was labeled with the Taco Bell logo, and his gloves and snowboard with a Target logo. Behind him, in the actual "space" of the Aspen, Colorado, run, Jeep and Mountain Dew had ad placement signage. The ubiquitousness and non-remarkability of such product-placement, only eleven years later, is stunning. Clearly, multinationals have come on board with a vengeance: and the individuality, self-determination, and spirit and ethos of snowboarding has been compromised.

This is corporatization *as we watch.* When a product (in this case, the product is extreme or action sport itself) is deemed (or created to be) faddish, stylish, cool, the massification of it, in a capitalist world, is nearly inevitable. The original intents are changed, for better or worse. But the quick feeling, the easy adaptability, of consumers, is also remarkable: consumers in the United States, at least, are trained and taught to live in the present.

It is not only that the present is celebrated as hip, cool, and fashionable, but that those who remember the past are maligned as "old school." In sport circles, if someone hearkens back to a (fairly recent) past, there is an easily applied label: they are "old school," they are not current. And multinationals, through their advertising efforts, have effectively quashed much of the resistance to their creeping capitalism with campaigns celebrating the current and criticizing the recollection of the past. Nostalgia, and nostalgic campaigns, play upon this dynamic: while it is cool to remember and celebrate the past, living in the present (without learning from the past) has much more cultural capital.

A Mountain Dew commercial implies, for instance, that having "done something" once, it has become blasé. Treading on the clichés of "been there, done that," Mountain Dew had a group of mountain bikers hovered over an enormous cliff:

Announcer: "Extreme mountain biking. . . forty-five miles an hour.
Biker #1: Did it.
Announcer: . . . sixty-five miles an hour.
Biker #2: Done it.
Announcer: . . .blindfolded.
Biker #3: Been there.
Announcer: . . . then, a four-thousand foot drop.
Biker #4: Tried that.
Announcer: . . . all while slamming a Dew.
Bikers: Whoa.
Announcer: Nothing's more intense than slamming Mountain Dew. Oh yeah—while watching *The eXtreme Games* on ESPN.
Biker #3: Decent. (Mountain Dew ad, ESPN, 24–30 June and 1–3 July 1995)

Obviously, one of the intents of this ad is to align viewers with the cool of ESPN, *the eXtreme Games*, and, primarily, Mountain Dew.

But it also confirms and instantiates, for *non*-power and performance sport athletes, what Coakley terms "the sport ethic": "a set of norms accepted as the dominant criteria for defining what is required to be defined and accepted as an athlete in power and performance sports" (2007, p. 161). Within this "sport ethic," four salient expectations are seen:

> 1. An athlete is dedicated to "the game" above all other things. . . . 2. An athlete strives for distinction. . . . 3. An athlete accepts risks and plays through pain. . . . 4. An athlete accepts no obstacles in the pursuit of possibilities. (Coakley, 2007, pp. 161–163)

In the case of extreme or action sports, multinationals have played upon the known and taken-for-granted logics of the sport ethic, and, in fact, are complicit with ESPN and the sport-purveyors in establishing extreme sport as aligned with "real" (that is to say, power and performance) sport.

The logics of so-called extreme sports (the activities that, prior to 1995's eXtreme Games, were still "lifestyle" and recreational activities) have thus been perverted. If it had been a gradual evolution conducted by the athletes themselves—done from the inside out—then most would agree that there was a sense of authentic change within the sport. But since these changes have been cynically promoted and overtly strategized by multinational corporations, the result is that there is a sense of inauthenticity to what remains of the "sports" *as* sports: therein lies some of the source of residual resistance to how ESPN and other transnational communications giants have exploited the ethos and the participants of these activities. But, portraying themselves as transgressive—to pull in an angst-filled market of pre-teens and teenagers—the multinationals have utilized quite conservative tools, hearkening back to successful formulae from previous generations of sports programming.

Thus, in 1995, the emphasis was on the tricks and skills athletes could perform, the fact(s) that they were performing such outlandish types of physical skills: much of the televised discourse included educating the audience as to what rules these "sports" consisted of (that they were even "sports" was contested). The artistic talents of these extreme sport "athletes" were conveyed. By 2007, however, the presence of adherence to Coakley's "sport ethic" was well established: there is, for example, a growing acceptance and glorification of pain and injury within alternative sport circles (cf., Walk, 2006).

The corporate model deliberately elided with the grass-roots activities in the mid- to late 1990s. The strategies of multinationals were to create a youth consumer who identified with anti-establishment values while deeply adhering to establishment consumption standards. By deliberately branding these activities to align them with more mainstream, successful sports, multinationals created a new market, selling to Gen Xers and Gen Yers. Thus, the tricky effects of branding worked nicely to establish a strong consumer base that was relatively uncritical of just what it was they were consuming. Though Fiske (1989) cautions us to be mindful of the agency of consumers and to be sensitive to consumers' ability actively to resist corporatization, youth are a particularly vulnerable segment of the population, especially vulnerable to the soft velvet noose that gradually constricts their ability to choose. As well, youth, grown up, are well-practiced consumers of a market economy: they have been taught to consume, they have been educated to accept "prefabricated desire" (Hughes, 2004, pp. 6–7). Whether the "cathedrals of consumption" are "re-enchanted" or not, they are still consumed (cf., Ritzer, 2005).

Living With the Present: Growing Up With Labels

According to Howe and Strauss, the strategy of marketers has in the past generally been to ratchet up generational disaffection. So it is no surprise that the image of contemporary teenagers ("Millennials," or "Gen Yers") is seen fairly simplistically by marketers as ". . . *über*-Xers. . . with lots more money to spend—$140 billion in total. . . or $4,500 per teenager per year" (Howe & Strauss, 2000, p. 264). With such a lot of spending cash at stake, marketers are fairly salivating over this group—with the strongest brand loyalties in magazines, music, and jeans (in Howe & Strauss, p. 271)—and clearly the sport branding market is riding this surge as well:

> Beneath the appearance of a diverse and chaotic marketplace lies the reality of big brands and new teen loyalties to them. Suppose a girl wants to dress in a way that appeals to her peer group. All she has to do is make one brand-name choice, one core style selection, and she can shop for nearly anything. There's an incredible variety, but it's the *same* variety her friends are wearing. . . . (Howe & Strauss, 2000, p. 270)

This *appearance* of fragmentation of the market is the core of branding, and youth these days are raised in an atmosphere of *apparent* choice, albeit real-istically-confined choices. The virtuality of branding makes perception one of the major keys to a successful brand and brand identification.

Grossberg (2005) sees "the withdrawal from the future and from imagina-tion [as having] placed kids in the crossfire" (p. 308). Certainly, corporate branding efforts replace imagination with programming, and concerns about the future with fulfillment of today's perceived needs—primarily centered on needs for the self. In extreme sport, in the mid-1990s, branding was an unknown. Skateboarders lead the charge toward combining their lifestyle with skating (their most salient role): many skaters began niche-market magazines in the 1980s, worked in skate shops, designed and built new trucks and boards, worked on artwork for boards, freelanced all over the world—in short, they did whatever they could to remain close to skating, to make it lucrative enough to continue to be able to be core members of the sub-culture (cf., Donnelly & Young, 1988; Hawk, 2000). Branding, during the 1980s and early 1990s, was largely in its infancy, yet "authentic" skaters imagined themselves as living the lifestyle of skating, imagined a future for skaters that would be inclusive and socially just. In the late 1990s, however, that imagination began to be co-opted by corporate branding strategies, so that kids have only seen the world as branded.

As the Millennial Generation—the Gen Yers—reached puberty, the si-multaneous omnipresence of brands, logos, and labeling reached a zenith. This served, simply, as a socializing mark and marker upon the blank slate of this generation. Logos, incessant labeling, and, particularly, branding efforts go unremarked-upon, simply because they have become unremarkable: the presence of the Taco Bell logo upon the "uniform" of a snowboarder; the Nike swoosh (or ACG logo) has become omnipresent, therefore invisible. As consumers, Millennials are less aware of the sneaking, creeping marketization of their sport forms, since they know and have experienced no other way.

The selling of a product is something that is blatant, something where seller and consumer have to overtly confront each other; the insinuation of a brand, on the other hand, into a consumer's life does not necessarily require the overt presence of a seller. In other words, marketers (particularly in sports marketing, lead by Phil Knight's Nike company during the decade of the 1980s) have receded from selling product, to merely offering an omnivorous and incessant choice of lifestyle locked within the purchase of product. This is a significant difference in approach—and in how the consumer sees her or himself in relation to a product and a brand. Georges Lewi says:

> . . . the major difference between the product and the brand is that the product is a matter of marketing, of selling, while the brand is the narration. In other words, the brand tells a story that appeals to both the mind and the heart and so, in fact, when we talk about the myth we are referring first to the beautiful story that is being told. And whether they are true or not, all major brands are beautiful stories. (in Pelletier, 2002)

Of course, one of the major purposes of creating this identification with brand is to inculcate in the consumer (in this case, youth who are "buying" sports lifestyles) a desire for satisfaction from aligning through the lifespan with the brand.

This strategy has been decried by the United States attorney general's office in regard to tobacco advertising targeted toward children. The seemingly-innocuousness of a cartoon-figured Joe Camel was revealed as an unfair advertising practice, targeting youth as lifelong consumers of tobacco products (cf., Levy, 1998). (It is interesting to note that the US-based multinational RJ Reynolds has successfully strategized toward, and penetrated, the Asian market.) Disney, too, has engaged in such practices, aiming much of its advertising dollars toward vulnerable youth (cf., Hiasson, 1998; The Project on Disney, 1999; Ritzer, 2005). As Giroux (2000) argues,

> Childhood innocence no longer inspires adults to fight for the rights of children, enact reforms that invest in their future, or provide them with 'the tools to realize their own political agendas or to participate in the production of their own culture.' On the contrary, as culture becomes increasingly commercialized, the only type of citizenship that adult society offers to children is that of consumerism. (p. 19)

The label culture, for most kids, is not a matter of agency: in order to dismantle the umbrella of consumerism, first they must become aware of the omnipresence of their being taught, in myriad ways, to become consumers—of sport, of teams, of renegade rebelliousness, and, perhaps most significantly, of lifestyle.

Conclusion: Consumable Sport, Non-Sustainable Humans

It is no coincidence that the strategies used by tobacco manufacturers to seduce the young into addictive behaviors are similar to the strategies used by multinational sport purveyors to seduce the young (and old) into sedentary viewing—and other participatory modes—within televised sport. But the strategies—and similarities—do not end there: while brands inculcate attached value to consumers aligning themselves with the product, they also work to create consumers who will return again and again, often for the same product/brand/attachment. Holt (2004) discusses ESPN consumers' brand loyalty in terms of "followers, insiders, and feeders" (p. 139):

> Followers. . . are those customers who identify strongly with the brand's myth. (p. 140) . . . Insiders are the gatekeepers to the brand's claims on the populist world. . . . They often hold the brand in considerably less esteem than do followers, partly because the brand competes with them for leadership within the populist world. (p. 143) . . . Feeders are those consumers of the iconic brand—often the majority—who thrive vicariously on the identity value that icons produce for their followers and (sometimes) insiders. Feeders have only a superficial connection to the values propagated by the icon through its myth. (p. 147)

One of the intentions of corporations within sport, leisure, and so-called "youth-oriented" kinds of lifestyle brands is to create a greater number of follower-type consumers. Niche-marketing will gain feeders, often slipping in and out of their roles, but followers become a loyal base for lifetime consumption.

Similar to the slow awareness of a cartoon dromedary—Joe Camel—who intentionally seduced youth into a lifestyle of smoking, alternative sport has been viewed and produced dominantly by much of the sports media and corporate world (who have a vested interest) as largely a positive influence for kids, at least in the United States. The "sport ethic" (cf., Coakley, 2007), now neatly elided with these formerly-resistant lifestyle activities, does not allow for resistance, questioning, or even discussion about the value(s) of sport. Holt's (2004) "insiders," however, might be a resistant strain within the consumer base that tends to prove the rule. Mainstream sport has actively been aligned with patriotism, activism, individualism, rugged individualism, and democratic ideals, and to criticize sport is taboo: thus, it isn't a far stretch to say that sport is anti-democratic values, anti-mindfulness. Action sport has been aligned, too, with this sport ethic, particularly in promoting healthy lifestyles, active physical participation, and risk-taking behavior, and most particularly for youth. To criticize the promotion of action sport is becoming taboo—and since many brands have infiltrated action sport and have begun to identify strongly with the action sport brand(s)—criticism of the brands has become taboo as well.

But what is wrong with people taking their minds off of daily problems and worries? What is so wrong with relaxing with a favorite team, sport, or individual—or, in fact, going out and doing the activity oneself? On the face of it, there is nothing wrong with those gestures. But the key is *mindfulness* in doing these things.

Jane Goodall, the ethologist of Gombe Stream Chimpanzee Reserve fame, may provide a way out for consumers: she proposes four "reasons for hope" that humankind may, in fact, be able to regain a sustainable conservation movement (2000; 2007). Grounded in the role of individual effort, her "reasons for hope" are altruistic and idealistic. Yet, they center social justice, renewal of energy resources, and a sustainable environment as keys to their success. Her listed "reasons for hope" may, in fact, be applied to a concomitant set of "reasons for hope" within sport and lifestyle consumerism:

> ... we can use our problem-solving abilities, our brains, and, joining hands around the world, find ways to live that are in harmony with nature. ... My second reason for hope lies in the tremendous energy, enthusiasm and commitment of a growing number of young people around the world. ... My third reason for hope lies in the indomitable nature of the human spirit. ... My fourth reason for hope is the incredible resilience of nature. (2007)

Similarly, applying these precepts to consumers' relationships to brands relies upon cognitive thinking, great energy, and an overabundance of individual agency. The alternative/action/ extreme communities have the wherewithal to mobilize against a steadily encroaching and disempowering corporate presence: but will they understand the possible ramifications of not acting?

Of course, criticism and positive critiques are exactly what might free action sport participants to regain the ethos that they have lost to multinational corporations. The interests of multinationals, whether participants rationalize it or not, are not consistent with the interests of self-determination, sustainability (both of the environment and of the self), and, at the very least, mindfulness. Thus, action sports, transnational corporations, and the consuming public will once again have to work to negotiate an uneasy—and probably capitalist-based—alliance. The seductions of capitalism, as enunciated by George W. Bush immediately following the tragedy of September 11, are, like corporations themselves, omnivorous and incessant.

Notes

1. The terms used by marketing academics are also interesting, especially in their alignment with bellicose and sexual language: we *target* consumers, *penetrate* new markets, *brand* corporations. But the language of angry corporate ethos is another essay, for another time.
2. For an extensive listing of "extreme/alternative/action" sports, see Robert Rinehart, "Emerging Arriving sport: Alternatives to formal sports," In J. Coakley and E. Dunning (Eds.), *Handbook of sport and society* (pp. 504, 519) (London: Sage Publishing, Inc., 2000).
3. The cynicism of this branding attempt is rather apparent when one traces ESPN's deliberate and self-conscious marketing of the very terms "extreme" and "X" by ESPN in describing their new alternative annual event. From year one (in 1995, "The eXtreme Games") to year two (in 1996), the name was changed, without remark, to "The X Games." One of their executives, Amy Cacciola, said that the use of the term "X," replacing "eXtreme," "had a mystique to it" (personal communication, October 4, 1996, cited in Rinehart, "Inside of the outside: Pecking orders within alternative sport at ESPN's 1995 *The eXtreme Games*," *Journal of Sport & Social Issues, 22*(4), 398-415 [1998]). See also Robert E. Rinehart, *Players all: Performances in contemporary sport* (Bloomington: Indiana University Press, 1998); Belinda Wheaton, "Introduction: Mapping the lifestyle sport-scape," in Belinda Wheaton (Ed.), *Understanding lifestyle Sports: Consumption, Identity and Difference* (pp. 1, 28) (London: Routledge, 2004).

References

Andrews, D. L., & Jackson, S. J. (Eds.) (2001). *Sports stars: The cultural politics of sporting celebrity.* London: Routledge.
Bush, G. W. (2001). News conference (O'Hare International Airport) (27 September 2001). Chicago, IL. Retrieved January 24, 2007, from http://transcripts.cnn.com/TRANSCRIPTS/0109/27/se.19.html.
Caillois, R. (1961). *Man, play, and games.* New York: Free Press.
Coakley, J. (2007). *Sports in society: Issues and controversies* (9th ed.). Boston: McGraw-Hill.
Donnelly, P., & Young, K. (1988). The construction and confirmation of identity in sports subcultures. *Sociology of Sport Journal, 5,* 223–240.
Fiske, J. (1989). *Understanding popular culture.* London: Routledge.
Giroux, H. A. (2000). *Stealing innocence: Corporate culture's war on children.* New York: Palgrave.
Goodall, J., & Berman, P. (2000). *Reason for hope: A spiritual journey.* New York: Warner Books.
Goodall, J. (2007). My four reasons for hope. www.janegoodall.org/jane/essay.asp Accessed 8 March 2007.
Grossberg, L. (2005). *Caught in the crossfire: Kids, politics, and America's future.* Boulder, CO: Paradigm Publishers.
Guttmann, A. (1978). *From ritual to record: The nature of modern sports.* New York: Columbia University Press.
Guttmann, A. (1994). *Games & Empires: Modern Sports and Cultural Imperialism.* New York: Columbia University Press.
Hawk, T. (with Mortimer, S.). (2000). *Hawk: Occupation: Skateboarder.* New York: ReganBooks.
Hiasson, C. (1998). *Team rodent: How Disney devours the world.* New York: The Ballantine Publishing Group.
Holt, D. B. (2004). *How brands become icons: The principles of cultural branding.* Boston, MA: Harvard Business School Press.
Howe, N., & Strauss, W. (2000). *Millennials rising: The next great generation.* New York: Vintage Books.
Hughes, G. (2004). *SportCo: Branding, management culture, and subjectivity in U.S. sports media.* Unpublished doctoral dissertation, University of California, Santa Barbara.
Katz, D. (1994). *Just do it: The Nike spirit in the corporate world.* Holbrook, MA: Adams Publishing.
Klein, N. (2000). *No Logo.* New York: Picador USA.
Levy, D. (1998). Documents show RJ Reynolds targeted teen smokers. *USA Today,* January 14, n.p.

Lyng, S. (2005). *Edgework: The sociology of risk-taking.* New York: Routledge.

Maguire, J. (2005). *Power and global sport: Zones of prestige, emulation and resistance.* London: Routledge.

Majors, R., & Billson, J. M. (1992). *Cool pose: The dilemmas of Black manhood in America.* New York: Lexington Books.

McLuhan, M. (1964). *Understanding media.* New York: New American Library.

Mickle, T. (2007). Dew Tour looks for leadoff site. *Street & Smith's SportsBusiness Journal, 9*(37), 7.

Nadeau, R. A. (2007). *Living brands: Collaboration + innovation = customer fascination.* New York: McGraw-Hill.

Pelletier, M. (2002). In brands we trust [videorecording]. Montreal: Locomotion Télévision, Inc.

Postman, N. (1985). *Amusing ourselves to death: Public discourse in the age of show business.* New York: Penguin Books.

Postman, N. (1994). *The disappearance of childhood.* New York: Vintage Books.

Pountain, D., & Robins, D. (2000). *Cool rules: Anatomy of an attitude.* London: Reaktion Books.

The Project on Disney. (1999). *Inside the mouse: Work and play at Disney World.* Durham, NC: Duke University Press.

Rinehart, R. (1998a). Inside of the outside: Pecking orders within alternative sport at ESPN's 1995 "the eXtreme Games." *Journal of Sport & Social Issues 22*(4), 398–415.

Rinehart, R. E. (1998b). *Players all: Performances in contemporary sport.* Bloomington: Indiana University Press.

Rinehart, R. E. (2000). Emerging Arriving sport: Alternatives to formal sports. In Coakley, J., & E. Dunning. (Eds.), *Handbook of sports studies* (pp. 504–519). London: Sage Publications.

Ritzer, G. (2005). *Enchanting a disenchanted world: Revolutionizing the means of consumption* (2nd Ed.). Thousand Oaks, CA: Pine Forge Press.

Shank, M. D. (2005). *Sports marketing: A strategic perspective* (3rd ed.). Upper Saddle River, NJ: Pearson Prentice Hall.

Walk, S. (2006). "Painography, risk voyeurism, and the near-life experience." NASSS Presidential Address (2 November 2006), Vancouver, British Columbia.

Wheaton, B. (2004). Introduction: Mapping the lifestyle sport-scape. In B. Wheaton (Ed.), *Understanding lifestyle sports: Consumption, identity and difference* (pp. 1–28). London: Routledge.

CHAPTER 5

To the White Extreme in the Mainstream
Manhood and White Youth Culture in a Virtual Sports World[1]

DAVID J. LEONARD

Despite the immense coverage afforded games like *Grand Theft Auto: San Andreas* (Rockstar Games, 2004) *Halo 2* (Microsoft Game Studies, 2004) or any number of war games (e.g., the *Medal of Honor* series)—and their attendant importance within cultural and political domains—the sports gaming industry continues to be the crown jewel of the video games world. In 2005, for example, when much of the industry faced losses in sales, sports games remained strong within the industry, accounting for more than thirty percent of all video games sales. That year, Electronic Arts, whose core market remained with virtual sports reality, generated $675 million in revenue during the second quarter alone, and later saw the 2006 version of *Madden: NFL*—its flagship title—take less than one month to become the top-selling game for year within North America.[2] In total, sports video games represent a $1 billion industry, a fact that demonstrates the economic power and cultural significance of sports video games (Schor, 2005).

While obviously crucial as a source of profit-making, the popularity and presence of sports simultaneously embodies a powerful racialized project, offering spaces of racialized play, fantasy and pleasure. Up against a perceived erasure of whiteness from the sports world, video games offer a space of play for primarily suburban White males to transform themselves into virtual athletes, into authentic men who can dominate multiple landscapes. Whether reflecting the commodification of an imagined contemporary blackness defined by the aesthetics of hip-hop (gangstas) or bling-bling, as evident in games like *NFL Street* (Electronic Arts, 2004) or *NBA Ballers* (Midway, 2004) or efforts to colonize spaces with extreme sports games, sporting virtual realities require ideological and cultural examination.

Although in past articles I have examined the ways in which the virtual sporting world offers its primarily middle-class, White players the opportunity to experience the coolness, the imagined savagery, and animalism (athleticism) associated with White supremacist fascination with male bodies of color, the racial meaning of sporting games is not limited to virtual athletes of color. Likewise, past analyses (Leonard, 2003, 2005, 2006a) regarding the ways in which video games represent a site in which White hatred and disdain for blackness manifests itself alongside love and adoration for Black bodies has erased the racial signification of whiteness. The desire to be Black because of the stereotypical visions of strength, athleticism, power and sexual potency (Hoberman, 1997; King and Springwood, 2001) all play out within certain types of virtual sports games, yet the desire to be White and hyper-masculine directs play into another type of virtual sporting reality, one that we might call an alternative or extreme virtual sport reality. So, while "today's gaming resides squarely in mainstream America, and for them fantasy means Tigers and Kobes," it equally means being athletic and *not* Tiger and Kobe, but rather Tony Hawk or any number of White extreme athletes who push the assumed boundaries of masculinity, whiteness, and the athletic imagination (Ratliff, 2003, p. 96; Leonard, 2003) through the representation and virtual reconstitution of the white extreme sport athlete (Leonard, 2005).

The world of extreme sports games thus represents an increasingly popular genre, offering its participants the ability to embody a virtual White sports rebel (Leonard, 2005). While not at the level of *Madden* or *Grand Theft Auto* series, extreme sports have proven to be significantly profitable within the video game industry. The original four *Tony Hawk* games grossed close to $9 million dollars, while both *Tony Hawk Underground* (Activision, 2003) games amassed over $5 million dollars in sales. Moreover, during the aforementioned industry-wide slump of 2005, *Tony Hawk: Wasteland* (2005) generated significant financial benefits for game-maker Activision, which through the Hawk[3] series and its long list of extreme sports games, remained competitive within the marketplace falling short only to Electronic Arts in global sales.[4]

Given the increased value anointed to extreme sports athletes, who are celebrated for their whiteness, rule breaking, and masculinity (i.e. the ability to seduce "sexy" women or otherwise conquer available sexual objects), it should not be surprising that these games generate significant levels of economic success. Belinda Wheaton (2004) describes extreme sports in terms of its fetishization of "risk and danger," as well as its participatory ideology that "promotes fun, hedonism, involvement, 'flow,' living in the moment, 'adrenaline rushes,' and other intrinsic rewards" (pp. 11–12). Whereas traditional sports, marked by the dominance of Black athletes and cultural aesthetics, are defined by institutionalization, commercialization, rules, and competition, extreme sporting cultures identify alternative sports as not only oppositional but extreme in its challenge to contemporary understanding of sport and sporting identities.

The fall of Jim Crow within certain sporting contexts has, in similar fashion to Title IX and the growth in women's sports, eroded the power of sporting cultures in confirming White masculinist prowess. Extreme sports, and to a greater extent, extreme sports video games, fills this void, reinscribing White masculinity into a sports world defined by aggression and physicality, yet taken to the extreme in both constructing a world without people of color, who have increasingly been signifiers of athleticism, and women, except as sexual props of desire. Moreover, the reconstitution of this sporting context as the most authentic space of masculinity and one defined by athletes defining limitations and facing physical and mental dangers further reveals the power of extreme sports—as real and virtual—in celebrating White masculinity.

Amidst an imagined backlash against White males during the 1980s and 1990s (into today), the increasing popularity of the (virtual) White extreme sports rebel reflects an ideological and cultural response to the presumptive pollutant of blackness and femininity on White manhood. The cultural stature of specific extreme sports athletes (e.g., Tony Hawk, Dave Mira,[5] etc.) and the gendered approval given to mastery over the extreme represent two distinct cues as to why extreme sports games dominate the industry.

The world of virtual extreme sports games tends to imagine two distinct geographies: a dangerous urban ghetto and the dangerous wilderness. The use of ghetto locations emphasizes the defiance and creativity possessed by extreme sports athletes, demonstrating that extreme sports are as much about challenging the boundaries of the law and the geographies of America's violent and dangerous urban centers as overcoming the physical limitations of body and nature. Emblematic of the deployment of a particular understanding of White masculinity, extreme within virtual reality reflects gamers' willingness to accept any challenge from the law, a city's architecture, or the dangers presented by the residents of America's ghettos.[6]

As with extreme sports, the virtual incarnations additionally define this alternative sports world as a space of White masculine dominance, whereupon the entry of women results from male fantasies and sexual needs; moreover, the perceptual presence of people of color legitimizes the space. Hypermasculinity and an excessive female sexuality geared toward male pleasure define *Tony Hawk Underground* (Activision, 2003), *SSX Tricky*[7] and *Amped: Freestyle Snowboarding*.[8] With this in mind, I argue how extreme sports—particularly the imagined identities within virtual extreme games—construct a White masculinity through erasing people of color, commodifying inner-city spaces, offering opportunities to dominate nature, all the while rendering females as sexually appealing and sexually available "eye candy." These games personify a powerful racialized/gendered/sexualized project that provides commonsense ideas about race, gender, and sexuality. Both in textual utterances and contextual meaning, alternative sports games demonstrate that while extreme sports athletes tend to imagine themselves and their sporting culture as different, as ideological and practical challenges to mainstream culture and values, the world of extreme sports (both the real and virtual), and the "renegotiated identities" that inhabits this world, ultimately reproduce "traditional structures of social and cultural power and inequalities" (Wheaton, 2004, p. 21).

According to Kyle Kusz (1997, 2001), Robert Reinhart (2003), and others, the discursive focus and popularity of extreme sports reflects both the increasing visibility of "angry white male/white male backlash" politics and the increasing anxiety over the diminishing power and visibility of White athletes. Given the importance of American sporting spaces as a marker of masculinist prowess, the increasing dominance of African American athletes in the face of a disappearing White athlete, fears about White masculinity are reconciled within with extreme sports, whether on ESPN or through gaming opportunities from EA Sports and Activision. S. L. Price (1997), in "What Happened to the White Athlete?" identified extreme sports as a response to "the diminishing opportunities for athletic success" for White men in "mainstream" sports such as football, baseball, and basketball: "Unsure of his place in a sport world dominated by blacks . . . the young white male is dropping of the athletic mainstream to pursue success elsewhere . . . . He is increasingly drawn to . . . alternative athletic pursuits that are overwhelming white" (pp. 31–32). Kusz (2003) not only links this discourse to those of "white male as victim," but to a desire to assert a particular vision of white masculinity that imagined white athletes (men) in a "superior and dominant position" (p. 166).

In examining these dimensions, this chapter equally gives voice to the narrative options of these games, in that players can simultaneously engage in a world of extreme sports, challenging mental creativity through imagined stunts, and enter into a world of hypersexuality, in which success leads to the opportunity to consume virtually naked females. In exploring these various narratives, I theorize the ways in which race, gender, and sexuality play into these available choices, each providing pleasure, while accommodating White fantasies and affirming White privilege through virtual gaming. More specifically, and in connection to the themes and focus of this collection, I argue that video games, particularly extreme sports games, recreate a space of youth culture that imagines White masculinity as oppositional, cutting edge, aggressive, physically powerful, sexually dominant, and transgressive. These games provide (white suburban) youth, otherwise unable to conquer mountains or unwilling (unable) to "ride where they're not wanted, and in particular treat private space as public," and those who have "matured" to the point where youth culture is otherwise inaccessible the opportunity to participate in a cultural space that validates their youthful and White masculinity as natural and desired (Quart, 2003, p. 104).

Responding to the limited analysis of video game culture, particular in regard to race and gender, and the scant engagement with virtual sporting cultures (Leonard, 2006c), this chapter offers a narrow focus on the intersections of race, gender, and sexuality with extreme sports games. It accepts the task of examining the racialized/gendered content of extreme sports games, paying particular attention to how these games construct extreme sports as spaces dominated by an imagined White masculinity. Specifically examining the popularity of these games, the celebration of rule breaking, and the constructions of White "athletes" as courageous, cool, creative, and holding mastery over space/nature, this chapter will defamiliarize the racial construct of whiteness within extreme sports games, demonstrating that extreme culture as it appears within alternative sports games does not challenge the status quo, instead reproducing dominant understandings of race, gender, sexuality, and social relations.

What Happened to the Black Athlete?

People of color fill one of two roles within the virtual extreme sports world: 1) as virtually absent or lone tokens; or 2) as exotic, racist caricatures. The bulk of extreme sports games lack characters of color, despite their visibility within the world of American athletics and sports video games. Within a game like *Amped* (Microsoft, 2002) people of color are totally absent. The entire Tony Hawk series, which represents the cornerstone of the extreme sports games, offer a single character of color who reflects hegemonic visions of blackness. Kareem Campbell, a character based on an actual person, is "a well-honed version of the world's street dwellers; hopes to someday attain smart, real, and smoothed out style—without the R & B."[9] Unlike his peers who reflect the alternative lifestyles of extreme sports, Campbell embodies its "authentic" rhythms and hip-hop elements; he provides a bridge between the "fugitive culture" associated with working-class whiteness, and the transgressive culture associated with extreme sports and hip-hop, a powerful commodity within White suburban culture (Giroux, 1996; Boyd, 1997). Whether completely absent or existing as hip-hop tokens, the presence of blackness within extreme virtual sports solidifies the meanings of White masculinity.

Games like *SSX* (EA Sports Big, 2000) and *BMX XXX* (Acclaim Entertainment, 2002), each which contain several characters of color, do not unsettle this White masculine hegemony, as virtual athletes of color are defined by intensely racist caricatures that add to the exotic and alternative orientation of the extreme sports world. For example, both *SSX 3* (EA Sports, 2003) and *SSX Tricky* (EA Sports Big, 2001) offer extreme (racist) caricatures of people of color: the exotic Asian woman, the Latina (Native American) woman wearing war paint, and the hip-hop, bling-bling Black man. Their extreme presentation and stereotypical embodiment signifies the extreme elements of these games. In *Gravity Games: Street, Vert, and Dirt* (Midway Games, 2002) which interestingly positions the street and dirt as interchangeable dangerous obstacles, only one of the game's real-life characters—Andre Ellison—is a person of color. The game, however, offers fictionalized characters, which not coincidentally are disproportionately minorities. Renaldo Marcellus, who appears to be Latino, is a tough rider who dons dreads and an earring and has an enormous chest. Notwithstanding his talent, "he is shunned by sponsors because of his perceived negative image." The deployment of hegemonic racialized tropes is not limited to Renaldo; it is evident in several others, including Bird Brains and British Biker. Bird Brains is, in fact, a bird who comes from Africa. Arriving in the United States illegally, after stowing away within the landing gear of a commercial airplane, Bird Brains excels within extreme sports because of its "genetic make-up" that allows for massive jumps off the ramp. Bird Brains is joined by British Biker, another foreign transplant into the world of extreme sports. The insert for *Gravity Games* captures the ways in which extreme sports game use racialized difference to reify dominant understandings of White masculinity in its description of British Biker, who importantly appears to be Afro-British.

> Abused as a boy by seven older brothers and an ex-con mother in London's East End, British Biker profited just two things from his much-maligned childhood: a lack of a formal education (street smarts notwithstanding) and an accent so thick it rendered him virtually unintelligible…Running away to the mean streets of London, British Biker was forced to develop the aggressive disposition and attitude necessary to defend himself and his unique trademark. Now, years later, armed with raw talent, street savvy, an unbridled fearlessness and a move called 'The Bloody Brit,' British Biker has come to the new world and intends to find a place to plant his colorful flaw. (p. 18)

Reflective of widespread stereotypes within extreme sports games (as well a vast majority of games), the game's emphasis of extremity celebrates the ghetto childhood of British Biker and the prevalence of violence, ultimately demonstrating how little these games oppose dominant ideologies and common sense.

The "otherness" of these personages provides meaning to the White characters, who despite their alternative identities, are still clearly White. The baggy pants, defiance of rules, and extreme masculinity, raise little question as to the presence and meaning of their whiteness, given the presence of these stereotypical characters of color. The racialized other marks the visible as invisible, rendering White masculinity as the natural opposition to the exotic, functioning as a defining element in the world of extreme sports.

As a popular cultural site, extreme sports has become involved in a reactionary politics of representation which seeks to represent a "strong, proud, confident, unconstrained, and unapologetic white athletic masculinity whose characteristics, investments, desires and practices would appeal to whites" (Kusz, 2003, p 155). To Kusz (2003), extreme (virtual) sports filled a void, need or panacea to 1990s male anxiety, which "were said to have a crisis of confidence, self-esteem, social status and identity" (p. 155). Extreme sports games fill this persistent void while addressing this imagined crisis. In fact, this constructed world of virtual extreme athleticism offers an "unapologetic white masculinity, defined by alternative values, risk-taking, and extreme sexual prowess" (Kusz, 2003. p. 154). Notwithstanding the White masculinized orientation of extreme sports (in the real and virtual), much has been made about its racial (colorblind) and gender politics. Often described as a "racially mixed world," where race, class, and gender are insignificant given the importance of the values and identities that define extreme sports, part of against-the-grain or oppositional elements that put extreme sports at the extreme are its defiance for White supremacy and patriarchy. "In skating, there is no segregation. You don't look at other skateboarders and become aware of their skin color or the clothes they wear. It just doesn't matter. There aren't the biases that exist in other areas of life. It's like we are our own race" (Borden, 2001, pp. 140–141). Despite the celebration of extreme sports for its (imagined) transcendence of racial classification, given its integrative possibilities and its emphasis on extreme sporting identities being the only meaning identity, the evidence of persistent inequalities (i.e., police contact with Black and White youth who defy the law whether on skateboards or with spray paint), and the representations available within virtual reality offer little evidence toward celebration.

More powerful than its real-life brethren, extreme sports games leave few gaps or contradictions. With the ultimate reduction of femininity to sexuality and the complete erasure of men of color, extreme sports games are a space for, by, and about White men. Unlike the discourse surrounding real extreme sports games, which emphasizes the whiteness of this alternative world, the fantasy world inscribes people of color as scenery, as racialized caricatures. However, as with ESPN's X-Games or the coverage of extreme sports (see Rinehart, this volume), these games relate White masculinity to a position of normalcy, as the most desired sporting masculinity. Otherwise imagined as the pollutants and points of comparisons to a normalized White masculinity, the absence of people of color and non-sexualized women further allows for the production of a particular vision of White masculinity.

We Love the Ghetto, But We Hate Black People

While extreme sports games construct a world defined by White masculinity, a significant number of games take place within America's ghettos. The importance of dominating or mastering space is found in those games located within America's inner cities. Whereas hegemonic projects of the ghettocentric imagination (Watkins, 1999) systematically demonize inner-city communities because of the presence of people of color, these extreme sports games construct the ghetto without people of color. Resembling an array of popular cultural projects that glorify/fetishize ghetto spaces, *Tony Hawk Underground* (*Thug*), *Tony Hawk's American Wasteland*, and *BMX XXX*, define the ghetto through its aesthetics and an imagined hip-hop culture. Virtual extreme sports games erase "how segregation strips communities of resources and reproduces inequality" (Kelley, 1998, p. 18). They, in imagining the ghetto as a cultural signifier and an exotic tourist destination, deny "how the decline of decent-paying jobs and city services, erosion of public space, deterioration of housing stock and property values, and stark inequalities in education and health care are manifestations of investment strategies under de facto segregation" (Kelley, 1998, p. 18). Robin Kelley (1998) further demonstrates the power of conquering and consuming those spaces inhabited by America's racialized other as part of both an ideological and capitalist project:

> Nike, Reebok, L.A. Gear, and other athletic shoe conglomerates have profited enormously from postindustrial decline. TV commercials and print ads romanticize the crumbling urban spaces in which African American youth play, and in so doing they have created a vast market for overpaid sneakers. These televisual representations of "street ball" are quite remarkable; marked by chain-link fences, concrete playgrounds, bent and rusted netless hoops, graffiti-scrawled walls, and empty buildings, they have created a world where young black males do nothing but play. (pp. 195–196)

In other words, those living outside these communities whose privilege and power enables them to pathologize, demonize, and otherwise erase the ghettos from the mainstream imagination, find pleasure, power, and legitimacy in constructing and dominating these ghetto frontiers safely inside America's suburban dream; or, better said, virtually visit America's dangerous wastelands from their safely protected suburban reality (Leonard, 2003).

A central element of extreme sporting cultures and their virtual representations is its extreme opposition to rules and order. Its extreme nature does
not emanate from the verticality of jumps, the danger of tricks, or even the
potential for energy, but the risks of defying societal cultural norms and the
law in base jumping from buildings, or skating on public property. "Street
skating requires an urban setting with public spaces that are not supervised,"
write Becky Beal and Charlene Wilson (2004) in "'Chicks Dig Scars.'" They
note further, "In fact, risk-taking behavior is exemplified by street skating
because tax-paying citizens post signs against skating and police officers
enforce anti-skating laws. Street skating maintains its status as more 'core'
because it most strongly reinforces the ethos of the activities which values
physical and legal risk-taking" (pp. 48–49).

While erased within their own imagination, the whiteness of most extreme
athletes (in the real and virtual worlds) and its perception as a space of White
youth, allows them to see themselves as "anti-social" and violate societal
laws without consequences. The anti-social behavior and defiance not only
becomes a "positive attribute" within extreme sporting cultures, but one
without the potential for repression and violence that are often experienced
by youth of color who defy societal expectations.

While extreme sports games most certainly reflect similar understandings of extreme embodiments of White masculinist challenges and defiance
against the law, they tend to reveal a greater investment in emphasizing the
risks associated with driving, skating, or otherwise pushing the physical limit
inside America's ghettos. At the ideological core of virtual extreme sport is the
mastery and conquering of untamed space amidst the hegemony of popular
and political protests that imagine the ghetto as a threat to White masculinity.
Many games offer players the opportunity to play or dominate (Black) city
spaces in absence of people of color. Given the realities of segregation, ostensibly virtual extreme sports games provide White suburbanites the opportunity
to play from the "safety" of their homes, transported into a dangerous, yet
not *too* dangerous, ghetto experience that erases people of color.

The valorization of "overcoming one's fear and taking risks" within extreme
sport games is especially powerful within these ghettocentric games, in that
they allow players/game characters to conquer dangerous ghetto spaces
through performing an extreme, athletic, White masculinity. Kusz (2003),
in writing about BMX and extreme sports, elucidates this racial context, as
evident in both the real and virtual inscriptions of extreme sports. Dominant
discourses concerning extreme sports "represents the extreme athlete as an
offspring of the American frontiersman (racially coded as white) as both
are said to have an insatiable appetite for risk, a thirst for adventure, and a
desire to be the embodiment of strength, coolness and confidence" (p. 168).
Whereas the frontiersman defied the dangers of the unnamed wilderness

guarded by indigenous "savages," the extreme virtual skateboarder defies the dangers and geographic obstacles of America's ghetto, conquering this once dangerous space, demonstrating the ultimate "strength, coolness and confidence" of this White masculinity.

For example, *Tony Hawk's Pro Skater 3* offers a series of locations to which players attempt to perform lip tricks and crazy moves within urban centers and suburban locations. Players can skate in Canada or the suburbs. The game insert and visual demarcation of suburbia constructs a banal world without danger or threats: "Did someone say Ice Cream? Explore the neighborhood! Hit the rooftop, ledge grinds, trash the trailer park vert ramps and find your way into the haunted house . . . . Who knows, if you are good enough, you own one of these houses some day." The rest of the locations, however, are within city landscapes, offering dangerous and exotic geographies to physically conquer even without residents of color. In Los Angeles, skaters face the dangers of traffic, rather than a repressive state apparatus, with Tokyo affording players the chance to traverse the chaos of city life. As with outdoors extreme sports games, the urban extreme sport location exotifies the urban landscape as a culturally exciting yet dangerous place that challenge and tests the creativity, courage and masculinity of the extreme sports athlete.

Celebrating White Transgression: Urban Extremism and Celebration of (White) Law Breaking

No two games are more indicative of the importance of urban and racialized geographies within extreme sports games than *Tony Hawk Underground II (Thug)* (Activision, 2004) and *Tony Hawk's American Wasteland*. Each uses the racialized danger that festers within America's ghetto as part of their celebration of White masculine conquering of space. Following in the footsteps of the original, it allows players to conquer urban spaces through tricks and the physical domination of the skateboard. It, too, erases people of color and women, rendering the world of extreme sports as a space of Jim Crow: a virtual athletic world without the intrusion of the racialized other. It also imagines America's inner cities as spaces of White play, devoid of poverty, state violence or police brutality. Likewise, this game constructs the ghetto as a space of cultural difference, a destination of virtual tourists needing exotic and dangerous spaces to prove White masculine coolness, courage and domination. Unlike America's actual ghettos, where police brutalize and incarcerate people of color for graffiti, destruction of property, and other transgressions of the law, *Tony Hawk Underground II* celebrates these activities as part of an alternative or extreme lifestyle.

Tony Hawk's American Wasteland follows the template set by the previous installments, providing a story in which in a rural-based character arrives in Los Angeles in hopes of conquering the difficult skating world. In order to make it, you are forced to not only prove yourself to a group of local street legends, but also negotiate the obstacles and dangers offered in an urban setting. Moreover, like its predecessor, *Wasteland* transforms America's inner cities and their deteriorating infrastructures into a space of consumption and pleasure, so that the game's dilapidated and littered skate park offers a more challenging test to the skills and manhood of any skater. bell hooks (1994) describes this process in profound terms, noting how the process of reducing America's ghetto to barren "wastelands" of suburban play is not simply about tasting the danger of the other side of tracks, but contributes to a maintaining of the status quo: "The desire to be 'down' has promoted a conservative appropriation of specific aspects of underclass Black life, who in reality is dehumanized via a process of commodification wherein no correlation is made between mainstream hedonistic consumerism and the reproduction of a social system that perpetuates and maintains an underclass" (p. 152). The appearance of extreme culture or opposition ultimately contributes to reproduction of the dominant social system, especially as relationships are increasingly defined by consumption and consumerism.

Tony Hawk's American Wasteland does deviate from past versions in terms of its *celebration* of "law breaking" and "anti-establishment" behavior: graffiti, knocking over police officers, trespassing, loitering, and vandalism—what would be termed as criminal behavior in racialized virtual realities. The appearance of White youth—suburban no less—proved unsettling to hegemonic understandings of criminality. Yet, at the same time, media commentators and critics alike sought to differentiate between the behaviors endorsed and promoted within *Wasteland* and those marked visible in games like *Grand Theft Auto* and *True Crime*, describing them as youth angst, "anti-establishment" sentiment, or mere transgression that require parental curtailment (Leonard, 2006d). Media Wise, an initiative from The National Institute on Media and Family, one of the most visible reactionary media groups, describes *Wasteland* as an improved game that still requires some parental (not state) intervention:

> Parents should know that the game's story mode depends heavily on an "anti-establishment" sentiment. Players steal signature items from places around L.A. to build up the ultimate skate park, and attempt to run from the cops and security in order to do so. The can also make cash by spray painting graffiti on walls. In addition, the games outrageous moves lead to spectacular crashes, complete with blood. Finally, the game is online enabled, which means players can run into unpredictable language and behavior. (The National Institute of Media

and the Family, N.D.)

Mimicking the sentiment of game designers and the discourse surrounding extreme sports in general, such descriptions reinscribe the notion that these games sit outside the norm, that their extreme elements challenge conventional values and morals normally practiced and embodied by White youth. In other words, their subscription or promotion of an aesthetic or values associated with blackness demonstrate both the extreme nature and its potential threat to impressionable with youth. Ultimately their understanding of White masculinity, race, and the urban imagination, mirrors dominant discourses, celebrating the possibilities and prowess of White masculinity. As with the rest of the genre, the ghetto proves to be an obstacle and source of danger that White men can successfully transverse; in other spaces, it is the gauntlet White men must brave in order to prove the value and valor of their racialized manhood.

White Mastery: Controlling, Dominating and Conquering Untamed Space

Of central importance to the allure and performative attraction of extreme sports games specifically, and video games in general, is the opportunity to control, dominate, and conquer space. Henry Jenkins, director of Comparative Media Studies at MIT, reflects the scope and canonical themes within game studies through his use of longstanding colonial/racialized language to describe the cultural allure and immense potential of virtual reality: "Now that we've colonized physical space, the need to have new frontiers is deeply embedded in the games. [Video Games] expand the universe" (Jenkins, 2003). As the literature connects the popularity of video games to fantasy, "exploration and discovery," colonization and penetrating "the virtual frontier," as if each were raceless projects, it is important to link games and the surrounding discourse to historical projects of White supremacy, based on the power of becoming and occupying the other (Gee, 2003; Jenkins, 2003; Rheingold, 1993).

Additionally, the possibility of controlling and mastering untamed geographies reflects a profound masculinist project, which enables players inside the extreme sports genre to demonstrate their own physical/mental prowess through courage, creativity and physicality. Within both real and virtual extreme sports, representation characterizes White masculinity as "desiring a space where it can reconstruct a sense of superiority and psychic stability by investing in a cultural space and practice it can claim as its own" (Kusz, 2003, p. 167).

This emphasis on controlling and dominating space is especially evident within extreme sports games, which offer its primarily White male players the chance to become White male extreme athletes—the chance to master both nature and urban geographies. "All extreme sports are thrill-seeking activities to which psychologies of danger and excitement" guide performative masculinities (Rinehart & Sydnor, 2001, p. 12). As Rinehart and Sydnor (2001) note, extreme sports offer a space where courage "can be a vice" (p. 12). Yet Kusz questions how this emphasis on courage and danger reflects a project that seeks to legitimize White masculinity. "The white male [virtual] extreme athlete, being an instrument an effect of representational politics of the white male backlash, . . .appropriates the logic of identity politics, makes visible and invests in a particular vision of whiteness." It simultaneously "makes a claim to holding an authentic marginal identity, is figured as overcoming these feelings of fear and insecurity through this practice, which allows him to resecure his manhood and to once again see himself as superior in this racially homogenous cultural site of extreme sports" (Kusz, 2003, p. 170).

Within extreme virtual sports, the emphasis on danger and conquering untamed space is particularly powerful. For example, games like *SSX Tricky* or *Amped* not only provide players spaces to exert creativity with tweaks, spins, jibs, jumps, "and insane sick über tricks" (from *SSX Tricky*), but to face and ultimately conquer all that the wilderness has to offer. No jump is too high, no cliff is too dangerous, no 100-year-old tree is too big an obstacle, nor is the threat of avalanche a deterrent. Each represents a conquerable obstacle to the White male virtual extreme sports athlete. The instructions of *SSX 3* capture the essence of this element of the game:

> **Conquer the Mountain**: Overcome everything the mountain throws at you—from fierce snowstorms and breathtaking vertical drops to multi-path slope style courses and earth swallowing avalanches—on the quest for the ultimate adrenaline.

> **Uncover the Mountain's Secret**: Explore a huge world of open vistas covered with fresh powder, tick venues, rail parks, racecourses and half pipes with new tricks to master and leave new competitors in the dust. (p. 5)

SSX Tricky, the sequel of *SSX 3*, offers similar masculine, frontier-related, rhetorical devices that frame virtual extreme sports as a battle between man and nature. "All of your favorite *SSX* courses are tweaked for more speed, more elevation, and more insane thrills, plus two wild new tracks that will blow your mind. Hit the mountain harder with *SSX Tricky* and the sky is your stage." Offering a "mind blowing world," with "near vertical sections and huge drops," *SSX Tricky* validates White male masculinity as unmovable, courageous and up to any test. There is no physical or mental obstacle that the virtual extreme athlete cannot overcome; White masculinity is powerful in the face of a crisis that devalues the visibility of spaces that invoke the productive power of White men. In a sporting world defined by black athletes, and a virtual sports world dominated by these athletes, White virtual extreme sports games elucidate the prowess of White manhood while simultaneously invoking an "identity cloaked in the codes of cultural difference to relieve itself of its feelings of vulnerability, inferiority, and instability and to reclaim its imagined sense of cultural [athletic] superiority and normality" (Kusz, 2003, p. 167).

Winning a Gold Medal or a Hot Chick?: Conquer and You Shall Consume

Just as extreme sports construct a world of White masculinist domination over nature and space, they equally provide an opportunity to conquer women, not surprising given the ways in which youth culture dehumanizes and hypersexualizes women, particularly those of color. Given the fact that extreme sports represent a masculinist project, the emphasis on controlling or consuming oversexualized female bodies is of little surprise. In an effort to reconfigure the virtual extreme sport world as a White masculine performative space, females are either erased or reduced to sexual commodities.

Within games like *Tony Hawk* or *Sonny Garcia Surfing*, women are totally absent, virtually erased from this world despite their visibility in the X-Games or other extreme sports competitions. Unlike other sporting arenas, which have seen the partial entry of women or the impact of feminism (or at least the imagination of these changes), these virtual extreme worlds remain untouched by the physical or aesthetic presence of females. This erasure signifies the ultimate mastery that successfully conquers/maintains a sporting world without women.

Nonetheless, an intrusion of female bodies is evident within certain games. The inclusion of extreme female athletes in *SSX 3, SSX Tricky, BMX XXX* or a host of other games does not, however, unsettle the hegemony of White masculinity, in that these characters exist for the pleasure of both the male virtual athlete and the male game player. In *Gravity Games*, players can ride as "Hotty Babe," whose "hypnotizing beauty," large breasts, and "piercing green eyes," leave her as something out of the ordinary within the extreme sports world (at least that is what the game concludes), whose sexuality not only confirms the game's understanding of masculinity and femininity, but the place of gender within the transgressive possibilities of the game. Within its insert, the game celebrates "Hotty Baby," for "ripping free of the shackles of her ex-boyfriend" who would not let her ride, and the expectations of society for her as a sexualized woman. Replicating much of the discourse surrounding extreme sports, this game celebrates "Hotty Babe" for defying expectations through hard work and fearlessness, demonstrating that she is as extreme as any male. Of course, in the end, evident by her name, her inclusion in the game and the extreme sports world is contingent upon her breasts and sexuality rather than her acceptance of an alternative sports identity.

Females in these games serve as either the "spoils of victory" within the game itself or the source of pleasure for the game player. For example, games like *SSX Tricky* and *BMX XXX* offer females as prizes for success. In *SSX Tricky*, victories allow players to purchase outfits that are more revealing for its female players, accentuating the already large breasts of the characters. While White male athletes in *SSX 3* wear baggy pants (i.e., a standard snowboarder's uniform), the women wear tight, revealing clothing. Elise, who the game describes as 5′11″ and 120 lbs, wears an extremely tight one-piece snowsuit that shows off her large breasts. As the announcer introduces her to the fans, she rubs her hands up and down her sides in a highly sexualized way in greeting. In each of these extreme sports games, as with all video games, female athletes are represented by their breasts and tight clothing. Children Now, in one of the few quantitative studies concerning race and gender stereotyping within video games, found that 10% of female characters possessed excessively large breasts and nonexistent waists and that 20% of female characters had disproportionate body types. Moreover, 10% of female characters exposed their butts, and an astounding 20% of virtual women revealed their breasts (Children Now, 2001, pp. 13–14).

All of the women in both *SSX* games are large breasted, existing for sexual consumption of their bodies. Similarly, *BMX XXX* offers a strip tease for the completion of a particular mission. In each game, over-sexualized, large-breasted, sex-kitten women, disguised as extreme sports athletes, do not threaten this masculinist space, but rather solidify its orientation, as women function as sexualized window dressing and sources of sexual pleasure as trophies or "athletes." In fact, upon its release in 2002, *BMX XXX* was described as "lewd," "raunchy," and as having gone "too far" (Buchanan 2002, p. 2; Leahy, 2003, p. 46; Snider, 2002, p. D05). Levi Buchanan (2002) captures the essence of the reaction that followed the release of *BMX XXX*, which brought bike riding together with "virtual strippers, pimps, and hookers mouthing off" (p. 2). He further notes the monumental contribution of this game: "On November 19, one of the few remaining taboos in video games will be stripped away, quite literally. Acclaim's *BMX XXX* finally shatters an almost two-decade kibosh on nudity in console gaming, taunting moral watchdogs with plenty of the gratuitous stuff that pulls teenagers into movie theaters or MTV to watch such bizarros as 'Jackass'" (p. 2). Both celebratory and in disgust, the critical reception of *BMX XXX* failed to connect its representational strategies of extreme sports to its more subtle brethren.

While the ubiquitous outrage focused on the pornographic elements of the game, as well as the game's deployment of "inappropriate language" or its overt sexuality, very little of this condemnation focused on the rampant racial stereotypes and deployment of patriarchal construction of females/femininity within this imaginary world of extreme sports. Before *BMX XXX* even starts, its orientation is made clear, as a young woman gazes toward the game player. She is wearing pink shorts with her g-string peeking through, a white halter top that exposes her midriff and her erect nipples; she straddles a BMX bike, the lone sign of the forthcoming extreme sports game; pulling her own hair seductively, she exudes sexuality, almost seducing players to continue with the same. This is not the sole signifier of the game's inscription of female sexuality. Each page of the game's instructions contains a scantily dressed woman clearly marked as the prize of the game. *BMX XXX* even includes an insert (to pin on the wall?) of a blonde White woman wearing an almost see-through halter-top, sitting atop a BMX bike. This is no ordinary bike—it has no seat, but rather what appears to be a silver "stripper pole" in its place that strategically sits between her legs. The sexual tone and the clear markers of women as sexualized objects of male consumption are evident in the game's teaser and instructional materials.

The place and function of over-sexualized women is not limited to the enclosed materials and advertising but plays out in the game. Throughout *BMX XXX*, players are advised to complete missions ranging from dropping off prostitutes at a hotel (per request of a Black pimp) to picking up recyclable cans for a homeless person. Each mission offers an identical reward: a naked woman. In fact, the game functions with the single goal of accumulating as many points and coins as possible so you can enter Scores, the community strip club. While the Playstation2 version offers censored but still overtly sexual images of women donning halter-tops and thongs, the Xbox and Game Cube versions leave little to the imagination, with women stripping completely. Players can also create topless female riders after mastering tricks and obstacles provided by this urban space.

In *BMX XXX*, as with the bulk of extreme sport games, the virtual game playing space, as well as its performative possibilities, reflect a clearly masculinist space where women are permitted entry only if they are willing and able to elicit pleasure from the male participants. This reality reflects the larger discourse surrounding extreme sports, the historical context and agenda of extreme (virtual) sports to reclaim a sporting world without substantive numbers of men of color and non-sexualized women—a space to reassert the power of an authentic White masculinity.

The inscription of hyper-masculine identity and over-sexualized femininity is not limited by the game's narrative, but is evident in the character descriptions found within the game's instructions/introductions. Each of the female characters reflects a grotesque notion of hypersexuality; their inclusion in the game is clearly linked to their physique and the sexual desirability held by male game players. Mika reflects this prototype better than any of the characters, with her large breasts and exposed nipples and midriff. She exudes a sexuality that marks her difference from her male counterparts. Mika's desirability emanates from her breasts and sexuality, while other White riders are destined to be picked because of their skills or style.

The other female characters reflect this one-dimensional sexuality, albeit through distinct racialized bodies. La'tey and Joy Ride are both Black female characters. La'tey appears angry and muscular, exuding a rough sexual exterior. Joy Ride fulfills a similar representation of Black femininity. While her image leaves one wondering whether she is a prostitute, with blonde hair, pink shoes, a short mini skirt, leg warmers, and a halter-top that cannot contain her ample breasts, she embodies not just the hypersexuality of female characters, but the markers of racial difference as well. Karma, a South Asian or Hawaiian, equally reflects this sexualized racial difference. Unlike Mika, who despite the emphasis on her breasts wears biker gear, Karma wears surfer shorts and a halter top that not only accentuate her dark skin, but her large breasts. La'tey, Joy Ride, and Karma jointly reaffirm the normalcy and desirability of both White masculinity and femininity. The representation of women not only emphasizes their sexuality/body, clearly marking their inclusion as a result of their "assets." However, the game differentiates between the sexualized identity/virtual bodies of its White female characters and those characters of color.

Comparable depictions of masculinity define *BMX XXX*; White male characters wear "traditional" or "normal" bike-rider clothing as characters of color don almost clownish threads. Rave (mohawk, tattoos, Vans, and no shirt), Sketcher (cut-offs, sleeveless shirt) and Nutter (jeans, hoodie, green beanie) all reflect the prototypical (White) extreme athlete. They offer a positive, yet oppositional, vision of masculinity. The inscription of an extreme sports identity through representations of whiteness is most evident in comparison to the game's characters of color. Twon is the stereotypical Black hip-hop athlete (long purple shorts, bling-bling); Mavel is the proverbial scowling *vato* (baldhead, chinos, white shirt); Triple Dub adds additional flavor as the Rasta biker (dreads, Jamaican colors); lastly, Itch, the game's only Asian character, is non-descript yet clearly odd. Each of the characters of color seems out of place. *BMX XXX* uses both the hypersexual female character and racially stereotypical virtual athletes as a means to validate the physical and psychic superiority of White men. Through the naturalization of whiteness and the inscription of extreme sports as a White world, *BMX XXX*, unlike *Tony Hawk*, uses people of color to naturalize the physical and cultural superiority of the

White extreme sports athlete. The transparent inclusion of females, whether as prizes in the strip club or topless riders, further links *BMX XXX* to games like *Tony Hawk Underground* and *SSX Tricky*, for each uses both the erasure of women athletes and as appendages, i.e., exposed breasts to fulfill male needs and fantasies. As part of a larger project that validates White masculinity as daring, cool, fearless and able to master any space at the expense of men of color and women who are ridiculed and demonized as "hos," *BMX XXX* is not new, but more of the same.

Concluding Thoughts: Extremism in the Absence of Transgression, Pleasure in the Absence of Transgression

Even as I prepared to play *Tony Hawk's American Wasteland* to finish this chapter, knowing my argument and my claims about extreme sports games being a vehicle for White male dominance over "America's jungles" and nature, I still find myself enjoying these games.[10] Despite my "oppositional gaze," my tendency toward critique, and my disdain for extreme sports given its celebration of White masculinity, and the immense number of racialized and gendered stereotypes found in these games, I found myself engrossed with the game. Does my pleasure in playing these games reflect my own desire to feel the pleasure derived from the performative opportunities available through virtual extreme sports athletics? Does my excitement stem from the provided opportunity to partake in a virtual reality where White masculinity is validated and celebrated in athletic terms; do I play for hours and find myself wanting to conquer the biggest mountain or successfully transverse America's city because it valorizes my White masculinity and even celebrates anti-establishment identities, even as it reifies common sense understanding of White heterosexual masculinity? As David Rowe (1998) notes, "Its pleasurable rationale lies in the imaginary insertion of self into texts for which the subject matter is of proven popularity and for which the capacity for eliciting powerful affective responses is inherent in the excessive nature of the fan-sports-society-mythology nexus" (p. 358). Douglas Kellner further explains this process where even the most astute (and progressive) gamers are unable to resist their clichéd and reactionary ideological messages that necessitates acceptance of each game's conception of extremity, the enticing empowerment of an evidenced and performed White, masculine, athletic identity. "In general, it is not a system of rigged ideological indoctrination that induces consent to existing capitalist societies, but the 'pleasures' connected to 'media and consumer culture'" (Kellner, 1995, p. 3). None of the games discussed herein are over-the-top commentaries on whiteness or transparent denunciations of people of color. Nor are they polemics offering either the celebration of anti-establishment masculinity, or an obvious virtual festivity for a sporting culture without women or people color. Moreover these games do not "indoctrinate" their players into a single world-view. "Media entertainment is often highly pleasurable and uses sight, sound, and spectacle to seduce audiences into identifying with certain views, attitudes, feelings and positions. . . . Media and consumer culture work hand in hand to generate thought and behavior that confirm to existing values, institutions, beliefs and practices" (Kellner, 1995, p. 3). The power in extreme athletic virtual reality lies in its ability to define a youthful masculinity through danger and the ability of White male bodies to conquer dangerous urban space and the untamed wilderness, as a means to teach whiteness, masculinity and the desirability of an anti-establishment sensibility for White males, even as they underplay the importance of race and masculinity. Its power lies in its powerful discourses as it offers pleasure even to the most literate (white, male) gamer, even one who enters into this virtual reality with a protective armor made from an oppositional gaze and theoretical baggage. More significantly, it rests with the ability to transport White suburban males, many who have left behind their youthful diversions and spaces of play for "professional" and "family obligations," yet still are allowed to reinsert their virtual selves within spaces of youthful play; spaces defined by hypermasculinity, transgression (although uncriminalized) and hypersexuality.

> When I open *Vogue*, for example, I am simultaneously infuriated and seduced, grateful to escape temporarily into a narcissistic paradise where I'm the center of the universe, outrage that completely unattainable standards of wealth and beauty exclude me and most women I know from the promised land. I adore the materialism; I despise the materialism. I yearn for the self-indulgence; I think the self-indulgence is repellent. I want to look beautiful; I think wanting to look beautiful is about the most dumb-ass goal you could have. (Douglas, 1994, p. 9)

Released amidst a cultural and communal panic that bemoans the declining significance of White athletes, wonders about the affects of female athletes and those of color, and calls for the policing and control of urban spaces, virtual extreme sports games reclaim the dominance and importance of a White masculinity imagined as lost. Ultimately, their success lies in their ability to codify ideologies of whiteness, masculinity, and sporting cultures through a package that emphasizes extremity, opposition and anti-establishment identities, all the while maintaining dominant understandings of white masculinity that govern social relations inside and beyond a virtual sporting context. While video games and the world of the extreme purports itself to be outside the norm or the mainstream (much like other extreme movements—White nationalists—for example) this positioning ultimately rings hollow: in the end, its understanding of race, gender, and identity demonstrates that transgression of boundaries—or merely taking things to the extreme—take us on the logical center, where White supremacy and patriarchy remain intact, where the extreme merely resembles the mainstream. In other words, extreme sports video games offer a space of imagined transgression and opposition, aesthetics and practices reserved for (and by) White youth culture, in which challenging the limitations of one's body and the rules of law are not only acceptable, but part and parcel with youthful (and thus harmless) play. To be youthful is to be oppositional and countercultural but only if you are a White male is this harmless and non-threatening. To be White, male, and youthful is to be pleasantly undisruptive yet powerfully in charge of body, space, and future.

Notes

1. This chapter contains substantial parts of a prior essay written by the author entitled "To the White Extreme: Conquering Athletic Space, White Manhood and Racing Virtual Reality" which appeared in *Digital Gameplay: Essays on the Nexus of Game and Gamer* © 2005, edited by Nate Garrelts. Said prior material is included herein with the permission of McFarland & Company, Inc., Box 611, Jefferson NC 28640. (http://www.mcfarlandpub.com/)
2. Notwithstanding the success of *Madden*, EA found significant success with other reality-based sports games, too. During this same period, *NCAA Football 2006* sold over 1.5 million copies. In addition, EA reported that for 2005, *FIFA 06* was tracking sales number of more than 30% ahead of last year. Retrieved from http://www.gamespot.com/xbox360/sports/tigerwoodspgatour06/news.html?sid=6136992
3. A professional American skateboarder, he has long been the most recognized and popular (commodified) celebrities within extreme sports culture. While talent and business smarts have been important, his whiteness and presumed "suburban look" has been instrumental in his ascendance within the extreme sports world
4. To date, the series of platform skateboarding video games, which originated in 1999, has totaled eleven different installments. These games, supported by and named after Tony Hawk, because of his popularity and visibility amongst casual extreme sports fans, and developed by Never Soft and published by Activision, have grossed over $1 billion.
5. A professional BMX rider and an acclaimed X-Games competitor, he has taken home numerous medals, a vast majority of them gold, during his extreme sports career.
6. It is important to note, however, that extreme sports are not exclusively defined by the challenges of urban geographies, the dangers of avoiding the police, or the risks associated with America's ghettos, but those associated with the great outdoors. Those games located outside the city, within the "wild" or nature, offer similar ideological and cultural inscriptions, providing a space where an athletic white manhood is validated through domination of the physical landscape
7. An EA Sports snowboarding game released in 2001; it has been followed by *SSX 3* (2003) and *SSX on Tour* (2005)
8. Released by Microsoft in 2001, it has been followed by *Amped 2* (2003) and *Amped 3* (2006), all of which take players into the virtual world of freestyle snowboarding, in an "athletic" and "cultural" sense
9. Description that appears in game insert for Tony Hawk's Pro Skater 3, p. 9 (Activision, 2001)
10. This is not the first instance in which I have faced and written about my battle with pleasurable yet disturbing cultural productions. In "Is this Heaven?" White sporting masculinities and the Hollywood Imagination (In C. Richard King & David J. Leonard (Eds.), *Visual economies of/in motion: Sport and film* (pp. 165–194). New York: Peter Lang) I explore (among other things) my complex relationship to *Rudy* and *Hoosiers*, given their cinematic investment and

my personal connection (investment) to White athletic masculinity. In a similar regard, we must continue to contemplate our own relationship to popular culture, even those productions we might engage in a critical manner.

References

Beal, Becky, and Wilson, Charlene. (2004). 'Chicks dig scars:' Transformations in the subculture of skateboarding. In Belanda Wheaton (Ed.), *Understanding lifestyle sports: Consumption, identity, and difference.* (pp 31-54) London: Routledge.

Borden, Iain. (2001). *Skateboarding, space and the city; Architecture and the body.* New York: Berg Publishers.

Boyd, Todd. (1997). *Am I Black Enough for You: Popular Culture from the 'Hood and Beyond.* Bloomington: University of Indiana Press.

Buchanan, Levi. (2002). BMX breaks barrier with profanity, topless females." *Chicago Tribune,* November 4, section 5, p. 2.

Douglas, Susan. (1995). Where the Girls Are: Growing up Female with the Mass Media. New York: Random House

Gee, James. (2003). *What video games have to teach us about learning and literacy.* New York: Palgrave Macmillan.

Giroux, Henry. (1996; 2003). *Fugitive culture: Race, violence, and youth.* New York: Routledge. (Original work published 1996).

Hoberman, John (1997). Darwin's Athletes: *How Sport Has Damaged Black America and Preserved the Myth of Race.* Mariner Books, 1997.

hooks, bell. (1994). *Outlaw culture: Resisting representations.* New York: Routledge.

Jenkins, Henry. Voices from the combat zone: Game grrlz Talk Back. From *Barbie to mortal kombat: Gender and computer games,* Justice Cassell & Henry Jenkins (Eds.). Cambridge: MIT Press. Retrieved July 8, 2003, from http://web.mit.edu/21fms/www/faculty/henry3/gamegrrlz. html

Jenkins, Henry. "Complete freedom of movement": Video games as gendered play spaces. Retrieved July 8, 2003, from http://web.mit.edu/21fms/www/faculty/henry3/gamegrrlz/pub/complete. html

Jensen, Jeff. (2002). Video game nation. *Entertainment Weekly,* December 2002, 20–41.

Kelley, Robin. (1998). Playing for keeps: Pleasure and profit on the postindustrial playground. In Waheema Lubiana (Ed.), *The house that race built* (pp. 195–231). New York: Vintage Book.

Kelley, Robin. (1998). Integration: What's left. *The Nation,* December 14, p. 18.

King, Chares Richard, and Charles F. Springwood (2001). *Beyond the Cheers: Race as Spectacle in College Sport.* Albany: State University of New York.

Kusz, Kyle. (2003). BMX, extreme sports, and the white male backlash. In Robert E. Rinehart and Synthia Sydor (Eds.), *To the extreme: Alternative sports, inside and out* (pp. 153–178). Albany: State University Press of New York.

Kusz, Kyle. (2001). "I Want to be the minority": The politics of youthful white masculinities in sport and popular culture in 1990s American. *Journal of Sport and Social Issues, 25*(4), 390–416.

Leahy, Dan. (2003). BMX XXX: Topless chicks can't save hapless game. *Game Now,* February 1, p. 46.

Leonard, David J. (2006a). Not a hater, just keepin it real: The importance of race and gender based game studies," *Games and Culture, 1*(1), 83–88, http://gac.sagepub.com/cgi/content/abstract/1/1/83.

Leonard, David J. (2006b). "Is this Heaven?" White sporting masculinities and the Hollywood Imagination. In C. Richard King & David J. Leonard (Eds.), *Visual economies of/in motion: Sport and film* (pp. 165–194). New York: Peter Lang.

Leonard, David J. (2006c) "Untapped Field: Exploring the world of virtual gaming." In Art Raney and James Bryant, eds., *Handbook of sports and media* (pp. 393-408), Mahwah, New Jersey: Lawrence Erlbaum Associates.

Leonard, David J. (2006d) "Virtual gangstas, Coming to suburban house near you: Demonization, commodification and policing blackness," in Nathan Garrelts, ed., *Meaning And Culture of Grand Theft Auto: Critical Essays* (pp. 49-69). Jefferson, NC: McFarland Press.

Leonard, David J. (2005). To the white extreme: Conquering athletic space, white manhood and racing virtual reality. In Nathan Garrelts (Ed.), *Digital gameplay: Essays on the nexus of game and gamer* (pp. 110–129). Jefferson, NC McFarland Press.

Leonard, David J. (2003). "Live in your world, play in ours": Race, video games and consuming the other. *Studies in Media & Information Literacy Education (Simile)* 3(4) (November) http://www.utpjournals.com/simile/issue12/leonardX1.html

National Institute of Media and the Family (N.D.). Retrieved May 7, 2007 from http://www.media-family.org/kidscore/games_tony_hawk_aw.shtml)

Official U.S. Playstation Magazine. (2003). BMX PG-13, Did acclaim take things too far? Sony censors the racy BMX XXX. Issue 64, January 1, 60.

Price, S. L. (1997). What ever happened to the white athlete? *Sports Illustrated*, December 8, pp. 31–46.

Quart, Alisa (2003). *Branded: The buying and selling of teenagers.* New York: Basic Books.

Ratliff, Evan. (2003). Sports rule. *Wired*, January, pp. 94–101.

Rinehart, Robert. (2003). "Dropping into sight: Commodification and co-optation of in-line skating." In Robert Rinehart & Synthia Sydnor (Eds.), *To the extreme: Alternative sports, inside and out* (pp. 27–51). Albany: State University of New York Press.

Reinhart, Robert E., & Synthia Sydnor (Eds.). (2003). *To the extreme: Alternative sports, inside and out.* Albany: State University of New York.

Reinhart, Robert E. (1998). *Players all: Performances in contemporary sport.* Bloomington: University of Indiana Press.

Rheingold, Howard. (1993). *The virtual community: Homesteading on the electronic frontier.* Reading, MA: Addison-Wesley.

Rowe, David. (1998, November). If you Film It, Will They Come? Sports on Film. *Journal of Sport and Social Issues*, pp. 350–359.

Schor, Juliet. (2005) *Born to buy: The Commercialized child and the new consumer culture.* New York: Scribner.

Snider, Mike. (2002). Video games kicking the sex up a notch. *USA Today*, November 13, D.05.

Watkins, S. Craig (1999). *Representing: Hip Hop Culture and the Production of Black Cinema.* Chicago: University of Chicago Press.

Wheaton, Belinda. (2004). *Understanding lifestyle sports: Consumption, identity and difference.* New York: Routledge.

CHAPTER 6

"You Can Break So Many More Rules"
The Identity Work and Play of Becoming Skater Girls

DEIRDRE M. KELLY, SHAUNA POMERANTZ,
AND DAWN H. CURRIE

"This one guy came up to me. He's like, 'Oh, girls can't skate.' I'm like, 'What?!' And like yeah, so I showed him like all my tricks, and he's like, 'Oh, wow, that's pretty cool.'"

—Madeline, 16, skater girl[1]

The "non-traditional" sport of skateboarding has a rich and vibrant history (Beal, 1995, 1996), dating back to its original incarnation in 1970s Californian surf culture.[2] In the new millennium, many elements of the culture remain the same—a dedication to risk-taking, an affinity with punk rock (now splintered into pop punk, old school punk, hardcore, grindcore, and Goth) and more recently hip-hop, a love of baggy clothes, an interest in marijuana and "partying," a "slacker" reputation (think Bart Simpson from *The Simpsons*), and an anti-mainstream attitude. Given these defining features, it is interesting to note that corporate America has taken up skateboarding as one of its favorite marketing themes. Sports-oriented corporations, such as Nike and adidas, have worked hard to brand their products with skater "authenticity" in order to tap into the "cool" identity that many skaters cultivate. In response to this corporate branding, many skaters have opted to engage in fringe activities and cultural practices, including shopping at non-mainstream stores, participating in community-sponsored skate jams or competitions, reading on-line independent skater zines, and listening to "indie" or independent music.

Yet for all of skater culture's association with nonconformity and anti-mainstream values, it has been oddly traditional in its membership,

113

dominated by boys and men. Boys have been the actors; girls the watchers, admirers, and supporters. It has also been overtly sexist from its inception.[3] Skater girls regularly confront sexist assumptions about girls being unable to skate or as not having what it takes to be an "authentic" skateboarder. Skater girls are ignored, accused of merely wanting to boy-watch, insulted, and otherwise made to feel like outsiders in male-dominated skate parks. These sexist practices are corroborated in Beal's (1996) ethnographic study of a group of young male skateboarders in Colorado. Beal found that while the boys created an alternative, or more cooperative masculinity, it was still defined by "differentiating and elevating themselves from females and femininity," thus maintaining "the privilege of masculinity" (p. 204; cf. Borden, 2001, pp. 143–149).

Possibly as a result, girls have generally not taken up skateboarding in numbers large enough to count—making girls who decide to become skaters risk takers and rule breakers in more ways than one. As we have noted elsewhere (Pomerantz, Currie, & Kelly, 2004; Kelly, Pomerantz, & Currie, 2005), to be a girl skater is to resist what R. W. Connell (1987) refers to as "emphasized femininity."[4] In our interviews with skater girls in Vancouver, Canada, we found that girls gravitated toward skateboarding and other forms of alternative youth culture as a way of off-setting the oppressive rules girls felt they "had" to follow in order to be perceived as a certain kind of (popular) girl. Fourteen-year-old Sara explained that being a girl entails following "many" unspoken "rules"—rules which she felt were unfair and unnecessary: "That's why I like being alternative, because you can break so many more rules. If you hang out with the cliques and the mainstreamers and the pop kids, there's so many more rules that you have to follow. And if you don't follow [them] … you're no longer cool…"

In this chapter, we take Sara's words to heart by exploring the ways in which being a skater girl enables girls to break the rules of conventional girlhood by staking out an alternative identity. For us, alternative identities include the range of ways that girls consciously position themselves against what they perceive as the mainstream in general and conventional femininity in particular. Consistent with a cultural studies approach, we define identity as meanings attached to the self, where meaning is seen to arise out of social interaction and shared processes of meaning-making (Hall, 1996). In forging these alternative identities, we see girl skaters as actively challenging conventional girlhood through the bodily and cultural practices that participation in skater culture entails. These cultural practices involve work: risk, pain, fear, practice, and political struggle. But they also involve play or the enjoyment that comes from performing a skater identity. In this chapter, we thus highlight the work and play that negotiating a skater identity entails for girls through the categories of bodily comportment and motility, style, and political struggle. We conclude by exploring the ramifications of skater girl identities for girlhood in general.

Kickflipping Culture: Girls, Skateboarding, and Youth Culture Studies

Little academic research has been done on skateboarding as a youth culture or, conceived more fluidly, as a "cultural practice of youth" (Bucholtz, 2002, p. 539). Borden's (2001) architectural history of skateboarding includes a chapter on skateboarding as a subculture; Willard (1998) theorizes (male) skateboarders' appropriation and understanding of public spaces; and Beal's (1995, 1996) ethnography of 41 skaters (only four of whom were female) focuses on constructions of masculinity within skateboarding as a non-traditional sport and as an oppositional subculture. We know of no other study—whether empirical, historical, or textual—that focuses on skater girls or girls within the male-dominated skateboarding youth culture.

Several high school-based ethnographies with gender as their focus have identified "skaters" as a social group, but without exploring their practices in depth. Bettie (2003) highlights skateboarding under the wider umbrella of White and working-class social categories. In her ethnographic study of girls' identity negotiations in high school, Pomerantz (forthcoming) found that some girls took up the skater label in order to avoid what they perceived to be an oppressive form of girlhood, but battled the "poser" label. And Kelly (1993) found that girls who hung around boy skateboarders became known among their peers as skaters or "skate betties" (slang for girl skaters, a term often used derisively by boy skaters), whether the girls themselves skated or not (p. 147; cf. Beal, 1995, p. 265).

Feminist scholars dating back to McRobbie and Garber (1976) have critiqued youth cultural studies and school-based ethnographies for focusing either on the experiences and identities of boys or analyzing "youth" where the implicit referent is still male. Willis (1977), for example, represents girls in working-class "lad" culture as sexual objects for the more powerful boys. And in Hebdige's (1979) analysis of punk culture, girls appear merely as accessories to the "more" spectacular practices of their larger-than-life male counterparts. As Leblanc (1999, p. 67) notes, "[w]ithin the context of such male-focused and male-generated subcultural theory and research, girls who participate in youth subcultures have been described as passive, ancillary, sexual, and 'less resistant' than their male peers."

Recently, however, researchers have begun to address more adequately the role of girls in youth cultures. The studies most relevant to our inquiry focus on girls and the construction of femininities within male-dominated youth cultures. Given that skater culture has some of its roots in punk, Leblanc's study of punk girls' resistance within this subculture is especially pertinent. Based on participant observation and 40 interviews with punk girls in several Canadian and U.S. cities, Leblanc shows that the punk subculture is indeed coded as masculine. Being tough, cool, rebellious, and aggressive—traits associated with adolescent boyhood—is highly valued. She argues that this culture provides punk girls with the resources to develop a critique of traditional femininity and an opportunity to construct an alternative "form of self-presentation" (p. 142), which, in turn, enables them "to retain a strong sense of self" (1999, p. 13; see also Roman, 1988).

Bettie's (2003) ethnography of 12th-grade girls in a small town school in California describes two forms of what she calls "dissident" femininity among the "hard-living" working-class White girls. These girls belonged to a social group known variously as the smokers, the punk or grunge rockers, and White trash. The first form of dissident femininity, reminiscent of the style of Leblanc's punk girls, rejected traditional femininity outright by dressing in a more masculine style and avoiding "girly stuff" (p. 133). The second form rejected "school-sanctioned femininity" by exaggerating traditionally feminine ways of dressing and acting; the highly sexualized result was intended to shock school authorities (p. 133). Mendoza-Denton's (1996) study of Latina gang girls demonstrates how the capacity for violence, whether implied or carried out, was part of how girl gang-members constructed a non-dominant (or dissident, to use Bettie's term) form of femininity.

Given the lack of empirical work that focuses on girls within the male-dominated skateboarding youth culture, we were curious to explore the nature of their identity negotiations and their struggles to be accepted as legitimate participants in the culture by skater boys. Did the skater label enable them to enlarge their sense of who they could be as girls?

One way for girls to expand the meaning of femininity is to use the resources of what has been a male-dominated youth culture to make those norms and values their own. As we discuss, girl skateboarders in our study appropriated the traditionally masculine traits of physical strength and bravery, technical competence, physical risk-taking and stoicism, as well as non-sexualized androgyny (read: masculine dress style). Another way that skater girls defined an alternative girlhood was against other girls and women whom they perceived as embodying emphasized femininity. They did this by avoiding behavior they associated with dominant femininity and by participating in the politics of distinction, or rejection of an undiscerning mainstream ethos (Thornton, 1995) that characterizes skater culture.

In what follows, we explore the identity work and play of being a skater girl through interviews with 20 girls who identified themselves in some way as skaters.[5] The girls we interviewed ranged in age from 13- to 16-years-old. Had we been looking for young women between the ages of 17 and 25, we would have located a much larger sample. But finding girls under the age of 17 who identified as skaters proved to be difficult and took some time. Based on information the girls provided about their parents' occupations and educational backgrounds, and their current living arrangements, fifteen girls came from middle-class families and five from working-class families. The sample was racially diverse, reflecting the multiculturalism of the city of Vancouver. Eleven were White (European Canadian), four were Chinese Canadian, three were of mixed racial/ethnic identity, and two were Aboriginal.

The skater girls in our study participated to different degrees in skateboarding culture. We discerned three broad categories. The "hardcore" or serious skaters frequented skate parks, had mastered a number of tricks, and took obvious pride in knowing how to assemble and maintain their own skateboard. The "skaters" (the biggest category) liked the "lifestyle" but skated more infrequently, and they had usually mastered only the basics, although some knew a few tricks. The "skater affiliates," identified as, or were known as, skaters mainly because of their friendships with other skaters, an affinity for skater culture, or both.

"I Hate Sports! Skateboarding Is Not a Sport!": The Work and Play of Skater Bodily Comportment and Motility

In the minds of working-class skater girls like Grenn, to call skateboarding a "sport" seemed to associate it with the much-hated preps, who traditionally have used organized athletics, cheerleading, and dance squad as routes to social status within many North American schools (Eckert, 1989; Merten, 1997; Bettis & Adams, 2003; Milner, 2004).[6] Regardless of this distinction, skateboarding requires physical strength, balance, agility, and bravery. To skate is to know how to fall and how to attempt complicated and risky tricks. Even the most basic trick, the ollie—where a skater smacks down the end of her board, moves her foot forward to bring the board up into the air, then lands smoothly with her feet equally apart in the middle of the board—runs the risk of injury.

Ollies, kickflips, grinding, and carving are all skater tricks that must be performed with the full knowledge that falling is likely, especially for beginners. "First, you've got to get the balance," explained Tori. "And then you've got to be fearless as shit, because 24/7 … you're riding along cement. When you fall, it hurts. It doesn't just hurt a little bit—it hurts a lot. But in order to learn these tricks, you fall down a lot."

This kind of physical audacity is not generally associated with being a girl. As Iris Marion Young (1989) suggests, typical motility and spatiality for girls can be timid, uncertain, and hesitant, as many girls are not brought up to have the same kind of confidence and freedom in their movements as boys.

Young sees femininity as based on a particular bodily comportment that is restrictive of large movements and risk-taking. Girls are not often seen to be capable of achieving physical acts that require strength and power or handling the pain that such physical acts can incur. Willingly inviting pain is seen to be boys' territory. Boys are ascribed the kind of confidence and craziness needed to carry skater tricks through to completion. Girls are not.

Skater girls in our study were aware of this gendered notion of motility and bodily comportment. When asked why girls did not skate as much as boys, Onyx noted that girls might see skateboarding as "a guy thing to do. It is our thing to sit around and chit chat and gossip and stuff and watch them skateboard." Grover added, "Yeah, and some girls are kind of, like, scared." But Onyx retorted that she and her friends did not "think like that. We wanted to try it." Emily, too, reasoned that girls "don't want to continuously fall," and realized that skater boys are much less worried: "Like, guys there, they fall and they keep falling, but it's amazing, they always get back up and, like, try the same thing again."

By "doing" skateboarding, girl skaters engaged in a transgressive bodily comportment. They were willing to stand with a wide gait on their boards, dangle their arms freely by their sides, and spread out for balance. They knowingly made spectacles out of themselves, courting the gaze of the skater boys and other onlookers. While some beginners were not keen to wipe out, others reported being less afraid. Pete enjoyed the adrenaline "rush," and Zoey added, "The first time I wiped out, I was just, like, 'Whoa!' I fell really hard. I was, like, 'Aahh!' kind of. And then I just wanted to do it again, because it was like, 'Wow!'" Despite a major "face plant" the first time she skateboarded, Kate recalled telling a "freaked out" friend: "I'm back on there still doing like weird stuff." Like Kate, Lexi evinced stoicism about her inevitable injuries: "I'm not very good, but if I get scraped, I'm not going to whine and bitch about it. I'm just going to go, 'Oh, damn. Okay.'" Tori and Priscilla, visibly scraped and bruised at the time of their interview, saw "road rash" as a badge of honor. The skater girls' toughness and relative lack of concern about bruises, scrapes, and scars provide a sharp contrast with dominant images of femininity.

No doubt part of the rush some of skater girls felt came from knowing they were engaged in an activity that most girls (and boys) did not have the guts to try. As Amanda suggested, most boys at the skate park were more "risk taking" than girls. "They don't care if they, like, get bruises and stuff. They'll be, like, 'Yeah! Cuts!' And then girls will be, like, 'Oh no!'" But some skater girls willingly accepted the risks involved in skateboarding as a way of setting themselves apart from emphasized femininity. Such work entailed dedication on the part of girls who wanted to be identified as skaters. The constant practice that goes along with mastering even the most basic trick (let alone learning how to stabilize yourself on the board, whether in motion or not!) separated the serious skater girls from those who mostly enjoyed being associated with the culture.

But as the comments from the girls suggest, there was a great deal of play in this hard work. Girls who skated displayed pride in their skills and were delighted to regale us with their "war stories." During their interview, Tori and Priscilla could hardly contain their enthusiasm for skateboarding and continuously jumped up from their seats to show scars and ollie-tears in their sneakers or to demonstrate how they balance on their boards. Lexi and Grenn, as well, displayed delight in being able to talk about skateboarding in their interview, and gleefully stood up to highlight their stances. The hard work that these girls put into skateboarding gave them bragging rights, endless amounts of fun, and a feeling of pride at being able to enter the male-dominated skater world. To the girls we spoke with, such pleasure was well worth the work.

"A Lot of the Skater Clothes Aren't Slutty": The Work and Play of Skater Style

Style is one of the most immediate and accessible ways for girls to negotiate their identities and to gain some power over how others see them (Pomerantz, 2005, forthcoming). While skater girls might suggest that style is less important to them than to girls who sport more mainstream fashions, it is still a crucial feature to performing the skater identity. Across the 20 girls interviewed, a fairly wide variety of styles and attitudes toward dress were in evidence. Nevertheless, taken as a whole, the girls liked the casual, comfortable look of skater clothes: hoodies, t-shirts, baggy pants, sneakers, and many were quick to contrast skater style with what they saw as a more emphasized form of femininity: "revealing," brand-name attire that they associated with a certain type of popular, preppy, "boy-hunting" girl.

Some of the skater girls were clear that, through their style, they wanted to "be their own person," to "stand out" (by wearing all orange or safety pins as earrings) or to be "funky" (by dying their hair blue or wearing an "explosive shirt"). But they were equally clear that their primary purpose was not to attract the attention of boys, but rather to make a statement about their individuality and difference. In seeming protest of corporate consumerism, a number of skater girls said they shopped at Value Village and other second-hand clothing stores, and Tori designed her own clothes as a hobby. Pete noted about her skater friendship circle, "I think we're kind of the different, kind of alternate, creative group, because we're always making up our own clothes and trends." Rather than "making up" a trend of their own, Grenn and Lexi asserted that they were following "no fashion trend at all" and that this defined them as "weird" in the eyes of their more affluent, "preppy" peers. They paid a high price for their adherence to an alternative style, describing intense scenes of being mercilessly teased. But the lack of acceptance they felt from popular girls only hardened their resolve to steer clear of mainstream femininity and to thumb their noses at what "those kind of girls" thought about them.

Of course, in recent years skater style has been touted by marketing machines such as Nike and adidas, thus complicating the discussion of what is "trendy" and increasing the cost of skater clothes. This development angered a number of the girls, particularly the most hardcore skaters. Kate and Christine spoke derisively of "little posers" who wore skater clothes but did not really skate. Madeline said it "bugged" her that some girls at her school bought expensive stuff that they did not really "need." For example, they wore skate shoes that "aren't really great for skating; they're just kind of poser brands."[7] The increasing popularity of skater style affected the hardcore yet working-class skater girls like Tori the most strongly. "It bugs me 'cause you see all these preppy little kids and they are going and buying skate shoes and skate clothing, which makes the price go up for people like us who depend on that. Like my shoes have the biggest ollie hole in them, like you have no idea!" Tori went on to explain that she used to be able to replace her shoes for $30, but now the "cheapest shoe" cost her $120. Pointing to her skate shoe, she explained, "This piece in here gets thrashed the most because when you ollie, it rubs up against your board. So you want nice plastic in here and you want the lips to be up high, and in order to get that, you have to pay [a lot]."

Equally important to defining their alternative identities was the skater girls' rejection of styles favored by a certain type of popular girl: tight, expensive designer jeans or skirts, "really tight tank tops," and lots of makeup. As Zoey explained, "A lot of the skater clothes aren't slutty, so that's really cool…. That really tight stuff—those can get really annoying after awhile, and you can't do *anything* on a board in it." According to Grover, "bun girls" (her group's name for the sexy-dressing popular girls at her school, all of whom regularly wore buns in their hair) wear "tanks tops four seasons a year…. They base a lot upon their looks and what they think the guys will like." "They're not really their own person," added Onyx. As Zoey declared, her skater friendship group was "totally the opposite" of girls who dress "sexy" to "attract guys," and her co-interviewee, Pete, agreed: "Dressing sexy kind of, in my perspective, attracts the wrong type of guys for me. I'm not into those guys . . . that are attracted to sex appeal only [and not the brain]."

Forging an alternative identity through style was difficult work and often entailed defending one's choices against the mainstream trends. It also meant risking teasing from popular girls and the possibility of not being perceived as "dateable" by boys, some of whom were said to value overtly sexual style over an anti-mainstream, somewhat androgynous look. Grover liked a skater boy, for example, but noticed that his current girlfriend dressed in a traditionally feminine way. If "that's the type he likes," she noted matter-of-factly, "I wouldn't try to become a [sexy-dressing] bun girl just to satisfy him." The skater girls in our study were mainly interested in having boyfriends[8] but felt that such pursuits needed to be conducted on their own terms and with as little attention to emphasized femininity as possible. Nevertheless, this identity work also elicited a great deal of play from the girls, many of whom took pride in scouring second-hand markets and pushing the boundaries of their own well-defined looks. As well, sometimes the cultivation of an alternative style fostered other playful features of identity, such as the creation of neologisms, being in the know about certain kinds of music and films, and other elements of style, such as piercing, hair dying, and deck decoration. The work of forging an alternative femininity through style was rewarded by the enjoyment that embodying a creative and fun femininity brought to the girls.

The Park Gang Boycott: The Work and Play of Political Struggle

The following story exemplifies the political struggle and intense work that some girls endure *en route* to becoming a skater and the pride and pleasure that can come from performing an alternative identity that has been hard won. The "Park Gang" is the name we have given to a group of eight skater girls, all friends or acquaintances who hung out at one skate park in Vancouver.

When members of the Park Gang decided to try skateboarding, they ventured into the skate park with their boards, hoping to gain acceptance and practice. The skate park they selected was considered amateurish compared to the larger and more daunting parks downtown. It was connected to a community center in an affluent neighbourhood and was relatively clean and safe. But the park proved to be a location of struggle, dominated as it was by skater boys who gave the girls a hard time. The boys were always asking members of the Park Gang to show them what they could do and constantly questioning the girls' abilities. The boys often asked Zoey, "Why don't you skate more?" She admitted that, "sometimes we don't want to skate around them 'cause, like, they do really good stuff and we're just kind of learning."

The Park Gang quickly realized that being the only girl skaters at the park singled them out for some harassment. To the skater boys who dominated the park and acted as its gatekeepers, the park was their space—a space that left very little room for girls, unless they were watchers, fans, or girlfriends. Gracie theorized that girls skate less than boys due to this kind of territorial attitude: "some [girls] are kind of, like, scared, because of what people might think of them." When asked what she meant, Gracie noted that the lack of girls who skated at the park might make the boys question girls' right to belong. Onyx added that the skater boys viewed the Park Gang as "invading their space." Grover felt that the Park Gang threatened the skater boys "just because, you know, girls are doing *their* sport."

This struggle eventually created tension for the Park Gang. Grover, Gracie, and Onyx understood that the boys were threatened by their presence but wished the boys could appreciate how hard it was for girls to get started. They wanted the boys to see them as equals who deserved the same kind of camaraderie that they showed each other. But instead, the boys saw them as interlopers with no legitimate claim to the space. Some of the boys accused some of the Park Gang of being posers. A poser wears the "right" clothes but does not really skate. Although boys can also be posers, girls who attempt access to skate parks are often singled out for this derogatory title. It is assumed that girls hang around the park as a way to meet skater boys.

It was just such an accusation that prompted the Park Gang to take action collectively in order to prove the skater boys wrong. Zoey recounted the story.

> There's this one time where a couple of the guys thought we were just—they said it out loud that we're just there for the guys, and we're like, "No!" And they're like, "But you're here all the time, like almost every day, skateboarding, and so are we." So we did this whole thing where we didn't come there for quite awhile just to show [them]; and then we came back and they stopped bugging us about it.

The girls involved in the park boycott practiced away from the boys for two weeks. When asked what they had gained by boycotting the park, Zoey responded, "That we're not there just for the guys and we're not there to watch them and be around them." Suddenly the girls received more respect and experienced less harassment from the skater boys. Zoey noted a distinct change in their attitude. "I guess to some level, they treated us like an equal to them, kind of." Instead of harassing the girls, the skater boys watched the Park Gang in order to see "how they were doing." They suddenly became curious about the girls' progress. When asked if they thought they had successfully changed the opinions of the skater boys, Zoey enthusiastically replied, "Well yes!"

The girls involved in the boycott retreated to a safe space where they were not being monitored and then re-emerged—triumphant. Through the boycott, the Park Gang challenged the skater boys' power and the ways in which girls are constructed through sexist and oppressive discourses. Before the boycott, the Park Gang were thought of in a very specific way: posers, flirts, and interlopers. After the boycott, the girls altered how the boys thought of them and, more significantly, how they thought of themselves. Through this political struggle, the Park Gang carved out a space for girls where none used to exist. In this way, the Park Gang engaged in the real work of changing how boys (and others) think about girls. But such hard work also legitimated their fun and opened the doors for other girls to use the park. As Pete pointed out, "lots of girls have actually started [skating] because my group started and then they kind of feel in power. I think they kind of feel empowered that they can start now, that it's okay for girls to skate."

Where the Real Work Begins: Rewriting the Rules of Girlhood

This chapter has focused on the identity work and play that being a skater girl entails through the areas of bodily comportment and motility, style, and political struggle. As the story of the Park Gang and other examples show, being a girl skater, particularly under the age of 17, requires a great deal of commitment, fearlessness, and the ability to stand up to boys who may not be welcoming at the park. Yet in being a skater, girls not only forge powerful individual identities; they also create and take advantage of collective opportunities to rewrite the rules of girlhood.

In her study of bedroom culture in the new millennium, Anita Harris (2001) suggests that girls have developed "new forms of political expression" (p. 128) that take place in new spaces. Harris explores how girls "express their politics when the prevailing view is that they have no politics to speak of at all" (p. 139). Focusing on "gurl" webpages, alternative music spheres, and underground zines, she demonstrates "that young women are passionately engaged in social change agendas, but that these occur in marginal, virtual or underground places" (p. 139). The skate park is one such place, or the schoolyard, or the downtown streets, or anyplace where the unforgiving asphalt allows girls to slap their boards down and stake a claim. It is here, at the margins of space and place, where skater girls can have a radical impact.

We found that skater girls saw themselves as participating in an alternative girlhood, an alternative that was both oppositional to emphasized femininity and in resistance to oppressive discourses of sexism and girlhood. Such discourses operate as a wall that keeps girls out of particular sports, jobs, activities, spaces, conversations, hobbies, and modes of being that they might—if given the chance—find pleasurable. As the girls in our study suggest, creating an alternative girlhood is a great deal of work, but also a great deal of fun that makes the work worth it. Indeed, the fun is in the work itself: the pride of accomplishment and the thrill of going where so few girls have gone before. Alternative girlhoods enable girls to maneuver within and against conventional notions of how girls should be and act, opening up space where none previously existed. Skater girls are a part of this renegotiation of girlhood, grinding and carving their way through uncharted terrain, both concrete and ideological.

Notes

1. All names of skater girls are pseudonyms. Earlier versions of parts of this chapter appeared in Pomerantz, Currie, & Kelly, 2004 and Kelly, Pomerantz, & Currie, 2005. The work was supported by a grant from the Social Sciences and Humanities Research Council of Canada.
2. For a fascinating look at the beginnings of this sport, see the documentary *Dogtown and Z-Boys* (Peralta, 2001).
3. Corporate marketers feed back skater culture's masculinist image to would-be boy skaters through toys such as Tech Deck Dudes (http://www.techdeckdudes.com), books aimed to entice reluctant readers, and even learning to type software programs.
4. Emphasized femininity is a femininity based on women's "compliance" with their subordination to men and "oriented to accommodating the interests and desires of men" (Connell 1987, p. 183).
5. Field work occurred between 2001 and 2003. Shauna recruited the sample by hanging out at skate parks, talking to skater boys in order to learn which parks skater girls frequented, visiting community centers where skater girls were known to go after school, and through serendipitous encounters with girls who were carrying skateboards around the city.
6. Other girls we interviewed were more than happy to call skateboarding a sport. For a social class analysis of this split, see Kelly et al., 2005, pp. 240–242.
7. Bettie (2003, p. 127) analyzes these types of competing "claims to authenticity" as displaced class antagonism.
8. One girl in the study identified as bisexual, and the other 19 implied or stated that they were heterosexual.

References

Beal, B. (1995). Disqualifying the official: An exploration of social resistance through the subculture of skateboarding. *Sociology of Sport Journal, 12*(3), 252–267.

Beal, B. (1996). Alternative masculinity and its effects on gender relations in the subculture of skateboarding. *Journal of Sport Behavior, 19*(3), 204–220.

Bettie, J. (2003). *Women without class: Girls, race, and identity.* Berkeley: University of California Press.

Bettis, P. J., & Adams, N. G. (2003). The power of the preps and a cheerleading equity policy. *Sociology of Education, 76*, 128–142.

Borden, I. (2001). *Skateboarding, space and the city: Architecture and the body.* Oxford: Berg.

Bucholtz, M. (2002). Youth and cultural practice. *Annual Review of Anthropology, 31*, 525–552.

Connell, R. W. (1987). *Gender and power.* Stanford, CA: Stanford University Press.

Eckert, P. (1989). *Jocks and burnouts: Social categories and identity in the high school.* New York: Teachers' College Press.

Hall, S. (1996). Introduction: Who needs identity? In S. Hall & P. Dugay (Eds.), *Questions of cultural identity* (pp. 1–18). London: Sage.

Harris, A. (2001). Revisiting bedroom culture: New spaces for young women's politics. *Hecate, 27*(1), 128–139.

Hebdige, D. (1979). *Subcultures: The meaning of style.* Toronto: Metheun.

Kelly, D. M. (1993). *Last chance high: How girls and boys drop in and out of alternative schools.* New Haven, CT: Yale University Press.

Kelly, D. M., Pomerantz, S., & Currie, D. (2005). Skater girlhood and emphasized femininity: "You can't land an ollie properly in heels". *Gender & Education, 17*(3), 129–148.

Leblanc, L. (1999). *Pretty in punk: Girls' gender resistance in a boys' subculture.* New Brunswick, NJ: Rutgers University Press.

McRobbie, A., & Garber, J. (1976). Girls and subcultures. In S. Hall & T. Jefferson (Eds.), *Resistance through rituals* (pp. 209–222). London: Hutchinson.

Mendoza-Denton, N. (1996). "Muy macha": Gender and ideology in gang-girls' discourse about makeup. *Ethnos, 61*(1/2), 47–63.

Merten, D. E. (1997). The meaning of meanness: Popularity, competition, and conflict among junior high school girls. *Sociology of Education, 70*(3), 175–191.

Milner, M., Jr. (2004). *Freaks, geeks, and cool kids: American teenagers, schools, and the culture of consumption.* London: Routledge.

Peralta, S. (Writer) (2001). *Dogtown and Z-Boys* [documentary film]. Culver City, CA: Sony Pictures Classics.

Pomerantz, S. (2005). "Did you see what she was wearing?" The power and politics of schoolgirls style. In Y. Jiwani, C. Steenbergen, & C. Mitchell (Eds.), *Girlhood: Redefining the limits* (pp. 173–190). Montreal: Black Rose Press.

Pomerantz, S. (forthcoming). *Girls, style, and school identities: Dressing the part.* New York: Palgrave.

Pomerantz, S., Currie, D. H., & Kelly, D. M. (2004). Sk8er girls: Skateboarders, girlhood, and feminism in motion. *Women's Studies International Forum, 27*, 547–557.

Roman, L. G. (1988). Intimacy, labor, and class: Ideologies of feminine sexuality in the punk slam dance. In L. G. Roman, & L. K. Christian-Smith, with E. Ellsworth (Eds.), *Becoming feminine: The politics of popular culture* (pp. 143–184). London: Falmer Press.

Thornton, S. (1995). *Club cultures: Music, media and subcultural capital.* Cambridge, UK: Polity Press.

Willard, M. N. (1998). Seance, tricknowledgy, skateboarding, and the space of youth. In J. Austin & M. N. Willard (Eds.), *Generations of youth: Youth cultures and history in twentieth-century America* (pp. 327–346). New York: New York University Press.

Willis, P. (1977). *Learning to labour: How working class kids get working class jobs.* Farnborough: Saxon House.

Young, I. M. (1989). Throwing like a girl: A phenomenology of feminine body comportment, motility, and spatiality. In J. Allen & I. M. Young (Eds.), *The thinking muse: Feminism and modern French philosophy* (pp. 51–70). Bloomington: Indiana University Press.

CHAPTER 7

"Take the Slam and Get Back Up"

Hardcore Candy *and the Politics of Representation in Girls' and Women's Skateboarding and Snowboarding on Television*

MICHELE K. DONNELLY

The television program *Hardcore Candy*[1] is described as having been created with "the aim of exposing adventurous role models largely ignored by
the media [...] It's time this exciting and visually stunning world of women
in extreme sports is documented. We want to tell the stories of our hidden
heroines" (http://www.hardcorecandy.tv). In spite of claims—made in commentary during major events, interviews with athletes, articles in skateboarding and snowboarding magazines, and academic articles—that skateboarding
and snowboarding are intentionally alternative to dominant sports (like
baseball, basketball, and football), with respect to gender relations, they seem
to maintain the status quo. According to these sources, skateboarding and
snowboarding subcultures are self-governed, anti-competition, informally
organized, and participant oriented (e.g., Beal, 1995, 1996; Borden, 2001;
Heino, 2000; Humphreys, 1997, 2003). Yet, like so many dominant sports,
these subcultures seem to be about (and for) boys and men. In light of this,
the creation of a television program dedicated to the "girls in action sports
and lifestyle", offers an interesting site of analysis.

Through an analysis of the representations of female skateboarders and
snowboarders on the first season of *Hardcore Candy*, I compared the representations of women participating in 'new' and 'alternative' sports with findings
from the existing literature on representations of female athletes participating
in mainstream sports. Within this literature, I found the general conclusion

that girls and women continue to be underrepresented in all media forms (newspaper, magazines, radio, and television), and when they are represented, their accomplishments have been "sexualized, commodified, trivialized and devalued" (Kane & Greendorfer, 1994, p. 36). A second body of literature that informed my analysis is the emerging literature on action or 'extreme' sports, particularly skateboarding and snowboarding, which provides insight into the lifestyle and subcultures associated with these activities. A small number of studies of skateboarding and snowboarding explore the negotiation of gender within these subcultures, and all conclude that skateboarding and snowboarding are associated with characteristics of hegemonic masculinity (independence, aggression, risk taking) and that boys and men continue to be considered the only 'authentic' participants.

In this chapter, I first introduce *Hardcore Candy*, by providing a detailed description of the program—focusing on the opening sequence, the layout of each episode, and the recurring segments and transitions. This also includes an analysis of language, and of the role of *Hardcore Candy*'s creators, producers, and hosts, Stephanie Drinnan and Zoe Flower. Following this is a discussion of a main theme from my analysis of representations of female skateboarders and snowboarders in *Hardcore Candy*: the relationship between maleness or masculinity and skateboarding and snowboarding. Through the use of particular representational (narrative and visual) strategies—reliance on male legitimation and focus on injury and risk—*Hardcore Candy* emphasizes the associations of skateboarding and snowboarding with hegemonic masculinity. Male legitimation is realized in the form of deference to male 'experts' and the consistent defining of female athletes' accomplishments by male standards. Focusing on injury and risk reinforces the masculine associations of skateboarding and snowboarding, and reaffirms male skateboarders and snowboarders as the only legitimate participants. I argue that these representational strategies can be considered to be at odds with the program's claims to promote and encourage women's involvement in action sports.

Welcome to *Hardcore Candy*

Hardcore Candy is a documentary style magazine show, infused with flirtatious animation, and highlighting stories about women athletes, entrepreneurs, musicians, and designers involved in action sports. (http://www.hardcorecandy.tv)

Based on their study of televised sport Gruneau, Whitson, and Cantelon (1988) concluded, any adequate understanding of sport television productions as texts had to begin with some attempt to grasp the basic rhythms and related elements of the program. In other words it appeared important to understand the internal composition of the program, especially with respect to the interrelations between the primary segments or blocs of movement within it. Here the notions of "composition" and "movement" offered greater purchase than the ideas of "structure" because they imply an active process rather than a fixed pattern or logic. (p. 273)

In order to read *Hardcore Candy* as a text, it is important to understand the composition of each episode and to identify the recurring segments and transitions. There are a number of similarities between *Hardcore Candy* and the traditional sport "variety" television program (as opposed to "live" game coverage), which is "dominated by studio and pre-packaged programming segments" (Gruneau et al., 1988, p. 274). *Hardcore Candy* relies on previously edited segments including interviews with athletes and coverage of events, and frequently uses "action" footage—most often, film of athletes snowboarding—from outside sources (e.g., sponsors, film production companies). As with sport variety programs, viewers of *Hardcore Candy* are guided through segments by the hosts. Stephanie Drinnan and Zoe Flower are the creators, producers, and hosts of *Hardcore Candy*. They also conduct the interviews, do much of the filming, and edit the program themselves.

An analysis of the program's name is particularly important: the word "hardcore" refers to both a style of music and a genre of pornography and, generally, is associated with intense, extreme, over the top, aggressive, obsessive, explicit, or crazy behavior or activity. These characteristics are most often associated with hegemonic masculinity, and it can be argued that in popular discourse being hardcore means being masculine. Adding the word "candy" to the title works to nullify or, at least, to modify the masculine connotations of "hardcore." Candy is sweet and consumable, and triggers associations with childhood and a lack of seriousness—candy is also enjoyable in the short term and does not connote a lifestyle or attitude, in the way that hardcore can. The potential sexual connotations of this word pair are apparent when they are entered into an Internet search engine.

The program's name and an accompanying graphic are the first image in the opening credits of *Hardcore Candy*. The graphic is a piece of hard candy (like a bon-bon) that changes to be a girl's smiling face (the candy's wrapper becomes pigtails). Her pigtails suggest youthfulness but also mirror the hosts' hairstyles in some episodes. The transformation from inanimate object to girl suggests a commodification and devaluing, and certainly an objectification, of women—although the graphic is clever and does work well (aesthetically) with the program's name.

Opening credits, used in each episode, include a visual sequence, music, and a voiceover introduction, and serve to set the tone for the program. As Duncan, Messner, Williams, and Jensen (1994) explain, the opening sequence is used to draw the viewer in; it frames the show and suggests the content (p. 254). Following the title and graphic, a voiceover promises "All girls and all action on *Hardcore Candy*." "Action" in this context is used to refer to the active participation of women in 'extreme' sports and the action footage that is a crucial element of the program. However, "girls" and "action" used together evokes a sexual connotation of "action," in the sense of "getting some action," or of the frequently used come-on on strip club signs. Using visuals and voiceover, three main segments of each episode are introduced during the opening sequence. The accompanying visuals include action footage (e.g., a skateboarder riding a halfpipe), and the voiceover often focuses on the physical appearance of the athletes. Words used to describe athletes in the introductions include: "beauty," "cutie," "hot," and "stylin." This trend continues throughout the program.

Throughout the opening sequence, images from the episodes and additional (action and non-action) footage of surfers, skiers, snowboarders, skateboarders, wakeboarders, and other athletes are flashed at the viewer, using MTV-style quick editing. Many of these images are of skateboarders and snowboarders (and a few other non-water related activities such as motocross, mountain biking, and base jumping), however, the majority of the images show girls in bathing suits (mostly bikinis). Some are action shots of surfers riding waves, or wakeboarders doing tricks, but there are also shots of girls in bikinis sitting on surfboards, and standing on boats and on the beach. The final image of the opening sequence is a snowboarder riding past the camera. As the rider turns away, snow sprays up at the lens, and the screen goes all white. After the opening sequence, the hosts, Stephanie and Zoe, describe the main segments of the episode and introduce the regular athlete profile segment, called the "*Hardcore Candy* Sweetspot."

The Sweetspot segment features a prominent woman action sports athlete. Of the 12 Sweetspot segments in the first season, one presented a professional skateboarder, and five highlighted professional snowboarders. A "sweet spot" often refers to the ideal place on something, particularly the best place to hit on a bat or a club, but the term also has sexual connotations especially in the context of representations of women (in part, due to its linguistic similarity to the term "g-spot"). The *Hardcore Candy* Sweetspot is composed primarily of the featured athlete's answers to interview-style questions, and comments of friends and family about her. Skateboarding and snowboarding are represented in *Hardcore Candy* through athletes in the Sweetspot, other segments featuring athletes, and segments featuring specific events. In addition to the six Sweetspot segments, four episodes include segments that showcase female skateboarders and snowboarders: an entire episode is devoted to the Boarding for Breast Cancer annual snowboarding event and related activities; one segment features the All Girl Skate Jam; another features the Slam City Jam skateboarding event; and, another segment is about women in action video games.

At the end of each episode, Stephanie and Zoe thank the viewers for watching and show previews of the next episode, followed by outtakes from the current episode. These are the only segments, in addition to the Sweetspot, that appear in every episode (the exception is the season finale). One of the outtakes from the first episode shows Stephanie messing up a line, laughing, and saying "Gotta give lots of material for the outtakes" (episode #1). *Hardcore Candy's* outtakes contribute to the sense that Stephanie and Zoe are friends in real life who are having fun making the program, and who are not perfect. This feeling is also fostered when the hosts, sitting on the rooftop patio, are shown speaking to each other and laughing before the program begins, and when they enter learn to ride programs for surfing and motocross. Viewers are invited to join in this relationship, and to share the program's understanding of the "world of women's extreme sports," through Stephanie and Zoe's consistent use of the term "we." Brundson and Morley (1978) refer to this "mode of address" as one that promotes the preferred reading by including the viewer in a sense of community. According to the *Hardcore Candy* website, this inclusive language is intentional: the program claims to offer "A unique behind-the-scenes approach [that] allows the viewers to connect with Zoe and Stephanie behind and in front of the camera" (http://www.hardcorecandy.tv). With this goal and using the strategies described, Stephanie and Zoe become more accessible and easy to identify with as personalities.

As the anchors for the program, Stephanie and Zoe facilitate transitions between the three or four main segments that make up each episode. While both are present for the episode introduction immediately following the opening credits, one or the other often introduces segments during the program (from the rooftop set location). Animated versions of Stephanie and Zoe are also used in transitions between episodes. In the first season, animated Stephanie and Zoe are more active (and more proficient) than 'real' Stephanie and Zoe. Only the animated characters are shown skateboarding and snowboarding—their real life counterparts do not participate in these activities. Through their animated selves, Stephanie and Zoe increase their presence on the program (and, to a degree, in the activities presented). Whannel (1992) argues, "In many ways the identity of the programme is built around the presenter[s]" (p. 107). Stephanie and Zoe's influence (as creators, producers, and hosts of the program) cannot be over emphasized.

Maleness/Masculinity and Skateboarding and Snowboarding

> the physical practice of snowboarding does not require the "masculine" strength and aggression that legitimize the exclusion of women in some sports… [However] through several social practices, snowboarders can make the practice of riding a board down a mountain into something that conveys their masculine status. (Anderson, 1999, p. 61)

Skateboarding and snowboarding—the activities and the subcultures associated with them—are considered 'masculine'. This is due, in part, to their history as activities whose participants were (and continue to be) predominantly male. The perception that skateboarders and snowboarders accept (and welcome) the high risk nature of their sports, and the resulting injuries, contributes to the masculine connotations of skateboarding and snowboarding. The representational strategies discussed reinforce the common understanding of skateboarding and snowboarding as appropriately masculine activities.

Male Legitimation—Legitimation by Males and Evaluation by a Male Standard

Hardcore Candy consistently relies on male legitimation of all aspects of women's participation in skateboarding and snowboarding. Male experts are used to lend legitimacy to women's events and a male standard of performance (the level of performance achieved by men) is used to evaluate everybody's skateboarding and snowboarding abilities. Gender marking enforces this reliance on male legitimation, and gender marking (of women's activities) happens continuously throughout the program, both verbally and through the use of graphics (Duncan et al., 1994). *Hardcore Candy* showcases *women's* extreme sports culture by presenting the best *female* action sports athletes: Vanessa Torres is the top skater on the *women's* tour; Cara Beth Burnside is an icon of *women's* skateboarding and snowboarding. Men's extreme sports are not gender marked, i.e., they are not referred to as "men's extreme sports," ensuring that "men's [activities] are presented as the norm, the universal, while the women's continually are marked as the other, derivative (and by implication, inferior) to the men's" (Duncan et al., 1994, p. 268). Graphics, especially the candy/face graphic, reinforce gender stereotyping and, in *Hardcore Candy*, so do the hosts. Because women's skateboarding and snowboarding are presented as derivative of men's skateboarding and snowboarding, male legitimation is necessary. Men's participation in skateboarding and snowboarding is considered more real or 'authentic'; male approval is sought to make women's participation more credible, and male standards of performance are the only ones considered.

Deference to male experts is a strategy used repeatedly in *Hardcore Candy*. A male 'expert' is called upon in almost every segment featuring a female skateboarder or snowboarder and in the segments presenting skateboarding and snowboarding events. In this context, "expert" is a loosely defined term. Some of the men are professional skateboarders and snowboarders. For example, professional skateboarder Tony Hawk is interviewed during a segment on the All Girl Skate Jam, an all girls skateboarding event:

> I came to the All Girl Skate Jam mostly just to watch (laughs),' cause I've seen it grow larger and larger every year and I came last year and checked it out and this year it's at a bigger skate park and it's more girls and the skating level is better and it's just fun to see, 'cause I don't really get to see too many girl skaters, you know, there's only a handful at every location and here is when they all conglomerate (sic) and it's really fun to watch. (episode #2)

In a segment on the Slam City Jam skateboarding event, professional skateboarder Matt Dove is used to lend legitimacy to the women's competition. He describes the female competitors: "The girls ripping—Lin-z rolling in on that big thing is ridiculous, into backside airs; Jen O'Brien smooth front side grinds, front side ollies, back side ollies; Hilary, just burly; Jessica, gnarly, good, smooth style. It's awesome, it's good to see, everybody's ripping" (episode #5). Dove is in the foreground, facing the halfpipe behind him to the left; as he starts to speak, Lin-z Adams Hawkins rolls into the halfpipe on a very large ramp, and, as he mentions each rider's name, the viewer sees footage of that skater in the halfpipe. As he makes his final comment, the camera is on Dove. He smiles, and sounds paternalistic, like a parent or a teacher talking about a child. According to these two (male) professional skateboarders, girl's skateboarding is "fun" to watch. The way this is said, and by whom, reinforces the notion that women's skateboarding is less real than men's skateboarding—it is fun, cute, and entertaining to watch.

Technical knowledge, such as the descriptions and names of tricks, and information about equipment, is largely absent in the *Hardcore Candy* segments featuring skateboarding and snowboarding. Dove is the only person to name the tricks that women are performing while the viewer can see them performed. The lack of technical information on the program is replaced primarily by a focus on the personal lives of the female athletes. *Hardcore Candy*, like the television coverage of the women's college basketball championships analyzed by Duncan and Hasbrook (1988), overlooks and symbolically denies the "elements of physical skill, knowledge, and strategy" and, thus, constitutes a "denial of game" (p. 11). It is telling that the only reference to technical skills on *Hardcore Candy* is made by a male skateboarder—as an 'authentic' participant in skateboarding, Dove is allowed to (and expected to) demonstrate his technical understanding of the activity.

Another example of deferring to male experts occurs during a segment featuring Vanessa Torres. The interview with Torres is interspersed with footage of an interview with Andy Meade, manager of the team that she rides for. About Torres, Meade says: "Vanessa Torres is a girl that used to live in Riverside, California, a super cool little girl that skateboarded around the corner from her house all day long, every day and jumped into the All Girl Skate Jam [...] and ended up being one of the best and is one of the best top girls in the world cup standings right now" (episode #5). What Meade says about Torres is less important than the fact that she does not speak for herself; her answers to questions about her skateboarding skills, sponsorships, and successes are each punctuated by a confirming or reinforcing quote from Meade. Similarly, in the Sweetspot featuring Victoria Jealouse, Jealouse talks about being extra careful when she snowboards on big mountains. Jim Conway, a helicopter guide who has worked with Jealouse is used to reinforce this sentiment: Jealouse "was one of the best mountain people I ever went out with—heads up, smart about what's goin' on out there, ripper" (episode #5). Not only is there a sense that these women's words need support, they need support from a man—regardless of whether or not he possesses the same skateboarding or snowboarding skills that she does.

As mentioned, I use the term "expert" loosely. The expertise of some of the men used in this role is less apparent when their relationship to skateboarding and snowboarding subcultures is unclear (when they are not riders, guides, managers). For example, in a Sweetspot with Annie Boulanger, *Hardcore Candy* speaks to Alex Auchu, described only as "Annie's ami." Sitting with Boulanger and three other people on a terrace in Whistler, Auchu wears snowboarding (or skiing) attire, though there is no evidence that he snowboards himself. Despite this, he says about Boulanger, "When I met her, do you want to know, when I met her she didn't have a clue (laughs). She was going off the jump and doing a 720 [rotation] and she didn't have a clue where the landing was. But now she figured it out. She's good now (laughs)" (episode #1). The purpose of including Auchu's opinion is unclear as Boulanger describes her snowboarding results—including winning the U.S. Open and being featured in a snowboarding video—at different points during the Sweetspot. It seems that having a man say that a female snowboarder is "good" carries as much (if not more) weight as her results.

Using male experts to legitimate female participation in skateboarding and snowboarding is one strategy used in *Hardcore Candy* to respond to the "primary interpretation" of skateboarding and snowboarding as appropriately masculine activities. Hall, Critcher, Jefferson, Clarke, and Roberts (2000) show that "a primary interpretation on a topic 'commands the field' in all subsequent treatments and sets the terms of reference within which all further coverage or debate takes place" (p. 650). Representations of sport (and sport participants) offer as their primary interpretation the perspective that sport is 'a male preserve'. Most sports, including skateboarding and snowboarding, offer a framework for understanding that is male dominated—all discussions and representations relate to and work within this framework, even when their subject matter (women athletes) does not.

What is more important, "this initial interpretive framework [...] is extremely difficult to alter fundamentally, once established" (Hall et al., 2000, p. 650). Rather than attempting to alter the interpretive framework, *Hardcore Candy* works within the "primary interpretation" of skateboarding and snowboarding by referring consistently to a 'male' standard. This regularly takes the form of comparisons between women's skateboarding and snowboarding and 'real' (men's) skateboarding and snowboarding. Often, the skateboarders and snowboarders presented in the program are treated as exceptional because they are 'almost as good as the guys'. The result is a portrayal of these female athletes as an incredible, but unachievable, standard. Other women may choose to participate but cannot expect that they will ever be this good, it is an anomaly, not something to be emulated. According to Messner (1988), "The outstanding female athlete is portrayed as an exception that proves the rule, thus reinforcing traditional stereotypes about femininity" (p. 205). One example of this is a description of Cara Beth Burnside as a "skate and snowboard icon" (episode #4). In another episode, Jeremy Jones, a professional snowboarder, talks about riding with Victoria Jealouse: "When she's in the mountains she's one of the guys and we treat her that way, we maybe swear a little less around her. But when it comes right down to her she's riding the same stuff as us and gets no special treatment" (episode #5). In the accompanying visual, the camera stays on Jones until he talks about Jealouse's riding and then the viewer sees footage of Jealouse (by herself) on a clean mountain ride (making the first track down the mountain). Most interesting in this example is Jones's suggestion that Jealouse's status as female is suspended when she is riding (because she is good enough to ride with the guys), and the visual which the viewer assumes is Jealouse but, because of the distance from the rider and the non-gender specific look of snowboarding clothing, could be anyone.

The adherence to a male standard and the presentation of particular (female) athletes as exceptional means that when women's and men's skateboarding and snowboarding are compared, the women's activities are invariably deemed lacking. In a classic example of conspiring in their own subordination, women action sports athletes themselves reinforce the idea that emulating men's action sports is the ultimate goal for women. In response to a question, Vanessa Torres says, "I think girls' skateboarding will be up with the guys because it'll progress, it's progressing like really fast since this year, and last year, I think it'll, they'll be pretty close together" (episode #5). In a segment on the Slam City Jam skateboarding event, professional skateboarder Heidi Fitzgerald comments on the women's halfpipe competition, "It was fun, it was a good jam—8, 8 to 10 girls. The level and ability's getting really good" (episode #5).

There are, clearly, a number of excellent female skateboarders and snowboarders. Unfortunately, their skills are not evaluated against other female riders, instead, these women are consistently compared to male skateboarders and snowboarders. Vanessa Torres' comment that girls' skateboarding is "progressing" sounds a lot like the commentator for the men's skateboard vert final at the 2003 Gravity Games: "Once you stop learning, you stop progressing. And that's what skateboarding is all about." As women start to perform bigger tricks, and gain recognition as 'better' skateboarders and snowboarders, their male colleagues will also be pushing the limits of their sports. Ultimately, it seems almost impossible for girls and women (as a group rather than a few exceptional individuals) to achieve the male standard to which they are constantly compared—and to be accepted as 'authentic' participants. Consequently, female skateboarders and snowboarders appreciate being included at the men's events. Professional skateboarder Jen O'Brien refers to girls now being included at the Slam City Jam event and it is clear that women do not make this decision. It seems that many women and men see women's skateboarding as the little sister of real (or men's) skateboarding. While women are present as athletes in *Hardcore Candy*, their continued exclusion from the position of 'expert' (even about the activities in which they are participating at a very high level) demonstrates that *Hardcore Candy* serves to reinforce the "primary interpretation" of skateboarding and snowboarding as masculine activities, and as male preserves.

Focus on Injury and Risk

A constant topic in the *Hardcore Candy* segments on skateboarding and snowboarding is injury and, by extension, risk. Some athletes are asked specifically about injuries they have sustained, and others are asked to speak about their biggest fears, which often leads to a discussion of injury (or the potential for injury). Injury, as a topic in the context of interviews with female skateboarders and snowboarders, reinforces the element of risk associated with action sports. A willingness to voluntarily subject oneself to risk and pain in the pursuit of an athletic endeavour is generally considered a masculine trait. According to Jefferson (1998), the embodiment of masculinity is as much mental as physical. Physical toughness in the form of strong muscles is only one side of the equation. Men who come closest to achieving an ideal masculine identity do so through their "willingness to risk the body in performance" (p. 81). Associations with masculinity in skateboarding and snowboarding relate more to the mental toughness that Jefferson discusses (than to physical toughness). Part of the rejection of 'mainstream' sports by skateboarders and snowboarders takes the form of rejecting routinized training schedules and/or physical training such as weight training (though this is not the case for all skateboarders and snowboarders). Instead, skateboarders and snowboarders demonstrate their physical toughness by recovering from big crashes and coming back from serious injuries, rather than through large muscles and 'hard' bodies. In pursuit of bigger and better tricks and runs, skateboarders and snowboarders consistently "risk their bodies in performance"—and, in this way, the association of their activities with masculinity is reinforced.

As a result, the focus on injury and risk in *Hardcore Candy* suggests that girls and women participating in skateboarding and snowboarding have accepted the masculine nature of these activities, and also a male standard of pain and injury. At the least, *Hardcore Candy* is framed to encourage the viewer to work from this position. According to Tony Hawk,

> The whole action sports genre never really was welcoming for women. For the most part because people thought it was a lot of risk for injury and, now, frig, you know, that mould's been broken with so many girls surfing, and so many girls snowboarding, and skating's just the natural progression and the, you know, girls take heavy falls now and they get back up, get right back on so that's not even an issue anymore. (episode #2)

As Hawk is speaking, a young skater makes two attempts at dropping into a street course and falls each time; a different, and clearly injured, skater hobbles over to a wall to sit down; a skater falls in the halfpipe; two separate skaters fall on the street course; and a final skater falls from a rail slide as Hawk says that "injuries aren't even an issue anymore." Hawk seems to be suggesting that action sports have become more accessible to women because they (girls and women) are willing to "take heavy falls". He does not mention any other changes in the genre that might have contributed to greater female participation (and he does not mention that male skateboarders also fall and get hurt). At the same event, Cara Beth Burnside says, "I know that girls can skate and take the slam and get back up, you know, there's girls out there that wanna skate and have a lot of potential, they just need like positive, positive support" (episode #2). Girls and women are consistently being told that in order to participate, they must be prepared to get hurt. *Hardcore Candy* presents injury as something that ends your riding. However, in other media forms presenting skateboarding and snowboarding (to primarily male audiences), crashes, injuries, and the (male) athletes involved are glorified.

The athletes, for the most part, speak about their injuries with pride—as a demonstration of their ability to hack it in male dominated sports, as battle scars they can share with other skate/snowboarders, and, generally, as something that is inevitable when you choose to be a skate/snowboarder. In a Sweetspot, Annie Boulanger talks about her biggest fear: "Biggest fear probably for all snowboarders is just to get injured. And then you try not to think about it because that's how you do get injured. Two years ago I blew my knee in January so I wasn't able to ride that entire year and then I've had just little injuries like broken hand, broken thumbs, shoulders wrecked, and little things like that" (episode #1). The camera is on Boulanger speaking and then cuts to footage of her doing a big trick and falling very hard (her goggles fly off and she bounces down a hill). As she describes the "little" injuries, Boulanger holds out her hands and points to her shoulder. A sense of 'macho' bravado pervades her reference to broken bones and "wrecked" shoulders as "little injuries". Sometimes entire events are framed in ways that focus on injury. For example, the All Girl Skate Jam is described as "an event where the pros and amateurs get together to celebrate skater chicks who aren't afraid to hit the concrete" (episode #2). Again, the message is: doing these sports can be painful; women must be willing to accept this in order to participate.

Injuries, for some athletes, are both an unavoidable aspect of their career choice and a source of pride. In the Sweetspot with Tara Dakides, she is sitting on the deck of her home in Mammoth Lakes, California and admits, "I'm injured right now, I'm just not wearing my brace and my crutches are inside" and the viewer sees her crutches propped against the wall inside the house (episode #9). According to Messner, Dunbar, and Hunt (2000), "Heroically taking risks while already hurt was a constant theme in Extreme sports commentary [...] Athletes appear especially heroic when they go against doctor's wishes not to compete" (p. 388). This was not often the case in *Hardcore Candy*. Instead, most athletes referred to multiple injuries and time spent recovering from them. Dakides talks about coming back from an injury as though it is something she has done more times than she can remember, "It's always harder to come back mentally than physically but I have confidence in myself that I am a mentally strong person so I just know that I'll come back and I'll be okay. I've done it so many times" (episode #9). The warning for viewers seems to be that multiple injuries and lengthy recovery times are to be expected if you want to be as good as these women. While this is probably true, *Hardcore Candy* frames the topic of injury exclusively as a (warranted) deterrent to women's participation. Injury is represented differently in media coverage of men's 'extreme' sports—it is often glorified and associated with an athlete's commitment to the lifestyle.

Even the exceptional athletes presented in the program talk about the risks they face, and the injuries they have suffered. Victoria Jealouse admits, "I'm not ever completely comfortable because there's always this element of risk that, um, you just don't know for sure. You can always run into something like, you know an avalanche, you can always trigger something" (episode #5). Following this discussion with Jealouse, we see footage from a helmet camera she wore during a run in Alaska. Jealouse is going through a very narrow passage on the mountain and breathing heavily—her movements suggest that she is not entirely in control, and snow slides out from under her with each move. With some concern in her voice she says, "Holy, that was a little narrow. Oh brother". Natasza Zurek is also very honest when she says, "In myself I'd like to change—I wouldn't be so afraid of injuries and of dying. I'd like to not be completely brainless but to at least be more fearless than I am now" (episode #7). As she says this, no action footage is shown—simply Zurek walking up a hill carrying her snowboard behind her back. Finally, Shannon Dunn-Downing talks about being a character in a snowboarding video game, "I kinda like being a video game character because I get to do stuff that I don't know how to do (laughs) and it makes me look pretty good, and when I fall it doesn't hurt, so it's like the ultimate thing" (episode #8). The suggestion is that crashing is inevitable, at least when you are a video game character, it does not hurt. While crashing might be an inevitable part of the skateboarding and snowboarding experience, the constant focus on injury, to the exclusion of more positive aspects of the experience, seems to work to deter viewers rather than promote their participation. Simultaneously, focusing on injury validates the achievements of these women in the context of mainstream (not just 'extreme') sport discourse.

Throughout *Hardcore Candy* a contradictory message about risk and injury is presented to the viewer. 'Experts' like Tony Hawk and Cara Beth Burnside claim that women are more willing than ever to assume the risks associated with action sports and that ideas about injury are not the barrier to women's participation that they once were. At the same time images on the screen show women falling, crashing, and getting hurt while skateboarding and snowboarding. Hawk and Burnside both say that girls now can fall and "get back up," as though (for an unidentified reason) they could not do this before. However, it is clear in the visuals that the girls shown falling *are* hurt (or injured). The camera stays on them, showing that they have not gotten up, that they are holding injured body parts, and that they are grimacing in pain or crying. In one case, an injured skateboarder is shown limping over to a wall to sit down but the cause of her injury is not shown. The images that accompany discussions of injury are at odds with the narrative. *Hardcore Candy* reinforces characteristics of hegemonic femininity by representing injury and risk in this contradictory way. While the narrative tells viewers that female skateboarders and snowboarders are 'tough enough' for these sports, the accompanying visuals, particularly of girls crying, reinforce the athletes' femininity (and suggest that they are not 'tough enough').

Contradictory narrative and visual presentations are quite common in televised women's sports. Analyzing television coverage of a surfing competition, Duncan and Hasbrook (1988) found: "Television's message was indeed contradictory. The audio said that women are capable, strong, talented athletes who were participating in an exciting sport; the video said that women are passive, decorative objects who beautify a nonsport. Presented in this light, female surfers cannot be taken seriously" (p. 14). In spite of *Hardcore Candy*'s efforts to encourage female participation in action sports, the emphasis on injury in the segments on skateboarding and snowboarding sends a strong message—you can participate if you want to, but participation in these activities can (and will) hurt you.

Injury is also a common theme in coverage of skateboarding and snowboarding directed at a male audience. Sydnor and Rinehart (2003) argue, "shocking up-close scenarios of sport-induced injury, illness, or crashes— tend to predominate in [media coverage of] extreme sports" (p. 7). In men's extreme sports, the emphasis on injury and risk calls attention to attempts by skateboarders and snowboarders to land huge tricks and it reinforces their commitment to the lifestyle. In *Hardcore Candy*, however, the contradictory narrative and visual presentation of risk serves as a warning: while they say that girls and women can take the falls, there is no visual evidence of female skateboarders and snowboarders getting up and continuing to ride (or even walk away) from the crashes they are shown taking.

Conclusion

Hardcore Candy's coverage of female skateboarders and snowboarders uses two particular representational strategies—reliance on male legitimation and focus on injury and risk—that emphasize the associations of skateboarding and snowboarding with hegemonic masculinity. Both strategies are borrowed from mainstream representations of female athletes (in all sports, particularly those that are male dominated), and may serve, in spite of claims to the contrary, to marginalize and deter women's participation. *Hardcore Candy* relies on and reinforces the ideology of gender difference as it identifies particular behaviors and activities as feminine or masculine. Investment in promoting the ideology of gender difference is necessary because, without it, there would be no "women's extreme sports culture" to showcase. A television program like *Hardcore Candy*, framed as it is, is only necessary if one believes in essential gender differences, i.e., *Hardcore Candy* justifies its own existence by insisting that women and men have essentially different experiences of 'extreme' sports. This would not be the case if *Hardcore Candy* presented a social, cultural, or historical context for women's participation in skateboarding and snowboarding. Instead of focusing on how girls and women negotiate a space for themselves within these male dominated subcultures, the discourse of *Hardcore Candy* implies that essential gender differences explain the exclusion and/or marginalization of girls and women within them.

Hardcore Candy is not, however, the only 'extreme' sports venue selling the ideology of gender difference. An industry is being built on the premise that boys and girls, men and women, learn and participate in skateboarding and snowboarding in *essentially* different ways. Clothing companies and equipment manufacturers are launching new lines created specifically for girls and women. Girls and women can pay to attend female only camps and learn to ride programs (often taught by female instructors). And various skateboarding and snowboarding companies, as well as other commercial sponsors, are getting on board to promote women's only events like SG's "Queen of Skate" or Shannon Dunn's P!Jamma Party. Women-only camps and events have the potential to be positive spaces where female skateboarders and snowboarders develop a sense of community, and escape—even if it is only temporary and incomplete—male domination of these sports. However, when these spaces are framed in ways that appeal to characteristics of hegemonic femininity, the potential for female empowerment is diluted.

All of the parties, including *Hardcore Candy*, involved in promoting gender differences to sell skateboarding and snowboarding products, experiences, and events emphasize girls' and women's position as *others* in skateboarding and snowboarding subcultures. The result is a reinforcement of boys and men as the only authentic participants—a message clearly sent by subcultural media sources such as skateboarding and snowboarding magazines and videos. And while the existence of girls-only clothing lines, camps, and events may lead to increased participation by girls and women, it has the potential to marginalize that participation by relegating it to the consumption end of the subcultural equation. Girls and women will continue to be marginalized in those media sources considered authentic and excluded from participating in the construction and reconstruction of the subcultures.

Hardcore Candy, like media coverage of the 1999 Women's World Cup of soccer, presents women's participation as "a new era for women's empowerment […] packaged to resonate with and appeal to women. Part of the real contradiction of the games, however, may be that the Women's World Cup was also packaged to resonate and appeal to men […] This representation appeals to the hopes of women while perhaps assuring the men that nothing has really changed" (Christopherson, Janning, & McConnell, 2002, p. 184; see also Metz, this volume). *Hardcore Candy* does not address only girls and women; the program is framed in ways that appeal to boys and men as well, assuring male viewers that their privileged position within skateboarding and snowboarding subcultures remains largely unchallenged. *Hardcore Candy*—a television program produced by women, about women, and for women—has the potential to be an alternative to representations of women in mainstream media sources. But, rather than offering an alternative, *Hardcore Candy* reinforces the messages about female skateboarders and snowboarders (and women athletes in general) that are produced by mainstream and subcultural media sources. The simple fact of *Hardcore Candy's* existence reminds us that girls and women continue to be *other* to *real* skateboarders and snowboarders.

Note

1. Girlsroom Productions created two seasons (13 episodes each) of *Hardcore Candy*, a half hour series hosted and produced in Canada. The program was broadcast in Canada on OLN and the Women's Television Sports Network (WTSN), both of which are part of the Bell Globemedia conglomerate. Internationally, *Hardcore Candy* was broadcast on KDOC in California, FUEL (a Fox Cable Networks channel) in the United States, the Australian Broadcasting Network, and Extreme Channel Digital in the United Kingdom. *Hardcore Candy* included segments on a wide variety of 'action' sports, and each episode consisted of stories about: (North American) athletes; learn to ride surf, ski, and motocross programs for women; and women's competitions and events.

References

Anderson, K. L. (1999). Snowboarding: The construction of gender in an emerging sport. *Journal of Sport and Social Issues, 23*(1), 55–79.

Beal, B. (1995). Disqualifying the official: An exploration of social resistance through the subculture of skateboarding. *Sociology of Sport Journal, 12*, 252–267.

Beal, B. (1996). Alternative masculinity and its effects on gender relations in the subculture of skateboarding. *Journal of Sport Behavior, 19*(3), 204–220.

Borden, I. (2001). *Skateboarding, space and the city: Architecture and the body*. Oxford: Berg.

Brundson, C., & Morley, D. (1978). *Everyday television: Nationwide*. London: BFI.

Christopherson, N., Janning, M., & Diaz McConnell, E. (2002). Two kicks forward, one kick back: A content analysis of media discourses on the 1999 women's world cup soccer Championship. *Sociology of Sport Journal, 19*(2), 170–188.

Duncan, M. C., & Hasbrook, C. A. (1988). Denial of power in televised women's sports. *Sociology of Sport Journal, 5*(1), 1–21.

Duncan, M. C., Messner, M.A., Williams, L., & Jensen, K. (1994). Gender stereotyping in televised sports. In S. Birrell & C. L. Cole (Eds.), *Women, sport, and culture* (pp. 249–272). Champaign, IL: Human Kinetics.

Gruneau, R., Whitson, D., & Cantelon, H. (1988). Methods and media: Studying the sports/television discourse. *Society and Leisure, 11*(2), 265–281.

Hall, S., Critcher, C., Jefferson, T., Clarke, J., & Roberts, B. (2000). The social production of news. In P. Marris & S. Thornham (Eds.), *Media studies: A reader* (2nd ed.; pp. 645–652). New York: New York University Press.

Hardcore Candy (2002). Girlsroom Productions. http://www.hardcorecandy.tv

Heino, R. (2000). What is so punk about snowboarding? *Journal of Sport and Social Issues, 24*(2), 176–191.

Humphreys, D. (1997). 'Shreadheads go mainstream'?: Snowboarding and alternative youth. *International Review for the Sociology of Sport, 32*(2), 147–160.

Humphreys, D. (2003). Selling out snowboarding: The alternative response to commercial co-optation. In R. E. Rinehart & S. Sydnor (Eds.), *To the extreme: Alternative sports, inside and out* (pp. 407–428). Albany: State University of New York Press.

Jefferson, T. (1998). Muscle, 'Hard men' and 'Iron' Mike Tyson: Reflections on desire, anxiety and the embodiment of masculinity. *Body and Society, 4*(1), 77–98.

Kane, M., & Greendorfer, S. (1994). The media's role in accommodating and resisting stereotyped images of women in sport. In P. Creedon (Ed.), *Women, media and sport* (pp. 28–44). Thousand Oaks, CA: Sage.

Messner, M. A. (1988). Sports and male domination: The female athlete as contested ideological terrain. *Sociology of Sport Journal, 5*(3), 197–211.

Messner, M. A., Dunbar, M., & Hunt, D. (2000). The televised sports manhood formula. *Journal of Sport and Social Issues, 24*(4), 380–394.

Rinehart, R. E., & Sydnor, S. (2003). Proem. In R. E. Rinehart & S. Sydnor (Eds.), *To the extreme: Alternative sports, inside and out* (pp. 1–17). Albany: State University of New York Press.

Whannel, G. (1992). *Fields in vision: Television sport and cultural transformation.* London & New York: Routledge.

Racialized Pedagogies

CHAPTER 8

Hostile Environments
*Anti-Indian Imagery, Racial Pedagogies,
and Youth Sport Cultures*

C. RICHARD KING

In the fall of 2001, Teresa Miller chose as one her first acts as Principal of Manhattan (Kansas) High School to propose ending the institution's use of American Indian imagery. Miller issued her proposal in response to the April 2001 statement of the U.S. Commission on Civil Rights condemning Native American mascots and a petition from indigenous students from the local university in the hopes of "educating each student to be a contributing citizen in a changing, diverse society." A heated public debate followed her proposal, revealing not only strong community support for retaining "the Indians" but also the pervasive resentment of multicultural pedagogies. While intentionality, tradition, and honor figured prominently in the debate, many boosters invoked education to advance their positions. Local resident C. Michael Smith (2001) suggested that the school district should seize upon the "honored school symbol and tradition as a teachable moment about people who were indigenous to North America." Retaining the mascot, he continued, would offer valuable lessons to "our students about how we respect and honor all elements of a diverse society, in order to progress together." Smith's commentary, an exemplary instance of neoconservative recodings of progressive movements for racial justice, is not about empowerment or enlightenment, but a hollow defense of the status quo. In fact, his editorial reveals something more as well: it directs attention to the increasingly complex articulations of race and pedagogy.

Focusing on Native American mascots in U.S. youth cultures—or, better said, the use of American Indian symbols, nicknames, and logos by high schools and their athletic teams, and the controversy surrounding them—this chapter explores the relationships between race and pedagogy in four distinct ways. After tracing the history of Native American mascots and detailing their initial emergence as well as more recent challenges to them, it elaborates both the manner in which pseudo-Indian imagery teaches students and citizens about race, culture, and history and the content and forms of such racialized lessons. Next, it directs attention to the hostile learning environments created via the use of Indian imagery by educational institutions and their athletics teams. Having established the deleterious effects of such symbols and spectacles, it engages the recent effort of mascot efforts to reframe Native American mascots as valuable teaching tools. In conclusion, it underscores the necessity of finding ways to challenge such popular pedagogy in the classroom, particularly if teachers wish to refashion education as a site of anti-racist intervention.

A History Lesson

Today, nearly 1,500 schools, including more than 75 colleges and universities, employ pseudo-Indian imagery (Rodriguez, 1998; Staurowsky, 1999). They have a long history, dating back to the late 19th and early 20th century. They developed in conjunction with the rise of intercollegiate and professional athletics, a crisis in White masculinity, the closing of the frontier, urbanization, industrialization, and the subjugation of Native America (Churchill, 1994; Deloria, 1998; Drinnon, 1980). Over the course of the 20th century, Native American mascots have become a taken for granted element of American culture, reflecting the pleasures, possibilities, and powers they have granted their Euro-American performers. In this context, pseudo-Indian imagery in athletics and education congealed for myriad reasons, including comments by fans or sportswriters, historic relationships between an institution and indigenous peoples, and regional associations. Over the past century, they have become institutionalized icons, encrusted with memories, tradition, boosterism, administrative investment, financial rewards, and collective identity (See Connolly, 2000; Coombe, 1999; Davis, 1993; King & Springwood, 2001b; Nussell, 1994; Vanderford, 1994).

Native American mascots rely on stereotypes and cliches. They reduce indigenous peoples to a limited set of cultural features: the feathered headdress, face paint, buckskin paints, warfare, dance, and the tomahawk (chop). They recycle these key symbols to fashion moving, meaningful, and entertaining personas and performances that many take to be authentic, appropriate, and even reverent. The condensed versions of Indianness rendered through such signs and spectacles confine Native Americans within the past and typically within the popular image of the Plains warrior. Pseudo-Indian imagery, then, confines indigenous peoples within overlapping tropes of primitive difference: on the one hand, romantic renditions of noble savagery conjure bellicose warriors like Chief Illiniwek and the Fighting Illini of the University of Illinois or the Seminoles with their Chief Osceola at Florida State University; on the other hand, perverse burlesque parodies of the physical or cultural features of Indians invigorate the basest visions of ignobility, such as Chief Wahoo of the Cleveland Indians or Willie Wampum at Marquette University (King, 2001).

Increasingly, Native American mascots have become subject to debate (King & Springwood, 2001b; Spindel, 2000). Activists protest at sporting events featuring teams with such team spirits, while students and citizens openly express concern about school symbols; in turn, political organizations, from the American Indian Movement to the National Congress of American Indians, have denounced pseudo-Indian imagery in athletics. Together, these public challenges have fostered heated discussions and policy reassessments. Some schools like the University of Utah have altered their mascots, while many others, such as Marquette University and the University of Miami, have ended their use of pseudo-Indian imagery. Likewise, many school boards—from the Minnesota Board of Education to the Los Angeles School District—have passed resolutions requiring that schools change the Native American mascots. In addition, religious organizations and professional societies—including the Unitarian Universalist Association of Congregations, the National Education Association, the United Church of Christ, the Modern Language Association, the United Methodist Church, and the American Anthropological Association—have condemned the continued use of pseudo-Indian icons in education and athletics. And at the national level, the United States Commission on Civil Rights and the Trademark Trial and Appeal Board have taken stands against Native American mascots. Over the past quarter century, the total number of symbols has dropped noticeably. By one estimate nearly 1,500 Native American mascots have been changed, retired, or reworked since 1970 (Suzan Shown Harjo, personal communication, December 2, 2001).

Miseducation

Although it may be easy to forget when witnessing thousands of fans do the tomahawk chop or when reading the highlights of a sensational game, Native American mascots actually perform a pedagogical function concerning race, culture, and history. Native American mascots are quite literally teaching machines. Playing Indian at half-time and the associated commercial products and cultural practices associated with it address citizen-subjects within a number of interlocking "sites of pedagogy" (Dileo, 2002), including sports stadia, pep rallies, parades, and half-time shows, the hallways and classrooms of countless schools, media coverage, commercial ventures between schools or teams and corporations, public appearances by embodied mascots, as well as, pennants, tee-shirts, and baseball caps worn by fans. Importantly, the use of anti-Indian imagery, names, and logos in association with athletics does not impart racial lessons in isolation. Instead, it teaches through complex intertextual, symbolic, and performative dialogues with other formulations of Indianness, such as movies, commodities and advertising, the news media, boy scouts and similar youth groups, biased historical accounts, and fiction (see Berkhofer, 1978; Bird, 1996; Whitt, 1995), and with constructions of other forms of racialized difference, especially whiteness and blackness (see King & Springwood, 2001a). Native American mascots educate, or, as Pewewardy (1991, 1998, 2001) and Staurowsky (1999) would prefer, *miseducate*, the public about cultural difference, history, race relations, and what it means to be a citizen-subject.

Obviously, as detailed above, the use of Indian imagery in athletics reiterates false renderings of indigenous peoples. It reduces them to cartoon characters and well worn cultural clichés of the Chief, the brave, the warrior, the clown. It traps Native Americans with the past, in perpetual, unwinnable conflict with the superior White man. It confines them most often to the horse cultures of the plain, adorned in flowing headdresses and beautiful buckskin. It misappropriates and reinvents indigenous spirituality, dance, and material culture for the pleasure of largely White audiences. In 1999, the Society of Indian Psychologists of the Americas outlined the consequences of such stereotyping:

> We believe that it establishes an unwelcome academic environment for Indian students, staff, and faculty and contributes to the miseducation of all members of the campus community…Stereotypical and historically inaccurate images of Indians in general interfere with learning about them by creating, supporting, and maintaining oversimplified and inaccurate views of indigenous peoples and cultures.

Perhaps most importantly, Native American mascots always have opened as occasions for the fashioning of the self as well as the Other: they construct White citizen-subjects as proud heirs of once great people sadly gone, reverent individuals who belong to community and nation, powerful conquerors and rightful owners of place and history, and men (and to a lesser extent women) privileged to honor and imitate imagined and invented alters, while rendering Indigenous others as inhuman objects and deaden masks, demonized threats to civilization and civility, romanticized containers of desire, liminal figures of (transgressive) possibility, and prized, profitable trophies testifying to the triumphant fatalism of EuroAmerican conquest.

Playing Indian at half-time not only communicates deeply held values about what it means to be a (White) man in a broader social community, but also rewrites the history of the social as well. In fact, such symbols and spectacles of Indianness alternately underscore EuroAmerican triumph and superiority (the metaphoric taking from the vanquished enemy, the Indian head as trophy, the Indian name as talisman) and actually narrates the past through ritual claims to culture and place, ranging from mimicking dance and dress to mockingly encoding historical peace offerings. In a very real way, Native American mascots foster the rote memorization of how to live as racialized citizen-subjects: who won the war, who is superior, who is a citizen (Strong 2004), who can take from whom, who can take pleasure in mimicking and mocking whom, what happened in the past, what is fun, and so on. Indeed, the continued use of Indian imagery in athletics offers lessons in White supremacy (Staurowsky, 2007).

Oddly, many Americans suggest that Indian imagery in athletics honors indigenous peoples. In effect, Native American mascots contribute to a dominant (mis)reading of race and racism that tends to suggest racism is negative, located in the past, discernible in the malicious and ill intentioned actions a few individuals, and not related to their beliefs and behaviors. In other words, such symbols and spectacles which evoke (White) tradition, often recycle gendered notions of valor, bravery, and strength, appear authentic, seemingly dignified, and above all else, look "positive" do not register as racial symbols for most EuroAmericans desperate to live in a color-blind society, but rather reaffirm for them a sense of belonging, pleasure, respect, and naturalness of difference. As a consequence, Native American mascots perpetuate what Joyce King (1991, 5) has dubbed dysconscious racism,

> an uncritical habit of mind (that is, perceptions, attitudes, assumptions and beliefs) that justifies inequity and exploitation by accepting the existing order of things as given. It involves identification with an ideological viewpoint which admits no fundamentally alternative vision of society.

Cornell Pewewardy (2001, 258) suggests that the ubiquity of mascots, their resonance with common sense, and the constant repetition of sanctioned and spontaneous antics associated with them numbs citizen-subjects, encouraging them to take for granted the existing social arrangements, while failing to equip them with the critical capacity or will to read them differently.

Ultimately, the lessons taught by Native American mascots are deeply anti-Indian. Anti-Indianism, according to Elizabeth Cook-Lynn (2001, xx), has four key elements:

> [I]t is the sentiment that results in the unnatural death of Indians. Anti Indianism is that which treats Indians and their tribes as if they do not

exist .... Second, Anti-Indianism is that which denigrates, demonizes, and insults being Indian in America. The third trait of Anti-Indianism is the use of historical event and experience to place the blame on Indians for an unfortunate and dissatisfying history. And, finally, Anti-Indianism is that which exploits and distorts Indian beliefs and cultures. All of these traits have conspired to isolate, to expunge or expel, to menace, to defame.

The continued use of American Indian imagery, nicknames, and logos clearly embody all of these elements. Of equal importance, so too do the practices and arguments employed by educational institutions to defend such symbols and spectacles of Indianness.

Learning Environments

Schools have perhaps always been spaces of terror for indigenous peoples. Indeed, educational institutions have sought to transform, if not destroy, native nations by instructing indigenous individuals, often quite purposefully stripping them of their languages, practices, and beliefs. This imperial project arguably reached its apex in off-reservation boarding schools, which for at their inception were guided by the motto, "Kill the Indian, save the man." At root, boarding schools sought, on the one hand, to assimilate and indoctrinate and, on the other hand, to undermine and expunge indigenous beliefs and behaviors. Students regularly traveled great distances from home, often against their wills, and entered total institutions in which they were forbidden to speak their native languages, at times given new, foreign names, forced to wear alien and uncomfortable clothing, required to change their appearance, most notably by cutting their hair, and taught the propriety of EuroAmerican actions, institutions, and values. Instruction stressed vocational training unsuited for their home communities, prizing military discipline over self-expression. Seventy-five years after the decline of the federal boarding school system, racial power and virulent anti-Indianism structures and animates educational institutions.

For the better part of a century, Native American mascots have kept alive the ethnocidal imagination that birthed the federal boarding school system. In fact, the persistence of such imagery has a deleterious impact on indigenous peoples and communities. It plays a major role in the low self-regard with which many Native Americans hold themselves and their societies. In turn, it contributes to the high number of Indian students who drop out of school, as well as the nihilism, alcoholism, and suicide rates in native communities. Native American mascots, Churchill (1994) and Pewewardy (2001) have argued, promote the annihilation of indigenous peoples.

Sadly, the terror associated with the use of Indian imagery is so ubiquitous as to be invisible. To be sure, most EuroAmericans cannot apprehend the traumatic effects of playing Indian because they have been miseducated (as outlined above), take for the granted the propriety of taking objects, ideas, and practice from indigenous people and remaking them as they please, and above all, enjoy White privilege. The countless reiteration of anti-Indianism include, in addition to the use of sacred objects (feathers for instance) in half-time performances, tee-shirts, and ball caps bearing stereotypic images, artwork in hallways and gym floors that is false, team names, school songs (the scalp song) and improvised cheers (Sioux Suck!), newspaper headlines (Cowboys finish off the Redskins) and fans dressed in feathers, pep rallies, parade floats, and setting fire to effigies of Indians before big games. A bizarre mixture of hostility and pleasure marks mundane uses of Indianness in schools, an incendiary combination allowing the most perverse expressions of racial power:

- The 1987 Naperville (Illinois) High School yearbook detailed "87 Uses for a Dead Redskin." (Staurowsky, 1999)
- "In Bemidji, Minn[esota], at a pep rally at the Win-E-Mac High School teachers dressed as stereotypical Indians while another teacher waved his guns at them and told them to go back to the reservation. After the rally, Native students were assaulted in the alley behind the gym." (Rose, 2002)
- A banner at Pisgah High School in Canton, North Carolina: "Wipe out the Warriors"…animal paw tears open the gut of a skinny, seemingly unclothed figure discernible as Native American only because of cultural clichés that suggest that his headband and feather as well as his somewhat longish hair are markers of Indianness…genocide…removal.
- An history teacher at Anderson High School, Ohio, speaking in defense of the Redskins tradition gave voice to the underlying misunderstanding and hatred shaping the support of mascots when he cast American Indians as wild deviants who enjoy special privileges at the expense of EuroAmericans:

your people came here a few generations before from Asia. You are no more native than I am. You just got here first …. Mr. Jones, I saw the videotape from the first meeting, I'd like to just offer this: maybe it's time we both looked at our own houses. But I'll make this deal to most tribes in America [sic] live under the same laws I do: no more reservations, no more tribal law and tribal courts, no more gambling on reservations, no more dressing up tall blondes in little Indian suits to be waitress' at those gambling casinos; no smoking dope at your religious ceremonies ... no more killing whales or pillaging the salmon waters of the Northwest just because an old treaty says so. We both have a lot of things to fix. And I'll tell you what, I guarantee you I'll still teach good things. (http://www.geocities.com/CapitolHill/1364/nmascots.htm)

In a very real sense, accepted, official, and everyday uses of Indianness transform classrooms into hostile environments (Baca, 2004).

Increasingly, educators have begun to recognize the consequences of such hostile environments for learning. For instance, teachers at Erwin High School in Buncombe County, North Carolina, supported calls to remove Indian imagery from the institution, including murals and an immense statue, and to rename the sports teams, then dubbed the Warriors and the Squaws, in part because of curricular concerns. In remarks before the school board, David Voyles invoked the district's highly touted character education program, noting "We are teaching our students the importance of virtues such as, honesty, integrity, respect, and fairness, but our teaching will be hollow and meaningless if we, as educators, do not practice what we preach." Anti-Indian imagery in youth sport cultures works against the ideals of educational institutions. It produces false knowledge, fosters hostility and discomfort, and undermines the creation of inclusive, democratic learning communities. For educators, as the faculty at the University of Illinois make clear, racialized sports mascots place them in an impossible position, compromising their roles as scholars and teachers.[1]

Teachable Moments

Increasingly, sports fans, administrators, pundits, and students also recognize the pedagogical power of Native American mascots. In contrast with opponents who stress the false and harmful elements of such racialized learning, supporters have seized upon the rhetoric of education to reclaim the propriety, privilege, and pleasures of playing Indian at half-time. In fact, defenders of such mascots reframe them as teaching tools, symbols, spectacles, and sites with the potential to convey insights into Indian cultures and histories, while imparting deeper, truer understandings of the human condition.

While debates over the use of Indian imagery by educational institutions frequently have torn communities apart, in Sioux Falls, South Dakota, the controversy over the Washington High School Warriors and their logo fostered a project to teach greater respect and understanding (Hetland, 2001). Rather than end local tradition, the principal opted to invest $15,000 in artwork for the school. A portion of these funds were spent to paint two portraits of Hollow Horn Bear on the gym wall; the famed leader, whose visage appears on the buffalo nickel and a postage stamp, replaced a more traditional and stereotypical figure. A new logo, dubbed the "Circle of Courage—a circle with two eagle feathers, and the letters WHS in the center" accompanied the appearance of Hollow Horn Bear (ibid.). The remainder of the monies were spent on a 250 foot long mural depicting a number of diachronically arranged scenes meant to celebrate the warrior (Indian and otherwise), including the historic life of the Lakota, complete with teepees and horses, famed indigenous warriors Big Foot, Red Cloud, and Sitting Bull, children from a range of ethnic and racial groups under Mount Rushmore and the planned Crazy Horse monument, the raising of the flag at Iwo Jim and other moments from World War Two, and the climatic panel picturing the events of September 11, 2001, and the subsequent military actions. While the mural was designed to allow the largely White student body, in the words of the coordinator, Art War Bonnet, "to learn about tolerance" (ibid.), the project had a more ambitious objective. In common with mascots of old, together, the new imagery, according to Principal Carla Middlen, "represents what our whole educational philosophy is about...developing in young people independence, mastery, belonging, courage" (ibid). An indulgent, shallow, and colorblind multiculturalism, pivoting on the erasure of race and power in deference to diversity and tolerance, legitimates the legacies of conquest and the privileges of whiteness that historically underwrote Native American mascots.

The appeal to education has a national influence as well. Most prominently, conservative Comanche commentator David Yeagley has insisted that American Indian symbols, nicknames, and logos are teachable moments: "Mascots provide an opportunity to re-educate America, as well as Indians, on the virtues of being man" (2002). While Yeagley regularly has reiterated the pedagogic value of mascot, his rhetoric quickened after the events of 11 September, 2001. He let out a war cry, inflected with race and gender. Not content with the administration's action, he called for a stronger response, "We've heard glorified condemnations before. We're tired of hackneyed adjectives, and effeminate, poetic dramatizations...We want action" (2001a). He casts Bush as feminine, promoting a more bellicose reaction to the attacks. Oddly, symbols center Yeagley's call to arms; in particular, he sees the post-9/11 world as one primed for the proliferation of Native American sports mascots. "Where are the warriors? Since February [2001], I've argued that the warrior images of American Indian mascots should remain forever in American schools and universities. If ever there was a time warriors were needed, it's now! ...Keep every mascot there is! Make more of them! Educate the country about warrior-hood. Let the people know what the great Indian warriors did for their people. If Americans really want to use Indian images on army badges, helicopters, police cars, and sports teams, then let's remind them all what Indians really can be" (2001a, 2001b).

In each of these instances, the rhetoric of education endeavors to shift the ground of the debate about Native American mascots. On the one hand, it seeks to depoliticize the use of Indian imagery, asserting that far from being racist or injurious such imagery actually performs a valuable public and pedagogic service. On the other hand, reframing Native American mascots in this fashion, despite supporters intentions to the contrary, reinvigorates the racialization and dehumanization central to playing Indian at half-time.

Conclusions: Unlearning and/as Anti-Racism

In this chapter, I have explored the increasingly complex articulations of race and education associated with Native American mascots and the struggles over them. I have endeavored to demonstrate that cultural symbols not only (mis)educate, strengthening racial ideologies and hierarchies, but that they also play a fundamental role in the creation of hostile learning environments. Moreover, I have suggested that rhetoric about education and learning clears a space to depoliticize and re-racialize signifying practices (like playing Indian at half-time).

Importantly, in response to these trends and tactics, students, teachers, parents, political leaders, activists, and scholars committed to social justice have embraced pedagogy as a means of challenging Native American mascots. They have devised a series of disparate strategies designed to foster the unlearning of the racist, anti-Indian lessons taught by such mascots; they have sought to call attention to the problem of anti-Indian racism embodied by such symbols and spectacles, to enlighten and empower individuals, and to transform social institutions. Efforts toward unlearning take many forms including protesting in the streets, at school board meetings, and outside of stadia, Web sites designed to problematize, contextualize, and politicize (see http://www.aistm.org), documentary films (most famously *In Whose Honor*, but also shorts like *I am not a Mascot*), scholarly writing and opinion pieces, petitions and policy initiatives, and teaching in the classroom. At their best, these struggles to re-educate a broader public about history, race, and power manifest a desire to make plain the processes and pain of racialization, humanize Native Americans, foster critical thinking, nurture empathy, and produce change.

Together, these emergent oppositional forms should remind educators dedicated to anti-racist work of the necessity of engaging popular forms and naturalized norms in the classroom. In the case of Native American mascots, this means more than encouraging students to grasp the positions taken in support and in opposition to such symbols and spectacles. It is not enough to teach tolerance as some would have it, what might be best described as pluralistic and superficial understandings of difference that celebrate diversity and too often dovetail with dominant interests and ideologies. Rather, as this case study reminds us, anti-racist pedagogy demands at least six inter-related undertakings to expose the intersections of signification, power, and race. First, teaching against racism means teaching about racialization, not simply race. That is, equipping students with the tools to recognize, engage, and challenge the (re)constructions of racial identities, ideologies, and hierarchies. Second, anti-racist teaching must be rooted in a pedagogy that is about more than difference or even stereotypes, a pedagogy that directs its attention toward the disruption of White supremacy as a structured social system. Third, as the use of Indian imagery in athletics powerfully highlights, it must deconstruct the institutions within which it housed; specifically, it must illuminate how racism and racialization shape and are shaped by schools. Fourth, it thrives only when it concerns itself with the sites of pedagogy that matter to those it seeks to hail in the classroom. Fifth, it has to be comparative, stressing the ways in which human communities, social problems, performative forms, cultural norms, corporeality, identity, possibility, pleasure, and privilege have been racialized differently for EuroAmericans, Native Americans, Asian Americans, African Americans, and Latinos. And sixth, anti-racist pedagogy can make the biggest difference when it teaches and passionately joins the key conflicts of the day.

Note

1. On February 16, 2007, the University of Illinois Board of Trustees announced the retirement of Chief Illiniwek as an embodied mascot, effective at the close of the 2007 home basketball schedule, suggesting that the educational institution may be prepared, thanks in large measure to pressure from the NCAA, to alter its use of Indianness, while possibly opening a space that would be less impossible for its faculty to work in.

References

Baca, L. (2004). Native images in schools and the racially hostile environment. *Journal of Sport and Social Issues, 28*(1): 71-78.

Berkhofer, R. F. (1978). *The white man's Indian: Images of the American Indian from Columbus to present*. New York: Vintage/Random House.

Bird, S. E. (Ed.) (1996). *Dressing in feathers: The construction of the Indian in American popular culture*. Boulder, CO: Westview.

Churchill, W. (1994). Let's spread the fun around. In *Indians are us? Culture and genocide in native north America* (pp. 65–72). Monroe, ME: Common Courage Press.

Connolly, M. R. (2000). What in a name? A historical look at Native American related nicknames and symbols at three U.S. universities. *Journal of Higher Education 71*(5), 515–547.

Cook-Lynn, E. (2001). *Anti-Indianism in North America: A voice from Tatekeya's earth*. Urbana: University of Illinois Press.

Coombe, R. J. (1999). Sports trademarks and somatic politics: Locating the law in critical cultural studies. In R. Martin & T. Miller (Eds.), *SportCult* (pp. 262–288). Minneapolis: University of Minnesota Press.

158 • C. Richard King

Davis, L. (1993). Protest against the use of native American mascots: A challenge to traditional, American identity. *Journal of Sport and Social Issues, 17* (1): 9–22.

Davis, L. R. (2002). The problems with Native American mascots. *Multicultural Education, 9*(4), 11–14.

Deloria, P. (1998). *Playing Indian.* New Haven, CT: Yale University Press.

Dileo, J. (2002). The sites of pedagogy. *Symploke 10* (1): 7–12.

Drinnon, R. (1980). *Facing west: The metaphysics of Indian-hating and empire building.* Minneapolis, MN: University of Minnesota Press.

Green, R. (1988). The tribe called wannabee: Playing Indian in America and Europe. *American Journal of Folklore, 99*(1), 30–55.

Harjo, S. S. (2001). Fighting name calling: Challenging "Redskins" in court. In C. R. King and C. F. Springwood, (Eds.), *Team spirits: Essays on the history and significance of Native American mascots* (pp. 189–207). Lincoln: University of Nebraska Press.

Hetland, C. Indian Logo used as Teach Tool. Retrieved June 15, 2004, from http://news.minnesota.publicradio.org/features/200201/21_hetlandc_logo-m/

King, C. R. (1998). Spectacles, sports, and stereotypes: Dis/playing chief Illiniwek. In *Colonial discourse, collective memories, and the exhibition of Native American cultures and histories in the contemporary United States* (pp. 41–58). New York: Garland Press.

King, C. R. (2001). Uneasy indians: Creating and contesting Native American mascots at Marquette university. In C .R. King and C. F. Springwood (Eds.), *Team spirits: Essays on the history and significance of Native American mascots,* (pp. 281–303). Lincoln: University of Nebraska Press.

King, C. R. (2002). Defensive dialogues: Native American mascots, anti-Indianism, and Educational Institutions. *Studies in Media & Information Literacy Education, 2*(1). http://www.utpress.utoronto.ca/journal/ejournals/simile

King, C. R. (2003). Arguing over images: Native American mascots and race. In R .A. Lind (Ed.), *Race/gender/media: Considering diversity across audiences, content, and producers.* Boston: AB-Longman.

King, C. R. (2004). Borrowing power: Racial metaphors and pseudo-Indian mascots. *CR: The New Centennial Review 4*(1), 189–209.

King, C. R., & Springwood, C. F. (2000). Choreographing colonialism: Athletic mascots, (dis)embodied Indians, and EuroAmerican subjectivities. *Cultural Studies: A Research Annual, 5,* 191–221.

King, C. R., & Springwood, C. F. (2001a). *Beyond the cheers: Race as spectacle in college sports.* Albany: State University of New York Press.

King, C. R., & Springwood, C.F. (Eds.). (2001b). *Team spirits: Essays on the history and significance of native American mascots.* Lincoln: University of Nebraska.

King, C. R., Staurowsky, E. J., Baca, L., Davis, L. R. & Pewewardy, C. (2002). Of polls and race prejudice: *Sports illustrated*'s errant "Indian Wars." *Journal of Sport and Social Issues 26*(4), 382–403.

King, J. E. (1991). Dysconscious racism: Ideology, identity, and miseducation of teachers. *Journal of Negro Education, 60*(2), 133–146.

LeBeau, P.R. (2001). The Fighting Braves of Michigamua: Adapting Vestiges of American Indian Warriors in the Halls of Academia. In C.R. King and C.F. Springwood (Eds.), *Team spirits: Essays on the History and Significance of Native American Mascots.* Lincoln: University of Nebraska Press.

Nuessel, F. (1994). Objectionable sports team designations. *Names: A Journal of Onomastics 42,* 101–119.

Pewewardy, C. D. (2001). Educators and mascots: Challenging contradictions. In C. R. King and C. F. Springwood (Eds.), *Team spirits: Essays on the history and significance of Native American mascots* (pp. 257–279). Lincoln: University of Nebraska Press.

Pewewardy, C. D. (1998). Fluff and feathers: Treatment of American Indians in the literature and the classroom. *Equity and Excellence in Education, 3,* 69–76.

Pewewardy, C. D. (1991). Native American mascots and imagery: The struggle of unlearning Indian stereotypes. *Journal of Navaho Education, 9*(1), 19–23.

Prochaska, D. (2001). At home in Illinois: Presence of chief Illinwek, absence of native Americans. In C. Richard King and C. F. Springwood (Eds.), *Team spirits: The Native American mascots controversy* (pp. 157–188). Lincoln: University of Nebraska Press.

Rodriquez, R. (1998). Plotting the assassination of Little Red Sambo: Psychologists join war against racist campus mascots. *Black Issues in Higher Education, 15*(8), 20–24.

Rose, C. (2002). Students and teachers against racism. Retrieved July 19, 2004, from http://www. racismagainstindians.org/STARArticle/Intro.html

Sigelman, L. (1998). Hail to the Redskins? Public reactions to a racially insensitive team name. *Sociology of Sport Journal, 15*(4), 317–325.

Smith, C.M. (2001, October 3). Removing mascot will be one more injustice. *Manhattan Mercury,* A6.

Society of Indian Psychologists of the Americas. (1999). Statement against the continued use of Indian symbols. Retrieved July 19, 2004, from http://aistm.org/society_of_indian_psychologists_.htm

Spindel, C. (2000). *Dancing at halftime: Sports and the controversy over American Indian mascots.* New York: New York University Press.

Springwood, C. F. (2001). Playing Indian and fighting (for) mascots: Reading the complications of native American and EuroAmerican alliances. In C. R. King and C. F. Springwood (Eds.), *Team spirits: Essays on the history and significance of Native American mascots* (pp. 304–327). Lincoln: University of Nebraska Press.

Springwood, C. F., & King, C. R. (2000). Race, power, and representation in contemporary American sport. In P. Kivisto and G. Rundblad (Eds.), *The color line at the dawn of the 21st Century* (pp. 161–174). Thousand Oaks, CA: Pine Valley Press.

Staurowsky, E.J. (2007). "'You Know, We Are All Indian': Exploring White Power and Privilege in Reactions to the NCAA Native American Mascot Policy." *Journal of Sport & Social Issues, 31*(1): 61-76.

Staurowsky, E.J. (2001). Sockalexis and the making of the myth at the core of the Cleveland "Indians" imagery. In C. R. King and C. F. Springwood (Eds.), *Team spirits: The Native American mascots controversy* (pp. 82–107). Lincoln: University of Nebraska Press.

Staurowsky, E .J. (2000). The Cleveland Indians: A case study in cultural dispossession. *Sociology of Sport Journal, 17*(3), 307–330

Staurowsky, E. J. (1999). American Indian imagery and the miseducation of America. *Quest,* 51(4), 382–392.

Staurowsky, E. J. (1998). An act of honor or exploitation? The Cleveland Indians' use of the Louis Francis Sockalexis story. *Sociology of Sport Journal, 15*(4), 299–316.

Strong, P.T. (2004). "The Mascot Slot: Cultural Citizenship, Political Correctness, and Pseudo-Indian Sports Symbols." *Journal of Sport & Social Issues, 28*(1): 79-87.

Vanderford, H. (1996). What's in a name? Heritage or hatred: The school mascot controversy. *Journal of Law and Education, 25,* 381–388.

Whitt, L. A. (1995). Cultural imperialism and the marketing of native America. *American Indian Culture and Research Journal, 19*(3), 1–31.

Yeagley, D. (2001a). Comanch war cry. *FrontpageMagazine.com* September 14. Retrieved July 31, 2002, from http://www.frontpagemagazine.com/Articles/Printable.asp?ID=1692. Accessed 31 July 2002.

Yeagley, D. (2001b). Make more Indian warrior images. Retrieved July 31, 2002, from http://www. geocities.com/americashauntedpast.htm

Yeagley, D. (2002). Where were the Fighting Whites? *FrontpageMagazine.com* May 1. Retrieved July 31, 2002, from http://www.frontpagemagazine.com/Articles/Printable.asp?ID=265

CHAPTER 9

Culture, Colonialism, and Competition
Youth Sport Culture in Canada's North

AUDREY R. GILES AND AVA C. BAKER

Caribou, moose meat, and muktuk!

If you're going to beat us, you're going to need luck…

Or a big truck!
>   —NWT's Swim Team Cheer at the 2002 North American
>   Indigenous Games

In this chapter we investigate youth involvement in sporting activities in the Northwest Territories (NWT) and Nunavut, Canada. Participant observation, semi-structured interviews, and archival research were used to collect data pertaining to Northern youths' experiences in local (community swim team), regional, and international (Dene games) sport contexts. While participation in these events provided youth with the frequently cited benefits of sport (e.g., sense of excitement, accomplishment, and fun), these sporting experiences also demonstrate the ways in which their participation in sport is informed by their Northern Aboriginal identities. As such, we argue that while sport can serve assimilationist and colonial agendas, it can also provide an avenue through which these agendas can be challenged and subverted, thus allowing Northern youth to assert and maintain identities that differ from other Canadian youth.

In recent years, images of Jordin Tootoo, a member of the National Hockey League's Nashville Predators, have been splashed across sports pages. Images of Tootoo carrying his younger relatives while leaping from boulder to boulder on the tundra and text reporting his love of country foods such as sun-dried arctic char (Allen, 2003) have been used to demonstrate the ways in which he was able to stay strong and obtain sporting success, despite hailing from remote Rankin Inlet, Nunavut. While these heavily stereotyped images have become well-known to the general public, sport in Canada's North has typically escaped the attention of those who theorize youth sport. Nevertheless, examinations of sporting practices north of the 60th parallel—that vividly imagined line that divides Canada's territories from its provinces—can provide powerful illustrations of the ways in which Northern Aboriginal youth can both adopt and challenge mainstream, or perhaps "whitestream" (Denis, 1997), sporting ideologies.

In her study of American high school students, Perry (2001) noted that White youth believe themselves to be "cultureless" and that they identify culture as something that exists only in and for non-white students. She identifies two cognitive processes that enable these beliefs: naturalization, "the embedding of historically constituted practices in what feels 'normal' and 'natural'" (p. 57); and rationalization, "the embedding of whiteness within a Western rational paradigm that subordinates all things cultural" produced a feeling of cultureless identity (p. 57). Certainly, we can identify these processes as being at work within sport, where, typically, competitive physical activities that are non-Eurocanadian in origin are seen as cultural activities, while competitive physical activities that are Eurocanadian in origin are seen as being legitimate sport (Paraschak, 1997). This legitimate sport/cultural activity binary is one that has been constructed out of colonial discourses that privilege European-based practices over all others. This binary requires deconstruction so that we can recognize that all forms of sport are reflections of the cultures from which they stem (Dyck, 2000).

Participation in sport is inherently cultural and political in nature, though both of these aspects are often obscured by processes such as those described above. The position that sport is apolitical and acultural is one that can only be taken by those who exist in the main/whitestream and are able to see themselves and their practices as being divorced from culture and politics because sport is congruent with their own particular cultural politics. Those who are marginalized, such as Northern Canadians, however, have no such luxury and, as such, sport becomes an important venue in which to take up cultural and political causes that have important implications, such as the fight against colonialism.

Sport in Canada's North needs to be understood as part of a larger colonial project. According to Johnston, Gregory, and Smith (1994), "[c]haracteristic features of the colonial situation include political and legal domination over an alien society, relations of economic and political dependence and exploitation between imperial power and colony, and racial and cultural inequality" (p. 75). In examining the history of the NWT, which included the region now known as Nunavut until separation occurred in 1999, it becomes clear that there have existed and continue to exist colonial relations between the Governments of the NWT and Nunavut and the Government of Canada. Coates (1985) finds that as a colony, the NWT has been developed according to the needs of the South—and, we would add, according to Southerners' perceptions of Northerners' needs—while Aboriginal peoples have had little opportunity for a say in the changes in the region. Colonial development cannot only be found in the ways in which previous governments have made decisions about governance in the NWT, but also in something as seemingly benign as youth sport. As such, it is critical to ask Northerners, and especially Northern youth, to reflect on their own experiences in order to allow for the development a better, less Southern-centric, understanding of youth sport culture in Canada.

According to Morrison (1998), "[b]eginning around 1850, Anglicans and Catholics engaged in a hot rivalry, a race for [Aboriginal] souls, [one] that would continue for many decades" (p. 55). Indeed, this rivalry extended into the education system, as it was these very missionaries who set up the first schools north of the 60th parallel (Morrison, 1998). Residential schools removed children from their families and systematically stripped them of their culture, practices, and language. These schools also resulted in the relocation of entire families from the land into communities that had educational institutions. These changes had a vast impact on traditional physical practices which had previously been engaged in on the land and during community gatherings.

The Government of Canada's Royal Commission on Aboriginal Peoples (RCAP; 1996) paints an unflinching picture of residential schools and the colonial project with which they were associated. According to the RCAP, the residential school system consisted of concerted efforts to rid Aboriginal peoples of Aboriginal languages, traditions, and beliefs; in short, to turn "savage" children into "civilized" adults who embodied the "Canadian way." Eurocanadian-derived physical activities and sport were included in such efforts:

> In school, in chapel, at work and even at play the children were to learn the Canadian way. Recreation was re-creation. Games and activities would not be the 'boisterous and unorganized games' of 'savage' youth. Rather they were to have brass bands, football, cricket, baseball and above all hockey 'with the well regulated and...strict rules that govern our modern games', prompting 'obedience to discipline' and thus contributing to the process of moving the children along the path to civilization. (Government of Canada, 1996)

The often forced relocation of children into residential and day schools resulted in many parents establishing more permanent residences in the communities in which educational institutions were located. As a result, physical practices that were heavily tied to life on the land were practised with less regularity or were banned by missionaries all together. This is the context in which sport was developed in the North.

Methods

Data for this chapter were gathered through participant observation, semi-structured interviews, and archival research in Canada's North between 2002 and 2005. The first author spent 3–5 months in each of Trout Lake, Jean Marie River, and Fort Simpson, NWT, while she also attended the 2004 Arctic Winter Games in the Wood Buffalo Region of Northern Alberta. The second author spent three summers, for a total of 11 months, in Taloyoak, Nunavut, though data were collected during the third summer. Prior to conducting this research, which was part of two larger research projects examining physical practices in Canada's North, extensive community consultations were held, and the requirements for Nunavut and NWT Research Licences and ethics approval were met. Participants were identified using purposeful and snowball sampling, and all interview transcripts were returned to participants in order to ensure accuracy and to provide participants with the opportunity to provide clarification or further information.

Dene Games

> [I]t was a residential school I went to [in Fort Simpson]; there were no traditional games, we weren't even allowed to speak our language. (D. Jumbo, personal communication, August 7, 2002)

The Dene live in Denendeh, which encompasses the southwestern and central-western portions of the NWT. According to *Dene games: A culture and resource manual* (Heine, 1999),

> There is a basic unity of Dene culture, and it is expressed by the way the people were connected to and survived on the land. What just about all groups of the Dene had in common was that surviving on the land meant travelling on the land. It was through their travels that the people most closely connected with the land. (p. 16)

Heine also notes that Dene games were heavily influenced by the connection between travel and life on the land. Strength, endurance, speed, and accuracy were necessary for travelling and hunting on the land and were often practiced by playing traditional games. Furthermore,

The close link between games and the traditional way of life is also shown by the kinds of equipment used in most games, that is, very little to none. On the trail, people relied mainly on their own strength. They were able to pack heavy loads, but not everything could be taken along...People generally knew how to make their own equipment for playing traditional games. (p. 137)

While Dene games were often played spontaneously on the trail or at community gatherings, in later years they became more organized and codified through the Mackenzie Regional Dene Games and the Arctic Winter Games (AWG). The Mackenzie Regional Dene Games began in the late 1970s and became established as an annual multi-community sport festival that rotated between communities. Events typically included: axe throw, bannock making, bow and arrow shoot, coin toss, canoe races, Dene baseball, dryfish making, fish filleting and frying, log splitting, spear throw, tea boiling, and tug-of-war. Beyond the Mackenzie Region, Dene games have also gained international exposure through their inclusion in the AWG.

Though the AWG began in 1970, the Dene Games component was not added until 1990. The games that were selected as Dene Games events at the AWG differ from the events at the Mackenzie Regional Dene Games and instead include finger pull, stick pull, snowsnake, pole push, and hand games. A category for Senior Men has been available since the addition of Dene games to the AWG, while a category for Junior Men was only added in 2002. A Junior Girl's category was added to the 2004 AWG, which were held in the Wood Buffalo Region of Northern Alberta.

Arctic Sports, otherwise known as Inuit Games, have been a part of the AWG since the early 1970s. According to Brian Walker, a coach for Team Alaska at the 2004 AWG,

[At the beginning, Dene Games] weren't real popular. The one foot and two foot [high kick, which are Arctic Sports] are really the crowd pleasers, so the Dene Games were kind of the poor cousins of the Games. So, I started making the division [between Arctic Sports and Dene Games] back when it was in Eagle River [in 1996]...we had our own medals, our own opening and closing ceremonies. And some people didn't like it, some people were against it. Um, but I didn't care. There are Indian Games and there are Eskimo Games and there has to be some sort of division there. We're a family, but there needs to be some sort of separation there. (Personal communication, March 3, 2004)

Though Walker speaks about Dene games in an American context, it is important to remember that current political boundaries do not reflect the political/cultural boundaries that exist between Indigenous peoples. Thus, we argue that his reflections can be used in the Canadian context with ease. Walker clearly illustrates the way in which Dene Games have been used to build and reinforce Dene identity. He further makes connection between Dene Games and youth identity:

> you get these kids and you get them to come out of that shell and start playing these games, and they start letting people know who they are, know what their games are, and then they're not so ashamed of being who they are, and it helps the non-Native kids say, hey, this is really cool, this is really fun. I want to do this! So it brings a pride to the kids. (Personal communication, March 3, 2004)

Adult coaches are not alone in identifying the ways in which Dene Games reflect youth identity, an important part of which is culture. Youth, too, have identified the linkages between Dene games, culture, and identity, framing it within struggles for self-governance, self-determination, and gender equity. As mentioned above, a category for girls for Dene Games at the AWG was only added in 2004, more than a decade after the category for men was added. Reasons for the recent emergence of competitive Dene Games opportunities for girls and women have been linked to a history in which Dene Games were typically, though not exclusively, played by men and boys (Giles, 2004, 2005a, 2005b). The addition of a category for girls has been primarily framed in two ways: a welcomed response to the need for gender equity; and the failure of AWG organizers to recognize the importance of maintaining Dene traditions.

Wesley Hardisty, a youth resident of Fort Simpson, NWT, sees the imposition of regulations concerning gender equity to be a manifestation of colonialism:

> I see it as a way of colonialism. We had our own rules and regulations set up before, traditional laws, and that's the way people governed their lives, by following these laws, guidelines, and protocols that were formed for everything that was set up. (Personal communication, February 12, 2004)

In addition, however, Hardisty also speaks to the complexities of maintaining certain traditions in contemporary times, which he views as demanding gender equality:

> The whole question of if women deserve to play because of the gender equality things is totally outrageous because, you know, women can do anything that a guy can do, as I can see, and I'd never say a woman can't do that because she's a girl, because that's the way things are now... It's tough because there are people who are really trying to

stick to traditional rules and games, and that's the way it was passed on then, and yet we're in a modern context. (Personal communication, February 12, 2004)

A member of Team NWT's Junior Girls' Dene Games team summarized the connection between women and girls' participation in Dene Games very succinctly. In response to the question, "Would it be good for women to play hand games [one Dene Game]?" she responded, "Yes, she can be our role model to be in a higher rank…That's just a step to getting closer to being leader" (A. Drygeese, personal communication, March 1, 2004). For this young athlete, who lives in a community where there has never been a female Chief, the road to having a woman leader in the community can be connected to participation in Dene Games.

Youth participation in Dene games is thus not merely about playing a sport, but also about cultural development and identity formation. Dene games occur within the highly charged political setting in the NWT, a territory that is attempting to come to grips with calls for self-governance and an end to colonial relations that continue to frame all aspects of politics and culture, including sport. As such, it should not be surprising that power relations and issues of cultural identity permeate youth and sport culture.

Community Swim Team

There's barely anything to do for the kids up here besides playing on the ice. There's barely anything up here to do for kids in the fall time or when there's no more sledding. (Chuck Pizzo-Lyall, personal communication, August 16, 2006)

The NWT Aquatics Program started in 1967 in an effort to bring leadership, recreation, and drowning prevention to Canada's North. Above ground pools, waterfronts, and bussing programs were established to enable Northerners, and especially Northern youth, to have exposure to aquatics-based recreation. At its height, this program operated in 41 NWT communities (Szabo, 2002). Despite the initial goal of training Northerners to offer aquatics programming, Northern communities have relied on Southern-based swimming instructors and lifeguards to facilitate programming across the North. As a result, dialogue concerning traditions and culture, which have often been marginalized by well-meaning swimming pool supervisors from the South, can play important roles in the creation of unique, culturally appropriate and meaningful aquatics programming for youth. An example of such a program can be seen in creation of a swim team in Taloyoak, Nunavut, which led to the development of the first ever Kitikmeot Regional Swim Meet, which was held in Cambridge Bay during August 2006.

Taloyoak, Nunavut sits on the Boothia Peninsula in the Kitikmeot Region of Nunavut. It is a small, closely knit community. In 2001, the population was just 720 people, and the majority of residents are Inuit (Community, 2001). The population is overwhelmingly young; 360 of the 720 residents were under the age of 19 in 2001. With such a large youth population in a small, isolated community, it is perhaps not surprising that available facilities are often inadequate for meeting Inuit youths' sporting needs. In 2006, the second author returned to Taloyoak for her third summer to not only work as the aquatic director, but also to conduct research on the community's aquatics programming.

Swimming programming in Taloyoak began in 1995 with the construction of the Moses Teelktaq Memorial pool. Scotty Edgerton, the Senior Administrative Officer for Taloyoak explained the reasoning for the swimming pool's construction: "We don't get rid of the ice here until generally the last week of July or the first week in August, so there's an issue there of safety. You go out there on the ice, and you could end up drowning" (Personal communication, August 4, 2006). Since the swimming pool's construction, pool supervisors for Taloyoak have been hired exclusively from Southern Canada and authority regarding programming has generally rested in the hands of these imported lifeguards, with little input or feedback from local residents. Generally, the creation of programs has relied on a model that where it is "good to have outside interests that bring in a different perspective" (S. Edgerton, personal communication, August 4, 2006). Additionally, many of the aquatic supervisors for Taloyoak were only employed for one summer; for example, a different aquatic director was hired for each summer session from 1998 to 2004, which led to a lack of continuity in programming.

The continual hiring of external swimming pool supervisors with little community training and input can be seen as a vestige of colonialism within daily life in the North; the establishment of Eurocanadian-styled aquatic programming without the opportunity for dialogue and feedback is a reflection of earlier colonial policies. For example, the construction of Inuvik, NWT, as a colony during the 1950s, was done in a deliberate and intentional order that became a template for many northern communities. "First came a machine shop, then a school with attached residence, then a nursing station, then a police post, then a power plant" (Ironside, 2000, p. 106). Each of these institutions is representative of a foreign cultural order that was imposed in northern communities in the mid-20th century, ignoring previously established Inuit systems of governance. In a similar fashion, ignoring community input into aquatic programming perpetuates the concept that Inuit ideas about their own community are inferior to those from the main/ whitestream, or even nonexistent.

The creation of the Hamlet's swim team and the members' participation in the regional swim meet are examples of programming that was developed in cooperation with and for Inuit youth, and is thus reflective of their sport culture. The swim team program is one of very few recreational sport programs not based in the school setting. Apart from the regional summer games and the Arctic Winter Games, in which only one or two athletes under the age of nineteen from the Hamlet are typically selected to participate, intercommunity sport and competition in Taloyoak is limited to sports programs within the school, such as soccer, volleyball, and basketball. An exception to this is the winter hockey program, which operate outside of the school setting and thus caters to all age groups. The separation of the swim team from the school was not an intentional split, but more a result of aquatic programming in Taloyoak occurring exclusively in the summer when school is not in session. This separation of school and sport, however, contributed to the strong practice attendance record by swim team members, as participation was not coupled with regulations concerning school attendance, nor the sometimes unpopular school environment. Instead of being billed as an instructional program, or a swimming lesson, the swim team was a collaborative effort between the swimmers and the second author. In fact, the creation of the swim team was suggested to her by students in the Junior High class at the Netsilik School with whom she spoke prior to planning the summer pool programs; this was done in an effort to ensure that the programs offered reflected the local youths' needs rather than the perceived needs that she might have projected onto them based on her own Southern experiences.

As swimming, swimming lessons, and competitive swimming were not common activities in the past in Taloyoak, they are not traditional Inuit activities; in fact, both swimming and competition can be considered relatively foreign ideals. Most of the Elders interviewed for this project told of how, as children, their grandparents and parents instructed them to stay away from the water. For example, Mary Karoo recalled how her great-grandparents used to keep her and her siblings away from the water:

> When my great-grandparents were around, we were told to never go into the lakes. They were afraid they might lose us by drowning, so I never experienced swimming in the lakes. We were told as little children not to go near the lake because we might slip in there and drown. They were afraid of losing us so we were always told not to go to the lakes. (Personal communication, June 25, 2006)

In addition to verbal warnings concerning the potential dangers posed by water, local children were told legends such as that of *Qallupilluit*, female monsters who grab children who wander alone on the sea ice (R. Karoo, personal communication, August 5, 2006). These local oral traditions were used to keep children from going close to the water's edge while their parents were involved with subsistence activities such as gathering food or drying meat. Thus, these oral traditions regarding swimming in Taloyoak are indicative of those in which Inuit youth approached and experienced both the swim team and sport practice in general, and how it differs from Southern-based non-Inuit youth.

One interesting phenomenon regarding Inuit youth sport culture in Taloyoak concerns the involvement, or rather lack thereof, of parents or guardians in a child's decision to become involved in sport. Interview participants repeatedly expressed that involvement in swimming lessons and the swim team was a result of the child's initiative, not the parents'. Rebecca Karoo, whose daughter Miranda was enrolled in swimming lessons, explained, "[I]t's the kid's idea, but I think that the parents have to agree" (Personal communication, August 5, 2006). In a small community like Taloyoak, parents are not required to transport their children to and from the swimming pool. Instead, children and teens can bike or walk to sport activities, leading to a relative independence in which what activities they participate.

One of the reasons that many participants identified concerning why teenagers took the initiative to participate in the swim team is the lack of other recreation facilities and programs. In Taloyoak, sport is one of the main forums for organized socialization for teenagers. With no mall, movie theater, coffee shop, or game hall around which teenagers can congregate, the hockey arena, baseball diamond, and gym serve as substitute locations. Informal sport, too, may serve as a "gathering point" for teenagers in the North. That is, if a community does not have recreational or sporting facilities, an impromptu golf course on the tundra might be an ideal place for teenagers to meet and interact with their peers, and may provide a venue for youth to interact independent of adult influences. Therefore, in isolated Inuit communities with few recreation facilities, the lines between youth culture and sport culture are blurred and the two concepts become almost synonymous.

Another distinctive aspect of Inuit youth sport participation pertains to the familial ties that exist between northern communities. The high cost of air travel in Nunavut makes regular travel between communities unattainable for many community members. However, travel for the purposes of intercommunity competition is often heavily subsidized and allows for interaction with teenagers outside one's regular social and family circle. At the regional swim meet, the nine Taloyoak participants were billeted with community members in Cambridge Bay. Almost every swimmer had relatives in Cambridge Bay with whom she or he could stay. Intercommunity competition thus provided the opportunity for family members to visit and re-connect with each other despite airfares that prohibit regular travel between communities. For example, while at the swim meet, one of the swimmers from Taloyoak's team stayed with her sister, whom she has not seen in two years due to the high cost of travel.

Beyond renewing familial ties, intercommunity socialization during regional events may be one of the contributing factors to the unique kind of competition in which Inuit youth participate. Richard Condon (1988) found that competitive sports are relatively new additions to Inuit culture, and he views this change as a concern to Northern residents. Condon argues that although traditional Inuit games tend towards collaboration and the enjoyment that lies within participation, "increased emphasis upon competition in teenage sports is…indicative of social and attitudinal changes occurring through the Arctic" (Condon, 1988, p. 126). Condon specifically points to Eurocanadian sport as being responsible for this shift: "increasing exposure to southern values and behavioural styles has made the overt expression of competitiveness more acceptable" (Condon, 1988, p. 127). Further, Condon specifically refers to aggressiveness and ordering in sport as being non-traditional, going so far as to assert that "young Inuit…are increasingly playing these games in a remarkably un-Inuit manner, with heavy emphasis on overt competition, explicit ranking, and physical confrontation" (Condon, 1995, p. 48). While it may be true that, historically, Inuit games were not played simply to determine a winner, but more as social activities or activities to practice land-based survival skills (Heine, 2002), Condon's view of competition as "un-Inuit" falls victim to a view that Aboriginal culture is a static entity and he thus denies the possibility of the emergence of a specifically Inuit brand of competition. This view has a negative impact on Aboriginal peoples, such as the Inuit, as it paints a picture of a culture that is literally frozen in time without progressing at all over the millennia.

The idea that culture is tied only to traditional activities is a fallacious view of both Indigenous culture and of culture in general. As Riphenberg (1997) explains,

> Culture is not static but is constantly changing: it is dynamic, perpetually adjusting to fit the current needs of the people. Moreover, culture does not exist independent of material factors but develops in response to a particular social and material environment. (pp. 45–46)

Therefore, the culture that exists among the Inuit youth at the time of any research is, in fact, the culture of the Inuit youth, not an "un-Inuit" bastardization of traditional practices. Through the second author's experience as the coach for Taloyoak's swim team, it became clear that Inuit youth culture in sport is distinct and is representative of an Inuit brand of competition. Condon (1995) points to fieldwork in Holman, now Ulukhaktok, NWT, between 1978 and 1980 as a baseline for Inuit youth competition in sport. He describes residents' behaviour as lacking explicit competitiveness and open conflict. He postulates that "the enjoyment of playing the game with friends and relatives was more important, it seems, than seeing which team could win" (Condon, 1995, p. 54). This spirit of non-competitiveness is still present among Inuit youth, as demonstrated through Taloyoak's swim team members. As part of the swim team program, the team created a list of expectations for themselves and for the coach. Expectations that the swim team participants produced included the trust that participants would not put each other down, that they would cheer "really loud" when they were racing, and that they would try and help each other swim faster. At the local swim meet, the second author was apprehensive about announcing the winners, who would go on to compete in the regional swim meet in Cambridge Bay, because she was anxious about behaviours that would typify poor sportspersonship. Instead, the team gathered around those who had won, shaking hands and offering congratulations and encouragement. While competing in the Regional Swim Meet in Cambridge Bay, the Taloyoak team offered cheers and support not only for their own teammates, but also for swimmers on the Cambridge Bay swim team as well. Further, when the swimmers had free time, the Taloyoak swimmers socialized and played with their rivals on the Cambridge Bay swim team. The demonstration of such a high level of sportspersonship and maturity among a group of individuals between the ages of 13 and 19 points to a youth sport culture that certainly differs from the typically hypercompetitive youth sport experiences found in Southern Canada.

Coda

Youth participation in both Dene games in the NWT and aquatics programming in Taloyoak, Nunavut illustrates the ways in which Northern Aboriginal youth create and reinforce their identities through sport. This sport culture, however, is not stagnant and preserved behind museum glass, but is instead re-established and re-created each time youth participate in sporting activities. For some, youth sport culture in Northern Canada may seem to be an unlikely arena in which on-going battles against Euro-Canadian cultural imperialism are fought. It is important, however, to remain cognizant of the ways in which sport and sport participation is, as we have argued above, inherently political and cultural in nature. Perhaps Felshin (1974) said it best: "Sport expresses the context of culture in its existence and modifies the culture by its existence" (p. 180); certainly, this is the case in Canada's North.

Note

1. The authors would like to acknowledge funding from the following organizations/granting bodies: the Social Sciences and Humanities Research Council (Doctoral Fellowship and Standard Research Grant), the Northern Scientific Training Program, Circumpolar/Boreal Ablerta Research Institute Grant, Aurora Research Institute's Research Fellowship and Research Assistant Grant, the Pan-Territorial Sport Strategy, and McMaster University's Arts and Science Experiential Education Travel Scholarship. The authors would like to acknowledge Gary Schauerte and Ian Legaree of the Government of the NWT for their ongoing support, Dr. Bob Henderson, Rebecca Karoo (research assistant extraordinaire), the Taloyoak swim team, and Sandy Oleekatalik. Finally, we would like to give our biggest thanks our research participants. *Mahsi cho* and *qujanamik*!

References

Allen, K. (2003). Skating across cultural gap. Retrieved December 6, 2006, from http://www.usatoday.com/sports/hockey/nhl/predators/2003-07-22-tootoo-cover_x.htm

Coates, K. (1985). *Canada's colonies: A history of the Yukon and the Northwest Territories.* Toronto: James Lorimer and Company.

Condon, R. G. (1988). *Inuit youth: Growth and change in the Canadian Arctic.* New Brunswick NJ: Rutgers University Press.

Condon, R. G. (1995). The rise of the leisure class: Adolescence and recreational acculturation in the Canadian Arctic." *Ethos, 23*(1), 47–68.

Community Highlights for Taloyoak. (2001). Retrieved December 6, 2006, from Statistics Canada, 2001 Aboriginal Communities Profile Web site: http://www12.statcan.ca/english/profil01/CP01/Details/Page.cfm?Lang=E&Geo1=CSD&Code1=6208087&Geo2=PR&Code2=62&Data=Count&SearchText=Taloyoak&SearchType=Begins&SearchPR=01&B1=All&GeoLevel=&GeoCode=6208087

Denis, C. (1997). *We are not you.* Peterborough, ON: Broadview Press.

Dyck, N. (Ed.). (2000). Introduction. In *Games sports and cultures* (pp. 1–12). New York: Berg.

Felshin, J. (1974). The social view. In E. W. Gerber, J. Felshin, P. Berlin, & W. Wyrick (Eds.), *The American woman in sport* (pp. 179–279). Reading, MA: Addison-Wesley.

Giles, A. R. (2004). Kevlar, Crisco, and menstruation: "Tradition" and Dene Games. *Sociology of Sport Journal, 21*(1), 18–35.

Giles, A. R. (2005a). A Foucaultian approach to menstrual practices in the Dehcho, Northwest Territories, Canada. *Arctic Anthropology, 24*(2), 9–21.

Giles, A. R. (2005b). The acculturation matrix and the politics of difference: Women and Dene games. *Canadian Journal of Native Studies, XXV*(1), 341–358.

Government of Canada. (1996). Royal Commission on Aboriginal Peoples. Retrieved November 20, 2006, from http://www.ainc-inac.gc.ca/ch/rcap/sg/sg28_e.html

Heine, M. (1999). *Dene games: A culture and resource manual.* Yellowknife, NWT, Canada: The Sport North Federation & MACA (GNWT).

Heine, M. (2002). *Arctic sportst: A training and resource manual.* Yellowknife, NWT, Canada: The Sport North Federation & MACA (GNWT).

Ironside, R.G. (2000). Canadian Northern settlements: Top-down and bottom-up influences. *Geografiska Annaler. Series B, Human Geography, 82*(2), 103–114.

Johnston, R. J., Gregory, D., & D. M. Smith (Eds.). (1994). *The dictionary of human geography* (5th ed.). Oxford: Blackwell.

Morrison, W. R. (1998). *True north: The Yukon and Northwest Territories.* Toronto: Oxford University Press.

Paraschak, V. (1997). Variations in race relations: Sporting events for native peoples in Canada. *Sociology of Sport Journal, 14,* 1–21.

Perry, P. (2001). White means never having to say you're ethnic: White youth and the construction of 'cultureless' identities. *Journal of Contemporary Ethnography, 30*(1), 56–91.

Riphenberg, C. (1997). Women's status and cultural expression: Changing gender relations and structural adjustment in Zimbabwe. *Africa Today, 44*(1), pp. 33–49.

Szabo, C. (2002). *NWT aquatics program: Brief summary.* Yellowknife: Government of the Northwest Territories.

CHAPTER 10

From Babies to Ballers
*Girls' Youth Basketball and
the Re-Becoming of U.S. Motherhood*

JENNIFER L. METZ

In J. K. Rowling's new classic of youth literature, *Harry Potter*, the mythical sport of Quidditch emerges as a powerful organizing agent for the lives of young inhabitants of the wizarding world. With everything from the Quidditch World Cup to fierce intra-school rivalries played out high in the air on super-charged broomsticks and beater bats, Quidditch provides the backdrop for much of what Harry and his friends do and think about when not fighting the evil wizard, Lord Voldemort. The students' intra-school Quidditch matches are full of rivalries, gruesome injuries, and last-minutes heroics by both girls and boys desperate to win the match for the honor and respect of their team and their house.

In this series, sport is a utopian fantasy of gender equality. Quidditch teams are unisex, they share dressing rooms, and there are no distinctions made between "male" or "female" style of play, or even star power—Gwenog Jones is just as popular as Victor Crum (perhaps this is how we know that Potter's world is one of fantasy).[1] In fact, the world of Potter is a place where young girls and boys both grow up admiring the (female) Captain of the all-witch Holyhead Harpies—Gwenog Jones—seems highly unlikely in a world where people are often confused and/or offended by Michelle Wie and Annika Sorenstam's attempts to integrate men's professional golf tournaments. And, moreover, statements that "they have their own team" act to reinforce the separate but (un)equal and very different attitude that has been the hallmark of girls' sporting experience in the United States. For while our young play on co-gender peewee soccer and T-ball teams, it does not take very long for them to learn that girls and boys playing together in team sports into puberty and beyond, like the land of Potter, is but a fairytale.

Thus, and within such an unequal historical present, the experiences of the professional athletes of the Women's National Basketball Association (WNBA) and Women's United Soccer Association (WUSA)—athletes who have grown up and matured within such a system of marginalization and latent exploitation—provide unique insight into the contemporary female athlete experience, particularly as related to its development from and location within youth sporting participation. It is their stories, often told as fairytales by an infotainment news media, that illuminate the ways in which girls' youth sport participation in the present—popularly imagined as the natural, empowered outcome of a post-Title IX generation—has been an uneven process of opportunity, struggle, and hardship.

For this chapter (which emerges out of a long-term study of the politics of racialized motherhood in the United States), I interviewed 11 WNBA players, all of whom were mothers: Annie Burgess, Pamela McGee, Joy Harris Holmes, Olympia Scott Richardson, Sheryl Swoopes, Niele Ivey, Nadine Malcolm, Natalie Williams, Jessie Hicks, Tracey Henderson, and Jackie Moore. All had been top collegiate players in the United States, with the exception of Burgess, who matriculated in Australia. The majority of the athletes are American by birth, with the exceptions of Malcolm, who is Jamaican, and Burgess. All but Ivey had played professionally in Europe. Most of the women intended to remain in the WNBA the season following my interviews; those who were not retiring or taking a year off to have children were planning to spend the winter season in one of the European leagues. Some of the athletes were members of the now-defunct American Basketball League prior to coming to the WNBA. Five of the athletes were married when they had their children, and three of the mothers are now either separated or divorced. Their ages ranged from 23 to 35 at the time of their respective interviews.

My aim was to examine their uniquely positioned views on the youth sport experience, how they viewed their current sporting participation, and what if any perspectives they had relating to their kids' future participation. In order to broaden my sample of professional female athletes, I secured two additional interviews with members of the now-defunct WUSA, Carla Overbeck and Danielle Fotopoulos (both of whom were members of the victorious 1999 U.S. Women's World Cup team). By interviewing players from two professional leagues, I attempted to get a cross-section of the experiences that a woman balancing professional athletics, motherhood, and socio-political gender and racial struggles would have. What follows is a (performative) distillation of these interviews and a discussion of my research findings.

Performing Motherhood/Performing Childhood

I arrive in Indianapolis on a breezy and bright May day. It is a clean city, newly gentrified and charmingly punctuated with a profusion of flags and flowers. I am staying at the Embassy Suites Hotel. Tonight, I will interview Cleveland Rocker's starting center, Tracey Henderson, and then in the morning I will visit with Olympia Scott-Richardson, the starting center for the Indiana Fever, at the Conseco Fieldhouse. Tomorrow evening I will watch as Henderson and Scott-Richardson square off in the opening home game of the season for the Fever.

I arrive at Conseco Fieldhouse about 45-minutes before the scheduled meeting time. It is all glass and dark brick with huge windows and enormous banners proclaiming its allegiance to the Indiana Fever. The sharp blue and red banners snap in the breeze and as I gaze at them and up into the sunshine I feel—hmm...excited, and slightly nauseated. From the outside, Conseco Fieldhouse is quite small, at least from a Chicago girl's standpoint. It has been newly renovated, fitting comfortably into the landscape of concrete and steel that surrounds it. The Fieldhouse has a distinct yet homey feel: styled as one of the retro-traditional stadiums, Conseco Fieldhouse's interior recalls, oddly enough, the baseball stadiums of yore. Looking to your right, you are reminded of a long-ago time of hotdogs and ballparks and cheap seats. To your left is the entrance to a modern athletic facility. The ticket counters on the right are trimmed in faux brick and are now covered with metal curtains. To the left is the opening to the stadium, and next to this entrance is a Willy Wonka-factory glass elevator floating over the steel girders that separate the public space of athletics and the private space of the *business* of athletics. Along the far wall is a glass window—wall, really—where the visitor has a bird's-eye view of the practice court below, which evokes a high school gym with its simple scoreboard, metal rack of balls, and humble, scuffed wooden floor. Onlooking fans can almost imagine themselves playing on this floor, and feel a synergistic bond between themselves and the athletes who practice and sweat on this surface. The floor is, of course, in sharp contrast to the glistening polished floors of the Fieldhouse's main floor, surrounded by thousands of metal-and-plastic seats, edged in skyboxes whose tops almost touch the banners waving and proclaiming the greatness of the teams that play within it: postmodernity, the clashing of genres, nostalgia for "the game" and a "better time," and the celebration of new technology are the hallmarks of this stadium and—perhaps, I think—women's athletics.

After a quick look around I realize I have a few spare minutes, so I choose between entering the gift shop and the ubiquitous Starbucks where the young and urbane urbanites read their newspapers and sip lattes at 1:30 in the afternoon. The gift shop is filled with toys, t-shirts, and paraphernalia. As it is the Fever's season, numerous jerseys and hats are given prominent display, although Indiana Pacers' (of the National Basketball Association) merchandise is certainly abundant. The black and gold of the Pacers' insignia blends with the red and blue of the Fever, and the shop is a cacophony of color and texture. The only thing restful to the eye here, I think to myself, is the slowly moving sales staff in their crisp white polo shirts and sharply-pressed khaki pants. I watch them saunter without any real urgency to help people.

Looking out over the shop, sitting high atop the merchandise, are three leather WNBA balls. Prior to this trip I had tried to purchase a WNBA leather basketball to have the athletes sign. This task proved nearly impossible. An official NBA leather ball can be located at almost any sporting goods store for about $75. Yet, when I inquired about a leather WNBA ball, a sporting goods store manager told me—in a voice as if they were an exotic spice—that "WNBA balls are only available on Ebay." (Turns out, it was hard too find them there, too!) Thus, seeing the three leather WNBA balls sitting high above the merchandise (I think more for aesthetics rather than sale), I quickly ask a sales clerk to get two of them for me. He seems a little surprised by the request but slowly complies, and $200 later I am the proud owner of two official WNBA leather balls. It is finally time to check in.[2]

I go to the check-in counter by the elevator and am greeted by an African American woman who is cheerily conducting the business of the fieldhouse. She is marking visitors in, answering questions, and charming all the passers-by. As I wait for Tom Savage, Director of Marketing for the Fever, my nausea returns. Finally, a few minutes after my appointment is schedule, the woman at the desk tells me that Tom will be down in a moment and she will need to give us passes. We march to the desk. She asks to see our IDs and then tells us she will need to search our bags. The cameras are shown and I open up my straw bag full of recording equipment. The woman at the desk and I are suddenly embroiled in a spirited discussion of summer bags—canvas versus straw—as she attempts to pick through my bag and the profusion of individual plastic market bags full of recording equipment. Realizing that this equipment may look menacing, I quickly tell her the bag contains two sets of recording equipment, two microphones, several tapes, and, of course, extra batteries. She smiles, mutters, "Ever since 9/11" under her breath, pulls out a bag with headphones in it and gently places it back in the bag with an aside statement that "I don't know what a bomb looks like, but I always look." It is a quintessential post-9/11 moment, a strange bond: a national tragedy as small talk.

Tom arrives, dressed in khakis and a navy polo shirt emblazoned with the Fever logo. He is a broad, fit-looking man. I am tense, and feel and know I must look awkward as I become uncharacteristically quiet. Tom leads me from the elevator into the bowels of the stadium into the Star Room (a 14

× 14-foot room with several mirrored vanities, a table, a couch, and several big armchairs). A few minutes later, I hear a knock on the door and Olympia and Tom enter. Olympia is a tall, elegant woman, with the thick thighs of a basketball player and the face of a model. Her short hair is a gamine cut that lies against her skull and accentuates her cheekbones. She has the tall and angular body with—in the parlance of my student-athletes—"jacked" (meaning well-defined) muscular but not bulky arms, and a lovely face; she is dressed in her practice gear—a mesh Indiana Fever jersey and sports bra and mesh Fever shorts. Her knees are wrapped in ice. She is still sweaty from practice but seems very at home, very at ease. She slides onto the couch and puts another set of ice bags on her knees. Introductions begin, with Tom standing nervously in the corner, indecisive over whether he should stay or go. I know this is a crucial moment. I want to speak with Olympia alone but I have no idea what form of self-presentation to make in order to get Tom to leave the room. I need Tom to trust me; after all, the Fever has one-third of the WNBA's mothers on their team. I smile and ask Olympia, "So how was your Mother's Day?" as she boldly scrawls her name on one of my newly-purchased WNBA balls. She glances up and says, "I was out of town but I got a card from a teammate and a present from my husband and daughter." "That's nice," I reply and then with a grin say, "Now let's talk turkey; what-cha get? Anything good? Is he a good shopper?" Everyone laughs; Olympia smiles, leans back into the couch, and says, "My husband can shop!" as she launches into a detailed description of her gifts. At that point, with the tension visibly released from the room, Tom deems it safe to leave, and he exits with "Well, I will leave you all to it" and a happy smile. Olympia is smiling and I'm laughing as I tell a story about my mother and Mother's Day gifts; next we easily shift into her experiences of playing in celebrity All-Star games and end with one of the formative discussions. Yet, the interview ends with one of the core bits of insights I received.

Jen: What would be some of the advice you'd give a young person—a basketball player?

Olympia: Well, just the song by Chaka Khan that also Whitney Houston remade—"I'm Every Woman"? That's from others. You have to be every woman. You have to be first a woman, then you're being a mother, then if you're a student or career-oriented; we can do all of those things. And I think, that's why I'm so excited about being a part of the WNBA, I'm a sociology major, so I'm going to be on a sociology tangent here, but we're redefining womanhood. Before they used to say that women couldn't work out because we physically weren't able to do all these things that we couldn't do. Now we're at the point where we are doctors, we are lawyers, we are musicians, we are professional athletes; we're all of those things, and we're still mothers at the same time. We're still wives. So just—that you can do it. That your mother before you did it and not to give up. And to understand, too, that whatever attitude you have is the attitude your child is being raised with. So if you're mad and upset and depressed all the time, that's how you're raising your child, in that environment. If you see my daughter, you would see my house as just Fun City, because she's always laughing. Just remember to have fun. Life is short, and just appreciate every day. You want to pass on the fun legacy. I know I can be a mean mom, don't get me wrong. I'm not saying it like that. But at the same time, just have fun. Life is short.[3]

A key moment in each interview was when my research participants revealed insights into their own youth sport participation. Initially, when I began the interviewing process, these moments were "ice-breaker" questions. I would query about the athletes' own youth sport participation background as a means of getting them relaxed and comfortable and thinking about their own social experiences within sport. For many of the interviewees, their sport participation emerged in a "haphazard" or "random" way. For example, they were asked by coaches in junior high school to try-out for the team because they were tall, or because friends were participating, or perhaps they had older brothers or male figure with whom they played informally at the start. This latter instance pertained to Joy Harris Holmes, where her father and brothers played a crucial role in the athlete sports participation:

Jen: When did you start playing basketball?

Joy: I started playing when I was about 13 years old. I was out in the backyard playing; I had three brothers. Since I started playing younger that helped, but…I didn't start playing organized ball until later.

Jen: With older players…and I include myself…they didn't have the teams to play for.[4]

Joy: I keep being surprised. They're really getting more opportunities, you know, basketball is really growing—college women's basketball, but professional basketball on television and there's so many great role models for us, so much more than what was available when I was growing up.

Jen: So who influenced you? You came from an amazingly athletic family.

Joy: I guess my family, they all had an influence—and I guess the one that pushed me over the edge is my dad. I was originally in cheerleading. I went out for freshman cheerleading and so my dad told me—why don't you just be in basketball, you're a freshman, if you don't like it, you can go ahead and be a cheerleader for the rest of your time in high school. So I thought I'd go ahead and give it a try. My freshman year we went 20–0. But my friend, she did the cheerleader thing all through high school and I did basketball.

Jen: What brought you to Purdue [University]? Obviously they recruited you, but I'm sure you had quite a few places to choose from.

Joy: I was not highly recruited out of high school.

Jen: Somebody made a big mistake...

Joy: I was not. You know what? I wanted to go to Ohio State so, so bad. I mean, that was like an hour from my home. Ohio State, Big 10 basketball, they just were not interested in me at all. Not at all. And I had just a couple of real small...they weren't even full scholarships offered me to come and play. But the last game I was playing, the All-Star game in Columbus, it was the Ohio North-South All-Star game and I remember we were sitting around the morning of the game, just stretching, and everybody's talking about what school they were going to—they were going to Ohio State, all these schools, these big schools that all of these girls are going to. I was just sitting there stretching. Finally they were like—Joy, where you going? I'm like—oh, I'm undecided. I hadn't decided yet. And I mean, these girls had signed back in the early signing period and this was like in April. And I was like—I'm undecided, I don't know. But the thing was I didn't have anything that I was really interested in. And it's not that my game really stood out, that I played, like, such an awesome game; it was typical of the way that I play. And the thing was that I hadn't had much exposure at all. And here are all of these college coaches here, watching these kids that they had already signed, and the assistant coach of Purdue was there and he always tells me, he's like—I'm flipping through them like—who is this kid?!? How come we don't know about her? So after that game I started getting a lot of calls and Purdue was like—we have a scout there today, we want you to come here to Purdue. I'm going to Purdue. And there were two other girls on that team who were going to Purdue, too, so there were two other Ohio guys there. Yes, it's amazing. I just keep thinking that that one game had just made a total difference in my whole life. You know, I went to Purdue, I met my husband at Purdue, we have a kid. I think—God, if I hadn't been to Purdue, what would my life be like today?

Likewise Scott-Richardson:

Olympia: Actually I was athletic when I was younger and I played a little bit
           at school but not really. But I played at the YMCA like twice with
           all the boys. But I was actually playing baseball first with all boys,
           and then going into high school, when I was 14 my freshmen year,
           I was already 6'2". So going in, you know I did my, um, interview
           from my high school. It was a Catholic high school so you had
           to do all this stuff. My interview was actually with the Dean of
           Students who was also the head basketball coach. So [laughter]
           right! Conveniently! So, um, you know, I knew I wanted to play just
           because I knew, okay, I'm tall and it's a fun sport. I didn't really have
           the skills to play because I hadn't played but…Just picked it up as
           I was going. And I think just my intensity level and aggressiveness
           kind of helped me play.

While Joy and Olympia seemingly grew up comfortable with their athleticism, still others struggled to come to terms with their participation. Jackie
Moore's story evidenced one particular experience that many young female
athletes have struggled with: negotiating the constructed tensions between
'attractiveness' and 'athleticism' existing side-by-side:

Jackie: When I was in high school—see, I didn't start playing until I was
          in 9th grade. People play when they're 5 or 10. I didn't start playing
          until I was in the 9th grade. Basketball wasn't even in my future.
Jen: Were you a volleyball player or track…?
Jackie: No, I was this girl who wanted to be cute all the time. One day I
          went to this tryout before my 9th-grade year in high school; my
          friend was trying out for the freshman basketball team and said,
          "Come with me; I'm scared." So I had this cute little skirt on, cute
          little tank top and my purse. I'm going to your tryout. So I'm there
          sitting down and being all cute and she's working out and the coach
          was like, "Yes—you—get up; you're tall, you can get up and work
          out." I had never touched a basketball in my *life* and besides—I'm
          not going to get my dress dirty! So he's like, come on, just get out
          here and try. So I'm out there in my skirt trying out for the team
          and not knowing [what I'm doing]. … I get a call—you're on the
          team. I'm like, oh-my-gosh! So I'm, like, okay, I can deal with
          this. [I went on to play] in high school all four years, get moved
          up to varsity, like, my sophomore year in high school. I'm like,
          okay, what am I doing out here . . .? But they really worked with
          me and then, okay, my plans after high school were to go to City

College and work; that was my plan. Because I didn't really start getting any letters from colleges or nothing so I figure—okay, well, basketball's not my future. And so I started filling out City College applications. And all of a sudden, my senior year—the last two months—I got all these college letters offering me scholarships. I'm like, oh-my-gosh, wow, where [did] this come from? So I didn't realize I was going to play in college. So I finally got the scholarship and in college, my junior year, I heard about the WNBA and I'm like—yeah, right, whatever. I'm not that good, whatever. Come to find out I was…So all these surprises just came about and I just rolled with them. I was, like, okay, I'll take it, it's there, so…I didn't realize I was going to be here, basketball wasn't even in my future. I went to school; my major's criminal justice and I want to be a homicide investigator. And I want to go to law school, so, of course, I have to find some time between, where I can take classes and stuff. But that's my true dream, my profession. But I'm here now and I'm just going to have fun while I can. While all these opportunities just keep coming up in my face, I'm just going to take them. And I personally think they're blessings to me and I never…It's not good to pass up a blessing because you don't know when it's going to come again, or if it's even going to come. So I'm just rolling with the punches right now as they come, I'm going to take it. I'm going to use everything to my advantage and that's how it is. Yes, basketball was not in my attention, there were not plans, they just happened. Okay, we'll do it.

Additionally, I found that the way many of the athletes currently make sense of childhood sport experience is both as a preamble to and a place of activism for their literacy in expressing how they wanted to empower *their* children (male and female) to a more gender equitable experience: their sport participation was not only deeply embedded in their *own* empowerment (broadly conceived), but in creating empowerment opportunities for young people who will come after them (be it their own kids or those who look up to them as role models). It is this overriding discourse of "empowerment" (often conceived of in terms of "social activism") that I want to focus on in the next section.

"They're so Wholesome!"
Swooping into Celebration

Deeply imbricated in the mediated presentation of professional female athletes as role models for America's youth, especially young girls 9 to 13 years of age, is the notion of "empowerment." In particular, this was promoted via the attendant role-modeling of "family values" that was actively conveyed under such a guise as part of core marketing strategies used by both the WNBA and the WUSA, as well as in advertising campaigns associated with Nike, adidas, and Gatorade (Banet-Weiser, 1999; McDonald, 2000; Giardina & Metz, 2005).

Thus did professional female athletes of the 1990s become the kinder, safer version of the [male] professional athlete. More specifically, the professional female athlete as *mother* became emblematic of the postfeminist ideal of heteronormative sexuality, emblematic of a successful career woman who did not abrogate her child-rearing responsibilities. As a representative figure of "proper womanhood" to be mimicked by "young (straight) girls", they functioned as a social mother embodying goodness and wholesomeness, offering sport as an activity that can be read as positive and family-focused. The female athlete is revered for her ability to be the "best" *and* for being the "best" of all women (McDonald, 2000; Metz, 2006).[5]

This strategy of celebrating female athletic participation and with it the (hyper) feminine female athlete is one of the central issues in my interview Sheryl Swoopes, who was perhaps the most mediated of all the athletes I interviewed. While all the athletes were deeply aware of the need to maintain the face of WNBA within their interviews, and many were veterans of the limelight (e.g., Pam McGee and Natalie Williams), Swoopes was the most invested in maintaining the "prototypical" WNBA mother—feminine and engaged in a celebration of women's sports as empowerment and a chance to celebrate femininity—in her interview. Swoopes used the absence of a support system for her sport participation as a springboard to celebrate the advancement of women's sport participation in general and as move a chance to celebrate femininity and empowerment through sport participation. It is the ultimate move in postfeminist rhetoric and yet, at the same time, *is* a celebratory moment for youth sport participation.

Sheryl: I don't think I really had anybody growing up that said... if this is what you want to do then you need to do it. I've wanted to play basketball and, at the time, it wasn't really the thing to do; for girls to play sports or girls to play basketball. So I didn't really have anybody that really encouraged me to keep doing it. I think it was more of a thing that people didn't think I could, didn't think I could be successful in it because it wasn't the thing for girls to do. I think somebody told me I couldn't do it because I was a girl so the more I wanted to do it and the harder I worked at it. And I think especially my mom and my brothers, after they saw that no matter what they did or what they said or how they treated me, I wasn't going to give up. At that point is when I started gaining their support and gaining their respect. [...] I've been playing since I was about seven, eight years old, but I didn't have my mom there right at the beginning saying hey or pushing me saying—if this what you want to do, go for it. My mom I think was like every other parent; she wanted me to play with my dolls and my dishes, the girly things. I just wasn't interested in that. That's not what I wanted to do with my life. I didn't want to play with dolls or dishes or things like that; I wanted to play with my brothers and I think it's okay that girls can see that. You know, like: This is how Sheryl is, she grew up playing with the boys and she is a great athlete, she's great at what she does.[6]

Swoopes continues her discussion of childhood sporting experience but shifts focus and uses her experiences as a vault for the celebratory rhetoric around the role of femininity and sport. Her commentary resonates with the famed Nike campaign of the early 1990s ("If you let me play") and with the belief that American women are both still asking permission to be active and still located outside traditional gender norms. In one breath she celebrates her rejection of norms while advocating for them as an adult.

Sheryl: But when that's over with...I'd like to think that I'm still very feminine when I'm on the court but when I'm done with that—it's all about me and taking care of myself. I like to get my nails done, my feet done, my hair done, wear makeup, dress up, wear high-heels. And it might sound funny but I think a lot of times girls are really struggling with that or they're confused...I've either got be very feminine and not play sports, or play sports. I think they need to know that it's okay to do both, and you can do both.

A Whole New Ballgame?

"Wholesome" may well have been the buzzword for women's sports in the 1990s, as women's sports were good for more than just girls; they were also seen as being good for (the health of) the nation. Female sport participation was no longer seen as a slippery slope from the All-American golden girl becoming large and bruising Communist-like bodies with "dangerous" sexual affiliations (see Cole, this volume); rather, women's sports were popularly imagined as a safe haven in which women were women and they were—thankfully—different than men. In fact, women's sports were celebrated for their ability to be a "kinder" brand of sports. These women exemplified what it was to be a female athlete as opposed to the male athlete that everyone both revered and despised. In the 1990s, men's sports were positioned as dangerous and criminal. Profligate, as everywhere from the local newspapers to *Sports Illustrated* was decrying the state of male athletics in America.[7]

Meanwhile, women's sports were being celebrated for their return to the "good ole days of sport" where athletes were heroes and glad to get a paycheck. In the 1990s athletes like Latrell Sprewell and Allen Iverson came to represent the new breed of sports anti-heroes: "thugs" with game. These athletes were the icons of this generation's new "street" athlete and everyone's greatest fear: a 1997 *USA Weekend* poll found that 86% of 51,285 of respondents found that misbehavior by players on the field and off is the biggest problem plaguing sports today (Goldberg, 1997, p. 39). In comparison, female athletes, whether the topic was parenthood or salaries, were held up as examples of athletes who truly played "for the love of the game." Female athletes like the members of the Women's World Cup team were applauded for their positive attitude, patriotism, and willingness to take a smaller paycheck:

> In an era when the egos of male athletes are dwarfed only by their paychecks, the World Cup women, minimum wagers by pro-sports standards, reminded the country that sports superstars can be gracious and grateful. On the field, the team showed us leadership and teamwork and they kicked butt. ("It Went Down," 1999, p. 46)

Meanwhile, the WNBA showed that an athlete could be a parent, and a woman could have it all, when Swoopes (then the marquee player in the league) returned to her team and the inaugural season just *six weeks* after giving birth to her son. Swoopes's return was seen as "one of the most compelling sports stories of the year. For those wondering whether women really could have it all, here was Swoopes balancing motherhood and a professional basketball career like a ball spinning on her index finger" (Whiteside, 1998, p. 39). Professional women's athletics provided a space where the postfeminist vision of the Supermom had actually occurred.

How, then, are we to make sense of this reiterative frame? Or, put differently, what is the purpose of youth sport and what is the meaning of making mothers and making families *through* youth sport? I would contend that the mediated celebration of women's sports as a place for (hetero)-social mothering offers an alternative script to the taken for granted celebratory logics of empowerment (or, to use one of the more popular 1990s catchphrases, "Girl Power!"). That is, how is the "proper" family being produced, and how is each performance therein enacted from such a social scriptology?

In her magisterial text on contemporary motherhood, *Making Parents*, Charis Thompson (2005) deploys the term "ontological choreography" as a means for explaining the dynamic coordination of the technical, scientific, kinship, gender, emotional, legal, political and financial aspects of assisted reproduction technology clinics. These elements, she argues, have to be coordinated in the assisted reproduction clinic to preserve the (natural) meaning of "family" and how it is created through societal and medical intervention and meanings. This same type of choreography, I contend, is sutured throughout the fabric of youth sport participation rites and rituals and images that give meaning "girls" and "women" in the historical present.

The images of WNBA stars as baby-toting, basketball-dribbling, career-oriented superwomen thrust forward the ideal of the "empowered [heterosexual] female" (athlete) in the mid- to-late-1990s, to the extent that they were to become in effect national hieroglyphs of proper forms of womanhood. As Lauren Berlant (1997) defines it, this national hieroglyph can be seen as being representative of "both the minimum and maximum of what the dominating cultures will sanction for circulation, exchange, and consumption" (p.104). Such hieroglyphic markings of athletes such as Mia Hamm, Brandi Chastain, and Swoopes are meant to represent the achievement and progress of a still very sexist and racist country where women remain underpaid, underadvertised, and limited by repressive gender ideology.

Middle America's active embrace of athletes such as Swoopes and Chastain also signals the limits of its acceptance of female athletes. Whereas the aggressive, empowered female athlete on the field should be celebrated, the female athlete who maintains this empowerment off the field is often still very unsettling. Thus, in order to be successful, the narrative goes, the female athlete is asked to utilize typical displays of femininity and hetero-normative behaviors—husband, children, ponytails, curves—to be accepted as a marketing tool and a cultural icon. She is always being reminded to play hard on the field, and look good off the field.

From this perspective, the success—socially, culturally, politically, and economic—of the WNBA, WUSA, and female athletes in general allows the American public to engage in a self-congratulatory rhetoric of "Look, I'm a good person; I support female athletics. I watched the Women's World Cup, the WNBA, etc." This course of action of supporting women's issues through athletics is particularly enticing to many women for, as bell hooks (1999) writes, "marginalized groups deemed Other, who have been ignored, rendered invisible, can be seduced by the emphasis on Otherness by its commodification, because it offers the promise of recognition and reconciliation" (p. 183). In other words, the seductive appeal of such seemingly "empowered females" works precisely because these athletes operate as iconic minority figures. As Berlant (1997) further explains,

> these luminaries allow the hegemonic consuming public to feel that it has already achieved intimacy and equality with the marginal mass population; as minority exceptions, they represent heroic autonomy

from their very "people"; as "impersonations" of minority identity, they embody the very ordinary conditions of subjective distortion that characterizes stereotypical marginality. (p.104)

How is this largely White, middle-class, heterosexual, pony-tailed group a "minority?" Berlant continues,

the national minority stereotype makes exceptional the very person whose marginality, whose individual experience of collective cultural discrimination or difference is the motive for his/her circulation as an honorary icon in the first place. (p. 104)

Thus do the women of the WNBA and WUSA operate as a celebration of all the mothers who have achieved and survived. Their success—commercial, social, cultural, or otherwise, is seen as a grand achievement for all and another step in the Title IX dream (see Giardina & Metz, 2005).

Correlatively, it is female athletes' reading as safe, heterosexual people that provide them with their success in the media. Rick Reilly's column in *Sports Illustrated* regarding the Women's World Cup of Soccer captures the essence of the discourse of how America makes sense of female athletes when he wrote,

You figured when a U.S. women's team finally broke through, one that made even the truck care, it would be a bunch of women with Bronco Nagurski shoulders and five o'clock shadows. Well, the revolution is here and it has bright-red toenails. And it shops. And it carries diaper bags. The U.S. women's soccer team is towing the country by the heart in this Women's World cup and just look at the players. They've got ponytails! They've got kids! They've got (gulp) curves! ... Whoever they are they are impossible not to watch. (p. 100)

If kids, ponytails, and curves are the requirements for making America "care" about women's sports, then it is unsurprising that both the WNBA and the WUSA mined the marker of motherhood and used it as both celebratory and emancipatory. (While at the same time, the dark underbelly of missed opportunities gets covered up in a Team USA soccer jersey or a Houston Comets sweatshirt.)

Concluding Thoughts

It's a sense of empowerment—that's the recurring theme for women's sports. We've got to look at women's sports as a sociological movement.—Brian Donlon, Vice President of Sports Programming at Lifetime Television[8]

Ten years have past since the 1996 Olympics—widely referred to as the "Games of the American Women"—and we have seen the birth (and, in some cases, utter demise) of several professional sporting leagues for woman. As a social body, we have further seen Title IX have massive effects on the experience of female athletes across this country. The effect of Title IX has been far-reaching and can easily be contextualized as a key factor in the emergence of the female athlete in the 1990s. For better or worse, Title IX has made a difference not only in the awareness of female athletes but in the type of structural and monetary support they receive from institutions and society. It is important to point out that Title IX, as a legislative act, did not have clearly measurable changes until the early 1980s. Also, as Cole (2000) argues, "Title IX has been, and is at best, unevenly instituted and enforced. Most universities have made minor and symbolic compromises while few have been penalized for persisting disparities" (p. 5). Despite the structural inadequacies of Title IX, it has to be positioned as a key player in the meta-morphosis of the female athlete's role in society. A review of the increased rates of participation since 1980 shows a dramatic difference in post-Title IX America. This phenomenon transformed the vision of the female athlete in society.

Women's high school and collegiate athletic participation has showed a steady and continual climb since 1972 and has continued to climb through the 1990s and even into the 2000s. According to the National Federation of State High School Associations (NFHS), from 1972 to 2000 the number of girls participating in high school athletics increased by 200% (NFHS Official Website).[9] While girls' sports showed a dramatic increase overall, girls' youth soccer participation rates skyrocketed during the 1990s. Girls' soccer participation increased 34% from 1991 to 1999 and reached a record number of 7.5 million soccer-playing girls and women in 1999.[10] The rise in high school sport has coincided with the development and expansion of college sport programs for women.

Collegiate sports have undergone a marked reconfiguration since the passage of Title IX. In a longitudinal study[11] done by the National Collegiate Athletic Association (NCAA), beginning in 1982[12] and still ongoing today, the NCAA found a dramatic increase in women's collegiate sports participation during the 1990s. In 1982, the NCAA found that there were 1,985 women's teams with 33,435 participants; by 1989, there were 2,262 teams 36,242 participants. These gains, while impressive, may seem insignificant when one compares the numbers from 1989 to 2000-2001. By 2001, there were 3,095 women's teams with 62,667 participants. From 1982-2001, the number of teams and participants in women collegiate athletics doubled. These numbers demonstrate the significant growth in female athletics in the United States during the 1980s and 1990s (NCAA Gender Equity Website).

Yet, as we reflect upon the changes and gains in women's sports and the impact it has had on the women and the children of the United States, we return to an old "feminist" campaign slogan, "We've come a long way, baby," and yet, the question remains, How far have we *really* come? As the athletes in these interviews reflect on their own experiences of getting involved in youth sport and through it and a series of political and social changes to careers in the professional basketball, we as a culture have to acknowledge the progress of women's issues. We have made progress. We are not nearly there yet, not even close, but we have created an opportunity that was not there before. Tracey Henderson, when asked if this is what she thought she would be doing, responded, "No, I thought I would be done playing basketball and I will have a family then. I never thought I would be in the WNBA raising a daughter…"

When Henderson was asked whether her two year-old daughter is playing basketball yet, she tells me:

> She wears her sweatbands, she looks like a million dollars, but no basketball yet. She loves basketball, she's got a basketball and dribbles a WNBA ball, she plays with it, but I know she probably won't play basketball but whatever she decides to do I will be happy.

What has Title IX and the 1990s created for our youth and what is the value of the WNBA and other professional leagues for women? They are opportunities for our children to be successful athletes and successful people. The leaps and strides made thus far tells us how far we have come, and now the real work begins to provide opportunity and success equally to all our daughters and to all of our women who want to play.

Notes

1. Take, for example, this passage:

   Harry stepped in, his head almost touching the sloping ceiling, and blinked. It was like walking into a furnace: Nearly everything in Ron's room seemed to be a violent shade of orange: the bedspread, the walls, even the ceiling. Then Harry realized that Ron had covered nearly every inch of the shabby wallpaper with posters of the same seven witches and wizards, all wearing bright orange robes, carrying broomsticks, and waving energetically. 'Your Quidditch team?" said Harry. "The Chudley Cannons," said Ron, pointing at the orange bedspread, which was emblazoned with two giant black C's and a speeding cannonball. "Ninth in the league" (Rowling, p. 40).

   Additionally, and mirroring a storyline from the film *Love and Basketball*, Harry Potter falls for his contemporary, the lovely and gifted seeker, Cho Chang, on the opposing Ravenclaws team. Harry admires her skill on Quidditch pitch as much as anything else.

2. In the years since this particular interview was conducted, WNBA leather basketballs have become far more readily available.

3. Later, when the interview is transcribed and my friends—most of whom are in their late-twenties and early-thirties—read it, they tell me they love it. Yet the critical theorist in me struggles to agree: I know that my colleague, Mary McDonald (2002), has critiqued this

celebratory rhetoric around motherhood and normative (White) femininity in the WNBA as a homogenizing and "Othering" agent for lesbians and women of color in women's basketball. Not surprisingly, when the interview airs on the radio, Olympia-Scott Richardson, a relatively unknown WNBA player, is adored. The listeners call in and say things like, "I love it. It is such girl talk. She is so real." This kind of commentary about the interviews never ends. Women call the radio station and say over and over again, "I never realized Sheryl [Swoopes], Olympia, etc." had so many of the same feelings I did." "Pam had breast cancer—I do too" or "I'm a single mom like Jackie" and "Oh, did I cry like Joy when I left my baby for the first time."

By gathering the voices of the women of the WNBA I hope I made them "more real" for others. I do so at the risk of hegemonically (re)-enforcing Berlant's iconic minority figure or the homogenizing and "Othering" effects that McDonald critiques. And yet, at times, I wonder if the very fact that these interviews are getting aired and being heard by women outside the "basketball" or even "academic" community is a good thing unto itself. By the same token, as women called and asked when I was going to interview "everyday" mothers (i.e., mothers who are not professional athletes, mothers who have no greater claim to fame then they have children and care for them) that I began to realize that everyone wants to know what the "other" mother is doing. The "Othering" of motherhood is often the poignant erasure of self for children regardless of your experience and it was those questions and those voices and desires that began to direct my project, and make me wonder if the stories themselves are just as important as the absences that exist within them.

4. Prior to turning to a career in academia, the author was a Division I scholarship basketball player.

5. The implication within this conservative family-values discourse is that these women are always and only heterosexual.

6. Likewise Jessie Hicks of the Orlando Miracle:

    Well I started at age 13. I wanted to start at 12, but I was too afraid and I had my sister at age 13 tell me a little bit about myself, saying that I was a little too tall and I needed to be doing something, so I figured basketball was the thing. And then I had a friend, too, to persuade me at age 13 to tryout for the middle school team. Ever since then, I've just been playing basketball playing in AAU [Amateur Athletic Union], playing like Richmond Youth Games, just all over high school, college.... I was like a tomboy. And I have twin brothers so I kind of grew up with them. Just playing with them all the time, doing different activities outside, running in the woods, I guess it just made me more athletic then. I didn't now what path I was going to take playing basketball, but just being a tomboy, that aggressiveness I have, I think I got it from my brothers.

7. See *Sports Illustrated* (May 4, 1998) cover "Where's Daddy?" and the coordinating feature article called, "Paternity Ward" by Grant Wahl and L. Jon Wertheim, which is an exposé about professional athletes and out-of-wedlock fatherhood. The article focuses primarily on African American athletes in the National Basketball Association (NBA) and the perceived notion that fathering out-of-wedlock children has become commonplace among athletes, many of whom seem oblivious to the legal, financial, and emotional consequences.

8. Cited in Bernstein (1999).

9. In 1972, there were 817,073 thousand girls participating in high school athletics; by 2000 there were 2,784,154 million, which is an increase of more than 200% (National Federation State High School Association (NFHS) Official Website).

10. This information can be found at http://www.sgma.com/press/1999/press986503572-9968.html.

11. The information cited here is part of the NCAA report on participation rates in intercollegiate athletics at the Division I through III levels. According to the NCAA, the information provided in this report "should offer a general overview of historical trends in participation and sport sponsorship by gender, sport and division" (http://www1.ncaa.org/). Additional information is available online.

12. The study began in 1982 because that was the year that the NCAA finally wrested control of women's sports from the Association of Intercollegiate Athletics for Women (AIAW). AIAW is a now-defunct organization that guided women's sport through the 1970s.

192 • Jennifer L. Metz

References

Banet-Weiser, D. (1999). Professional basketball and the politics of race and gender. *Journal of Sport and Social Issues, 23*(4), 420–430.
Berlant, L. (1997). The Queen of America Goes to Washington City: Essays on Sex and Citizenship. Durham, NC: Duke University Press.
Bernstein, A. (1999, July 23). Lessons from World Cup apply to all the sports world. *Washington Business Journal, 23*, 28.
Cole, C. L. (2000). The year that girls ruled. *Journal of Sport and Social Issues, 1*, 1–6.
Department of Health and Human Services. (2002). Girl Power! Retrieved 17 June 2006 from http://www.girlpower.gov/
Getting their kicks: Wherever U.S. soccer stars Joy Fawcett and Carla Overbeck go, their kids go too (1999, July 5). *People Weekly*, 171–175.
Giardina, M. D., & Metz, J. L. (2005). Women's sports in postmodern America: Body politics and the corporo-empowerment of "Everyday Athletes." In S. J. Jackson & D. L. Andrews (Eds.), *Sport, culture, and advertising: Identities, commodities, and the politics of representation* (pp. 59-80). London: Routledge.
Goldberg, K. (1997, February 17). Has old-fashioned sportsmanship gone the way of real grass?: Crass behavior of athletes reflects mores of US society. *Insight on the News*, 39–42.
hooks, b. (1990). *Yearning; Race, gender and cultural politics.* Boston: South End Press.
"It went down to the wire." (1999, July 19). *Newsweek*, 46.
Lafrance, M. R. (1998). Colonizing the feminine: Nike's intersections of postfeminism and hyper-consumption. In G. Rail (Ed.), *Sport and postmodern times* (pp. 117–142). Albany: SUNY Press.
McDonald, M. (2000). The marketing of the Women's Basketball Association and the making of post-feminism. *International Review for the Sociology of Sport, 35*, 35–47.
McDonald, M. (2002). Queering whiteness: The peculiar case of women's national basketball association. *Sociological Perspectives, 45*, 379–396.
National Federation of State High School Associations. Participation figure search. Retrieved August 2004, from http://www.nfhs.org/ScriptContent/VA_Custom/vim displays/contentpagedisplay.cfm?Content_ID=133&SearchWord=Title% 20IX
NCAA Gender Equity Homepage. Retrieved July 10, 2005, from http://www1.ncaa.org/ membership/ed_outreach/gender_equity/homepage.html
Patrick, D. (2002). Twenty years later, AIAW legacy lingers [Electronic version]. *USA Today Online*. Retrieved July 30, 2002, from http://www.usatoday.com/ advertising/orbitz/orbitz-window.html
Reilly, R. (1999, June). The goal-goal girls. *Sports Illustrated, 5*, 100.
Rowling, J. K. (1999). *Harry Potter and the chamber of secrets.* New York: Scholastic Press.
Thompson, C. (2005). *Making parents: The ontological choreography of reproductive technologies.* Cambridge, MA: MIT Press.
Tresniowski, A. (1999, July 26). Soccer's happiest feat. *People Weekly*, 52–59.
Whiteside, K. (1998). WNBA—A Celebration: Commemorating the birth of a league. With Foreword by Rosie O'Donnell. New York: Harper Horizon.

Coda
Youth Sport in the Shadows of American Vertigo

MICHAEL D. GIARDINA

Proem

We aren't kids anymore; we just act like it when it comes to baseball. From upstate New York hamlet to big-city metropolis, from East Coast port city to east-central Illinois college town, the recent Farrelly Brothers' baseball-themed remake of Nick Hornby's classic soccer novel and film, *Fever Pitch,* rings all-too-true. In the film, *Saturday Night Live*-alum Jimmy Fallon portrays public school teacher Ben Wrightman, a long-suffering Boston Red Sox fan. The film's narrative arc follows Ben from childhood and his first game at Fenway Park with his uncle, Carl, on through to his present-day connection to the team and its tradition, which culminates with [I still can't believe I'm writing this] the Red Sox winning the 2004 World Series and putting an end to their 86-year championship drought. While the film is a charming romantic comedy that pits Ben's fanatical baseball obsession against the personal relationship ambitions of his pragmatic new girlfriend and baseball neophyte, Lindsey Meeks (subtly played by Drew Barrymore), the bond shared between Ben and his friends through the cultural performance of baseball fantasy and nostalgia is my inspirational focus here.

Stop. Think. Reflect. What was the first major sporting event you went to as a kid? Where was it? Who took you? Where did you sit? What did you eat? Mitch Robbins (a.k.a. Billy Crystal) remembers his:

> Seven years old and my dad takes me to Yankee Stadium. My first game. We go in through this long dark tunnel underneath the stands, and I'm holding his hand, and we come up out of the tunnel, and into the

light. It was huge. How green the grass was, the brown dirt, and that great green copper roof, remember? And we had a black and white TV then, so this was the first game I ever saw in color. I sat next there the whole game next to my dad. He taught me how to keep score... Mickey [Mantle] hit one out...I still have the program.[1]

So does Ben Wrightman:

When I was a kid, I moved here from New Jersey...and I didn't have any friends or anything...so my Uncle Carl started taking me to Fenway Park. I just...I got lost in the game. I mean, the ballpark and the people. The color, the sounds. The smells.

And so it went for my college friends and myself, too, where the 1996 ESPN commercial tag line "You don't mess with tradition" was always met with its flip rejoinder, "Well, not around here, you don't," in perfect rhythm by any who essayed to stroll through our dorm room during the 6:00 p.m. weeknight edition or 10:00 a.m. morning replay of the late-night version ("The Big Show" with Dan Patrick and Keith Olbermann, as that particular installment of *SportsCenter* was then known). While on any given day the small 19-inch TV in the background could be tuned to college basketball, pro football, or even ice hockey (long-suffering Los Angeles Kings, Boston Bruins, and New York Rangers fans amongst our group), it was baseball most of all—and following W. P. Kinsella's Terrence Mann—that was to become for us the "constant through all the years," a "part of our past" that "reminds of us all that once was." And in fact, when we get right down to it, to misquote *Bull Durham*'s Annie Savoy, baseball might just have been to us "full of magic, cosmic truth, and the fundamental ontological riddles of our time." And, who knows, *maybe it still is.*

In the introduction to a previous book (Giardina, 2005), I wrote an off-hand footnote explaining the tension between writing a critical exposition on popular sporting culture operative in the global arena whilst being, ostensibly, a "fan" of the same. It went something like this:

As I'm writing this Introduction, it is Major League Baseball's 2004 Opening Day. The Cubs/Reds game plays on television in the background and, between breaks in my thoughts, I send Instant Messages to a former college housemate in Boston, bantering back and forth about the chances of the Red Sox and Angels this year [who would have predicted a Red Sox World Series victory? Not us], as well as espousing our takes on Michael Lewis's (2003) Sabremetriffic bestseller *Moneyball* (a book that my friends and I have a definite love–hate view of, in the sense that we'd probably each give an arm and a leg to be Billy Beane, Paul DePodesta, or J.P. Ricciardi). (p. 22)

More importantly, perhaps, is that the game and its connections to and through us helps to keep us young, to turn us into kids once more (even when we *recognize* the racialized narratives, hyper-sexualized images, or economic puerilism running rampant throughout). Reworking Sarah Vowell (2002), perhaps baseball and its soap operatic ebbs and flows has no point at all.[2] But that, for some of us, may just be the point, for our life is full of points—"the deadlines and bills and recycling and phone calls." And against all that, maybe we've come to "appreciate, to depend on, this one dumb-ass little passion" (p. 65). But a passion nonetheless. A complicated one. One that touches our souls, gets inside of us, keeps us young at heart, even as we work to expose it for all of its failings. (Recall Ben Wrightman's story of seeing an aging Ted Williams being carted in a wheelchair out to the mound for a pre-game ceremony at the 1999 All-Star Game in Boston: "I was there. I was 10 feet away from him. Old men crying. Tears. Tough old guys. I even started to lose it, ya know. I got the program. I could show you."[3])

Such are the kinds of tensions at play in the modern world that I find myself, as someone writing on sport and the consumption of sporting culture from an academic perspective—but also having worked in sport on the professional side, not to mention having played sports all my life—confronting at nearly every turn in my *scholarly* life. To be honest, it's an odd relationship. A colleague of mine once said, "You have a deep 'love-hate' relationship to the products of popular culture you write about, don't you?" At the time I was dismissive of her comment but, in retrospect, I think she was/is right. As Jim Denison and Pirkko Markula (2003) write in their call for a departure from "traditional" practices of sporting scholarship and representation, "More than anyone…we [sport scholars] are aware that sport and movement experiences can be elusive, bodily, intense, and contradictory" (p. 9). It is this very contradictory nature of sporting culture that a great many of the few who dare write on sport—challenging at every step the normative frameworks that we have come to know since childhood, in essence disavowing all that we had taken on face value about the "unquestioned" and positive role of sport writ large in our daily lives, while at the very same time being able to surrender ourselves to the passion of a playoff hockey game or the light-hearted nature of a cousin's youth soccer match or the unbridled joy that is a Cubs game at Wrigley Field on a mid-summer's afternoon with your partner in crime—must come to terms with if we are to move the field forward and realize its promise, not just in words but in actions (see especially Giardina, 2005).

Performative Youth Studies

So, how do we go about doing this? How do we go about deploying a critical youth studies for the historical present, a critical cultural studies project that, in Norman K. Denzin's words, *matters*? While by no means universally Marxist in terms of theoretical and/or political underpinnings, there would seem to be a widespread consensus among those who critically study (youth) sport regarding the need to comprehend fully a sporting practice's necessary interrelation with the social formations in which it is located and contested (see Andrews & Giardina, in press). While some may engage in a form of willing suspension of cynicism when viewing or attending a sporting event (for example, when watching the Los Angeles Angels of Anaheim play the New York Yankees, or the University of Illinois throw down with the University of Wisconsin, or the Steeltown Tank Girls defeat the Hamilton Harlots), in the academic sphere sport has been *outed* as the labrynthine and multifaceted social, cultural, political, and economic institution that it is (Andrews & Giardina, in press). According to Grant Jarvie and Joseph Maguire (1994), there has been

> a transcendence of a general belief that sport and leisure were somewhat autonomous or separate from society or politics or problems of social development…[which] gave rise to a growing recognition that sport and leisure were far too complex to be viewed as simple products of voluntary behaviour or totally autonomous entities. (p. 2)

Or, as George Sage (1998) outlined with respect to analyzing sport in the United States:

> Sport is a set of social practices and relations that are structured by the culture in which they exist, and any adequate account of sport must be routed in an understanding of its location within society. The essence of sport is to be found within the nature of its relationships to the broader stream of societal forces of which it is a part. Thus, a real necessity for everyone trying to understand the sociocultural role of sport in American society is to approach sport relationally, always asking, "What are the intentions of sport to other aspects of American society?" (p. 14)

This recognition is a good first step. But it is not enough. We must push harder, further, against the boundaries of our inter/disciplinary walls, asking, What is to be the next "movement" of critical studies (particularly one oriented to critical youth studies, and sensitive to and imbricated within an historical present exemplified by neoliberal capitalism, global corporate dominion, and unilateral invasions of sovereign nations by dubiously elected U.S. presidents [read: George W. Bush])?

Recently, and under the umbrella of what one might term an "Illinoisian-inflected (performative) cultural studies," there has been a marked, para-digmatic shift toward a politically motivated, contextually relevant, and performatively rendered cultural studies project that interrogates the historical present.[4] Or, to put it another way, the deployment and (re)-realization of *a cultural studies that matters,* one that aims to produce the type of knowledge through which it would be in a position to intervene into the (broader social) world, and *make a difference.* A project, as Grossberg (1989) noted, that would be

> propelled by its desire to construct possibilities, both immediate and imaginary out of its historical circumstances. It has no pretensions to totality or universality; *it seeks only to give us a better understanding of where we are so that we can get somewhere else (some place, we hope, that is better—based on more just principles of equality and the distribution of wealth and power.* (p. 415, emphasis in original)

To be sure, and following Norman K. Denzin's poignant Foreword to this volume, this is an activist-minded project, a public intellectualism on the order of the kind Noam Chomsky advanced in his 1967 article "The Responsibility of Intellectuals," where he argued that intellectuals (i.e., you, dear reader) have a moral, ethical, and professional obligation to speak the truth, to expose lies, and see events in their historical perspective.[5]

Moreover, and following Cameron McCarthy and his collaborators (2007), this is a project that

> while mindful of the extraordinary venue that cultural studies has provided over the past few decades for theoretically-, empirically- and pragmatically-grounded investigations into the conditions of production and the forms of existence of the subjugated cultures of the Anglo-based Western industrial societies pertaining to the problematic integration of youth, women and minorities into modern social formations...seeks to both invade and surround cultural studies with the insistent, noisy demands of a polyglot world, putting new voices, new angles of view, new perspectives, new capacities, needs, interests and desires, and indeed, wholly new research objects onto the landscape of cultural studies. (p. 2)

For Bryant K. Alexander (2003), such a performative approach (to cultural studies) has the destabilizing potentiality to be an act of intervention "at the confluence of reflection and remembrance" (p. 105). Identities in this vein are marked, bent, remade, and restored (Schechner, 1998).[6] "Learning" history from a subjective, performative vantage point such as this "makes possible the construction of new historical ideas, images, and myths" (Garoian, 1998, p. 6) to emerge and disrupt the official mediated pedagogies of our historical present. That is, as Dwight Conquergood (1985) reminds us, the tacit understandings of culture, the dynamics of oppression and resistance, and the knowledge upon which we base these understandings have been shattered, helping us to "recognize the partial breakdown, renegotiation, and reposition of boundaries as fundamental to how pluralization is linked to the shifting nature of knowledge, identities, and the processes of globalization" (Giroux, 2001, p. 9).

With this in mind, and standing with Arundhati Roy (2004), it should be incumbent upon us to never complicate that which is simple, and to never simplify that which is complicated: "we should never let a little hunk of expertise carry us off to our lair and guard against the unauthorized curiosity of passers-by" (p. 120). Rather, we must do the opposite. "We must create links. Join the dots. Tell politics like a story. Communicate it. Make it *real*. Present impassioned polemics. And refuse to create barriers that prevent ordinary people from understanding what is happening to them" (Roy, 2004, p. 10).

In this vein, the performative pedagogy we might do well to subscribe to "is never neutral, just as it is never free from the influence of language, social, and political forces" (Giroux, 2000, p. 8). Not only does the linking of the performative and pedagogical "constitute a dialectical and dialogical process that instantiates a reciprocal exchange…that engages in the task of reframing, refunctioning, and reposing the question of understanding itself" (Kincheloe, 2003, p. 121), it "also suggests that cultural workers address critically how new modes of symbolic meaning and social practice necessitate a transformation in how we think about the relationship among knowledge, power and political agency" (Giroux, 2001, p. 9). The goal here is to foster an engaged social citizenship and promote a radically progressive democratic consciousness, in effect a version of what Peter McLaren (2000) refers to as a revolutionary pedagogy that

> creates a narrative space set against the naturalized flow of the everyday, against the daily poetics of agency, encounter, and conflict, in which subjectivity is constantly dissolved and reconstructed—that is, in which subjectivity turns-back-on-itself, giving rise to both the affirmation of the world through naming it, and an opposition to the world through unmasking and undoing the practices of concealment that are latent in the process of naming itself. (p. 185)[7]

Invoking Cornel West (1991, p. 36; 1989, p. 234), I therefore envision such a project as one whose underlying post-pragmatic political goal contributes to an awareness and understanding of greater individual freedom in the broader social order. Paraphrasing West (1991, 35–36), prophetic pragmatists as moral agents understand that the consequences of their interventions into the world are exclusively political, judged always in terms their contributions to a politics of liberation, love, caring and freedom (see Denzin, Lincoln, & Giardina, 2006).[8] As such, our larger aim must be directed at thinking through the "radical implications of cultural politics, the role of academics and cultural workers as oppositional public intellectuals, and the centrality of cultural pedagogy as a moral and political practice" (Giroux, 2001, pp. 5–6). It is a project that sees its pedagogy as a "kind of transformative intellectual practice that can encompass the variegated work of artists and critics, as well as researchers and educators" (Giroux, 2001, p. 3). This approach involves communicating the skills that will empower students and citizens alike to become more open to and cognizant of the popular politics of representation of race, class, gender, sexuality, and other cultural forms so as to empower individuals and promote radical, progressive democracy, what bell hooks (1997) refers to as a project of transforming consciousness and providing students "with a way of knowing that enables them to know themselves better and live in a world more fully" (p. 76).⁹ *This volume has been one step in that direction.*

Concluding Remarks

Writing in her homage to the radical Brazilian education, Paulo Freire, Antonia Darder (2002) speaks of a pedagogy of love, of a belief that "we are filled with a vision of a world where human beings will strive consistently to live a revolutionary solidarity, fueled by the integrity of our minds, hearts, bodies, and spirits" (p. 256). If we are indeed at one of the gravest turning points in the history of the world—as many activists, intellectuals, and everyday citizens contend—then it is incumbent upon us to reach out to as many people as possible, to sharpen our critiques without speaking simply to the academy, and to broaden our own disciplinary horizons by not shutting off those arenas which have historically been marginalized. In light of these uncertain and violent times, cultural studies scholars have a moral obligation to police this crisis; to speak to the death of people, culture, and truth; and to undo the official pedagogies that circulate in the media (see Denzin, 2007). We must seek non-violent regimes of truth that honor culture, universal human rights, and the sacred. We must seek critical methodologies that protest, resist, and help us represent, imagine, and perform radically free utopian spaces. And, as Judith Butler (2004) writes in her moral polemic *Precarious Life*, we must ultimately be committed to creating "a sense of the public in which oppositional voices are not feared, degraded, or dismissed, but valued for the instigation to a sensate democracy they occasionally perform" (p. 151).

Notes

1. Quote taken from *City Slickers* (1991).
2. Of course, to borrow from the 1990s primetime television drama, *Northern Exposure*, baseball might also be operating as an "antiphiliopietistic metaphor for America's role in post-Cold

War geopolitics" (qtd. in McGimpsey, 2000, p. 162).

3. Everything is always already interconnected: I recall watching this "filmic" moment (Williams at the "real" 1999 All-Star game) in Hoboken, New Jersey, whilst visiting friends who happen to appear in this text.

4. See, for example, Denzin (2007), Kien (2006), Guiliano (2007), McCarthy, Durham, Engel, Filmer, Giardina, & Malagreca (2007), Moreira (2007), Metz (2006), and Newman & Giardina (forthcoming).

5. Bratich (2006), in fact, argues that, for cultural studies to remain relevant, it must become *pro*-active rather than *re*-active.

6. We can carry this further, following Schechner (1998), to say that the way a performance is enacted both describes and reiteratively instantiates performatively rendered identity such that it becomes "increasingly difficult to sustain any distinction between appearances and facts, surfaces and depths, illusions and substances. Appearances are actualities" (p. 362). Performances can thus "reaffirm, resist, transgress, re-inscribe or passionately reinvent...repressive understandings that circulate in daily life" (Denzin, 2003, p. 10).

7. Such a pedagogical imagination understands that the classroom, curricular, and school structures in which teachers and educators enter are not neutral sites waiting to be shaped by instructors; rather, critical pedagogues maintain that every dimension of schooling and every form of educational practice are politically contested sites (see Kincheloe & McLaren, 2000; Kincheloe, 2003).

8. Following Collins (2000), Pelias (2004, p. 163), and Freire (1999), the moral inquirer enacts a politics of love and care, an ethic of hope and forgiveness. Love, here, to borrow from Darder and Mirón (2006),

   means to comprehend that the moral and the material are inextricably linked. And, as such, [we] must recognize love as an essential ingredient of a just society. Eagleton (2003) defines this concept of love as a political principle through which we struggle to create mutually life-enhancing opportunities for all people. It is grounded in the mutuality and interdependence of our human existence—that which we share, as much as that which we do not. This is a love nurtured by the act of relationship itself. It cultivates relationships with the freedom to be at one's best without undue fear. Such an emancipatory love allows us to realize our nature in a way that allows others to do so as well. Inherent in such a love is the understanding that we are not at liberty to be violent, authoritarian, or self-seeking. (p. 150)

   For more, see the collection of essays in Denzin & Giardina (2006, 2007).

9. Importantly, these critical methodologies

   must exhibit interpretive sufficiency; be free from racial, class, gender, or sexual stereotyping; rely on multiple voices; enhance moral discernment, and promote social transformation and critical consciousness... combin[ing] theoretical rigor with social *relevance*, moving critical, interpretive practices beyond the mandarin class of Ivory Tower specialists to the streets, the realm of the everyday, the battleground of heartfelt struggles springing forth with a pedagogy of love, not hate. (Denzin & Giardina, 2006, p. 8)

References

Alexander, B. K. (2003). Fading, twisting, and weaving: An interpretive ethnography of the black barbershop as cultural space. *Qualitative Inquiry, 9*(1), 105–128.

Andrews, D. L., & Giardina, M. D. (in press). Sport without guarantees: Toward a cultural studies that matters. *Cultural Studies/Critical Methodologies.*

Bratich, J. (2006). Apocryphal now redux. In N. K. Denzin and M. D. Giardina (Eds.), *Contesting empire/globalizing dissent: Cultural studies after 9/11* (pp. 213–230). Boulder, CO: Paradigm.

Butler, J. (2004). *Precarious life.* London: Verso.

Chomsky, N. (1967, February 23). The responsibility of intellectuals. *The New York Review of Books, 8*(3). Available online at http://www.nybooks.com/articles/12172

Collins, P. H. (2000). *Black feminist thought* (2nd ed.). New York, Routledge.

Conquergood, D. (1985). Performing as a moral act: Ethical dimensions of the ethnography of performance. *Literature in Performance, 5*, 1–13.

Darder, A. (2002). *Reinventing Paulo Freire: A pedagogy of love.* Boulder, CO: Westview Press.

Darder, A., & Mirón, L. F. (2006). Critical pedagogy in a time of uncertainty: A call to Action. In N. K. Denzin & M. D. Giardina (Eds.), *Contesting empire/globalizing dissent: cultural studies after 9/11* (pp. 136–151). Boulder, CO, Paradigm.

Denison, J., & Markula, P. (2003). *Moving writing: Crafting movement in sport research.* New York: Peter Lang.

Denzin, N. K. (2003). *Performance ethnography: Critical pedagogy and the politics of culture.* Thousand Oaks, CA: Sage.

Denzin, N. K. (2007). *Flags in the window: Dispatches from the American war front.* New York: Peter Lang.

Denzin, N. K., & Giardina, M. D. (Eds.) (2007). *Ethical futures in qualitative research: Decolonizing the politics of knowledge.* Walnut Creek, CA: Left Coast Press.

Denzin, N. K., Lincoln, Y. S., & Giardina, M. D. (2006). Disciplining qualitative research. *International Journal of Qualitative Studies in Education, 19,* 6, 769–782

Eagleton, T. (2003). *After theory.* New York: Basic Books.

Freire, P. (1999 [1992]) *Pedagogy of hope* (Robert R. Barr, Trans.). New York: Continuum.

Garoian, C. R. (1998). *Performing pedagogy: Toward an art of politics.* Albany: State University of New York Press.

Giardina, M. D. (2005). *Sporting pedagogies: Performing culture & identity in the global arena.* New York: Peter Lang.

Giroux, H. A. (2000). Impure acts: The practical politics of cultural studies. London: Routledge.

Giroux, H. A. (2001). Cultural studies as performative practice. *Cultural Studies/Critical Methodologies, 1*(1), 5–23.

Grossberg, L. (1989). The circulation of cultural studies. *Critical Studies in Mass Communications, 6*(4), 413–420.

Guiliano, J. (2007), *Educating the public: Sports mascots, history, and racial ideology.* Paper presented at the Third International Congress of Qualitative Research.

Jarvie, G., & Maguire, J. (1994). *Sport and leisure in social thought.* London: Routledge.

Kien, G. (2006). Postmodern gargoyles, simulated power aesthetics. *Qualitative Inquiry, 12*(4), 681–703.

Kincheloe, J. (2003). *Critical pedagogy.* New York: Peter Lang Publishing.

Kincheloe, J., & McLaren, P. (2000). Rethinking critical theory and qualitative research. In N. K. Denzin & Y. S. Lincoln (Eds.), *The handbook of qualitative research* (pp. 279–313). Thousand Oaks, CA: Sage Publications.

Lewis, M. (2003). *Moneyball: The art of winning an unfair game.* New York: W. W. Norton & Co.

McCarthy, C., Durham, A., Engel, L., Filmer, A., Giardina, M. D., & Malagreca, M. (2007). *Globalizing cultural studies: Ethnographic interventions in theory, method, and policy.* New York: Peter Lang.

McGimpsey, D. (2000). *Imagining baseball: America's pastime and popular culture.* Bloomington: Indiana University Press.

McLaren, P. (2000). *Che Guevara, Paulo Freire, and the pedagogy of revolution.* Lanham, MD: Rowman & Littlefield

Metz, J. (2006). "Babes, Balls, and Babies": A Critical Ethnography of Working Motherhood. Unpublished doctoral dissertation. Department of Kinesiology, University of Illinois, Urbana-Champaign.

Moreira, C. (2007) *Transgressive body, Transgressive scholarship: A fragmented life in so many acts.* Unpublished doctoral dissertation. Institute of Communications Research, University of Illinois, Urbana-Champaign.

Newman, J., & Giardina. M. D. (forthcoming). *Consuming NASCAR nation: Sport, spectacle, and the politics of neoliberalism.*

Pelias, R. J. (2004.) *A methodology of the heart: Evoking academic and daily life.* Walnut Creek, CA, AltaMira.

Roy, A. (2004). *The checkbook and the cruise missile: Conversations with Arundhati Roy (Interviews with David Barsamian).* Cambridge, MA: South End Press

Sage, G. (1998). *Power and ideology in American sport: A critical perspective.* Champaign, IL: Human Kinetics.

Schechner, R. (1998). What is performance studies anyway? In P. Phelan & J. Lane (Eds.), *The ends of performance.* New York: New York University Press.

Vowell, S. (2002). *The partly cloudy patriot.* New York: Simon & Schuster.

West, C. (1989) *The American evasion of philosophy: a genealogy of pragmatism.* Madison, University of Wisconsin Press.
West, C. (1991) Theory, pragmatisms and politics. In J. Arac & B. Johnson (Eds.), *Consequences of theory.* Baltimore, MD, Johns Hopkins University Press.

Contributors

David L. Andrews is associate professor of Sport Commerce & Culture and director of graduate studies in the Department of Kinesiology, and an affiliate faculty in the Department of Sociology, at the University of Maryland, College Park. He is the author of *Sport-Commerce-Culture: Essays on Sport in Late Capitalist America* (Peter Lang, 2006) and *Sport Culture: An Introduction* (Blackwell, in press), and the editor or coeditor of such books as *Michael Jordan, Inc.: Corporate Sport, Media Culture, and Late-Modern America* (Routledge, 2001), *Sport and Corporate Nationalisms* (Berg, 2005, with Michael L. Silk and CL Cole), *Sport Stars: The Cultural Politics of Sporting Celebrity* (Routledge, 2001, with Steven J. Jackson), and *Sport, Culture, and Advertising: Identities, Commodities, and the Politics of Representation* (Routledge, 2004, with Steven J. Jackson). He is assistant editor of the *Journal of Sport and Social Issues* and a member of the editorial board of the *Sociology of Sport Journal*.

Ava C. Baker is a graduate student in the Arts and Sciences Program at McMaster University, Hamilton, Ontario, Canada, where she is interested in issues related to Aboriginal health.

C. L. Cole is professor of Advertising, Sociology, Afro-American Studies, and Gender & Women's Studies at the University of Illinois, Urbana-Champaign. She is widely considered one of the leading figures of Sport & Cultural Studies research, serving as editor of the *Journal of Sport and Social Issues* and having published widely on feminist cultural studies, Nike, Inc., Michael Jordan, the National Basketball Association, and popular culture. She is editor of *Women, Sport, and Culture* (Human Kinetics, with Susan Birrell), *Corporate*

Nationalisms & Sport (Berg, with David Andrews and Michael Silk), and a forthcoming volume on body politics (with Grant Farred). She is also coeditor of the book series "Sport, Culture & Social Relations" (SUNY Press), and serves on the editorial board of *Cultural Studies/Critical Methodologies* and the advisory board of *GLQ*. Currently, she is completing a book on national popular culture, sport, and embodied deviance in post-WWII America, titled *Good Sports? The Boundaries of American Democracy.*

Dawn H. Currie is professor of sociology at the University of British Columbia, Vancouver, Canada. She is the author of *Girl Talk: Adolescent Magazines and Their Readers* (1999, University of Toronto Press), as well as numerous articles on gender, girl culture, and feminism, which have appeared in such journals as *Gender & Society, Youth & Society, Journal of Comparative Family Studies, Journal of Human Justice, Feminist Theory,* and *Feminist Review.*

Norman K. Denzin is distinguished professor of communications, College of Communications Scholar, and research professor of communications, sociology, and the humanities at the University of Illinois, Urbana-Champaign. One of the world's foremost authorities on qualitative research and cultural criticism, Denzin is the author or editor of more than two dozen books, including *Performance Ethnography, Reading Race, Interpretive Ethnography, The Cinematic Society, Images of Postmodern Society, The Recovering Alcoholic,* and *The Alcoholic Self.* He is past editor of *The Sociological Quarterly,* coeditor of the landmark *Handbook of Qualitative Research* (1st, 2nd, and 3rd editions, Sage Publications, with Yvonna S. Lincoln), editor of the *Handbook of Critical Indigenous Methodologies* (forthcoming, Sage, with Yvonna S. Lincoln and Linda Tuhiwai Smith), coeditor of *Contesting Empire/Globalizing Dissent: Cultural Studies after 9/11* (Paradigm, 2006, with Michael D. Giardina), coeditor of *Qualitative Inquiry and the Conservative Challenge: Confronting Methodological Conservatism* (Left Coast Press, 2006, with Michael D. Giardina), coeditor of *Ethical Futures in Qualitative Research: Decolonizing the Politics of Knowledge* (Left Coast Press, 2007, with Michael D. Giardina), journal coeditor of *Qualitative Inquiry,* founding editor of *Cultural Studies/Critical Methodologies,* series editor of *Studies in Symbolic Interaction,* and *Cultural Critique* series editor for Peter Lang Publishing. He is also the Founding President of the International Association of Qualitative Inquiry and Director of the annual International Congress of Qualitative Inquiry.

Michele K. Donnelly is a PhD student in the Department of Sociology at McMaster University, Hamilton, Ontario, Canada. Her research interests include sociology of gender and the body, as well as alternative and "extreme" sport, contemporary social theory, and qualitative methodologies.

Michael D. Giardina is visiting assistant professor of advertising and cultural studies at the University of Illinois, Urbana-Champaign. He is the author of *From Soccer Moms to NASCAR Dads: Sport, Culture, & Politics in a Nation Divided* (Paradigm, forthcoming) and *Sporting Pedagogies: Performing Culture & Identity in the Global Arena* (Peter Lang, 2005), which received the 2006 "Most Outstanding Book" award from the North American Society for the Sociology of Sport. He is also the coeditor of numerous books on cultural studies and qualitative research, including most recently *Contesting Empire/Globalizing Dissent: Cultural Studies after 9/11* (Paradigm, 2006, with Norman K. Denzin), *Qualitative Inquiry and the Conservative Challenge: Confronting Methodological Fundamentalism* (Left Coast Press, 2006, with Norman K. Denzin), *Ethical Futures in Qualitative Research: Decolonizing the Politics of Knowledge* (Left Coast Press, 2007, with Norman K. Denzin). His work has also appeared in scholarly journals such as *Harvard Educational Review, Cultural Studies/Critical Methodologies*, and the *Journal of Sport & Social Issues*.

Audrey R. Giles is an assistant professor in the School of Human Kinetics at Université d'Ottawa, Canada. Her research interests include: Aboriginal peoples' involvement in leisure pursuits, in particular, menstrual traditions associated with Indigenous women's leisure activities; the Dene Games; the Arctic Winter Games; the NWT Aquatics Program, the notion of gender equity and its impact on sport and recreation policy in Northern communities; contested understandings of "tradition"; cross-cultural examinations of understandings of gender, gender equity, and notions of leisure; feminist poststructuralism; and Indigenous leisure pursuits and their relation(s) to community health practices.

Deirdre M. Kelly is professor of sociology of education at the University of British Columbia, Vancouver, Canada. She is the author or editor of numerous books on the subject of critical youth studies, including *Pregnant with Meaning: Teen Mothers and the Politics of Inclusive Schooling* (Peter Lang, 2000), *Last Chance High: How Girls and Boys Drop In and Out of Alternative Schools* (1993, Yale University Press), and *Debating Dropouts: Critical Policy and Research Perspectives on Leaving School* (1996, Teachers College Press, edited with Jane Gaskell).

C. Richard King is associate professor of comparative ethnic studies at Washington State University. He is the author of *Colonial Discourses, Collective Memories, and the Exhibition of Native American Cultures and Histories in the Contemporary United States* (Garland, 1998) and *Beyond the Cheers: Race as Spectacle In College Sports* (with Charles Fruehling Springwood, SUNY

Press, 2001), and is the editor of *Native Athletes in Sport & Society* (University of Nebraska Press, 2005), *Postcolonial America* (University of Illinois Press), and *Commodity Racism: Representation, Racialization, and Resistance* (forthcoming). His work has also appeared in such journals as *Journal of Sport & Social Issues, Qualitative Inquiry,* and *Public Historian.*

David J. Leonard is assistant professor of comparative ethnic studies and American studies at Washington State University, where he teaches and researches on social justice movements and the racial logics of late-capitalism in a global context. He is the author or editor of numerous books, including *Race, Culture, and Power in the United States* (McGraw-Hill, 2006) and *Visual Economies of/in Motion: Sport and Film* (Peter Lang, 2006, with C. Richard King). He is currently completing two books, one titled *"No Jews and No Coloreds are Welcome in this Town": Constructing Racial Coalitions in Post/War Los Angeles* and one titled *A Culture War Inside America's Arenas: Race, Basketball, and a Battle for Power.*

Cameron R. McCarthy is research professor, communications scholar, and university scholar in the department of Educational Policy Studies at the University of Illinois, Urbana-Champaign. He has also been a visiting scholar and lecturer at the University of Cambridge, York University, the University of Newcastle, Monash University and the University of Queensland. Professor McCarthy has published widely on topics related to postcolonialism, problems with neo-Marxist writings on race and education, institutional support for teaching, and school ritual and adolescent identities in journals such as *Harvard Educational Review, Oxford Review of Education, The British Journal of the Sociology of Education, Studies in the Linguistic Sciences, International Studies in Qualitative Research, Qualitative Inquiry, Educational Theory, Curriculum Studies, The Journal of Curriculum Theorizing.* Professor McCarthy has authored or co-authored numerous books, including: *Race and Curriculum* (Falmer Press, 1990), *Race Identity and Representation in Education* (Routledge, 1993), *Racismo y Curriculum* (Morata, Madrid, 1994), *The Uses of Culture: Education and the Limits of Ethnic Affiliation* (Routledge, 1998), *Sound Identities: Youth Music and the Cultural Politics of Education* (Peter Lang, 1999), *Multicultural Curriculum: New Directions for Social Theory, Practice and Policy* (Routledge, 2000), *Reading and Teaching the Postcolonial: From Baldwin to Basquiat and Beyond* (Teachers College Press, Columbia University, 2001), and *Foucault, Cultural Studies and Governmentality* (SUNY Press, 2003).

Jennifer L. Metz is a visiting professor in the Department of Sport Sciences at the University of Iowa. Her work centers on the intersection of race, gender, and feminism in late-capitalism. She is currently completing a book entitled *Babies, Babes, & Ballers: A Critical Ethnography of Working Motherhood in the United States.*

Shauna Pomerantz is an assistant professor in the Department of Child and Youth Studies at Brock University, St. Catherines, Ontario, Canada. Her research focuses on girls and the construction of girlhoods through the intersecting lenses of sociology and cultural studies. Her past projects include *Girl Power*, a three-year study in British Columbia on girls' expressions of empowerment, and *Dressing the Part*, a year-long ethnography of how girls used style to negotiate their gendered, raced, classed, and sexual identities in an urban Vancouver high school. Her current research focuses on how girls navigate the "global social world," both in the school, where multiculturalism has created new avenues for identity, and on the Internet, where girlhood is open to cross-national interpretation, influence, and scrutiny.

Robert E. Rinehart is associate professor of Educational Leadership & Counseling Psychology at Washington State University, where he teaches courses on cultural studies, ethnography, and popular culture. He is the author of *Players All: Performances in Contemporary Sport* (Indiana University Press, 1998) and editor of *To the Extreme: Alternative Sports, Inside and Out* (SUNY Press, 2003, with Synthia Sydnor) and *Encyclopedia of Extreme Sports* (forthcoming).

Michael L. Silk is an associate professor and member of the Physical Cultural Studies Research Group located in the Sport Commerce and Culture Program, Department of Kinesiology, at the University of Maryland, College Park. His work is committed to the critical, multidisciplinary, and multi-method interrogation of sporting practices, experiences, and structures. He has published a number of book chapters and journal articles in *Media, Culture, and Society; Journal of Sport and Social Issues; Sociology of Sport Journal; International Review for the Sociology of Sport; Sport, Culture, and Society; Journal of Sport Management;* and *Media Culture: A Review.*

Ryan White is a doctoral candidate in the Department of Kinesiology at the University of Maryland, College Park. His work focuses on the intersection of sport, cultural studies, and popular politics in late-capitalism.

Index